MIRRORS of Love™

In Acts of COURAGE

To Bob,
As promised,
from my heart to yours.
With Warmest Wishes,
Cheri
12/02

CRITICAL ACCLAIM
for
MIRRORS of Love – In Acts of COURAGE

"It is an honor to be a part of this book. Cheri has a way of getting to the heart. Her writing goes much deeper than most. The description of the situations make me feel like I am right there in the moment."
>**Rachael Lampa**, Louisville, Colorado
>Top Christian Teen Vocalist

"Everyone wants more courage and by reading this book, your courage will expand instantly and dramatically."
>**Mark Victor Hansen**, Southern California
>Co-Creator, #1 *New York Times* best-selling series,
>*Chicken Soup for the Soul*®

"Cheri Lutton serves up an impressive roster of heroes who inspire by their courage and examples, making a positive difference in our world."
>**Dan O'Neill**, Bellevue, Washington
>President, Mercy Corps

"Cheri is a tremendous writer ...the words just flow beautifully from one thought to the next. An intimacy with Cheri is developed from the first page. WOW!"
>**Steve Siebold**, Boynton Beach, Florida
>Former Tennis Pro & President, Gove-Siebold Group

Critical Acclaim

"Cheri Lutton has written a book that you will not only enjoy reading, but it will help you to realize that courage exists in people from all backgrounds. By reading of the courage of others, it will help each of us to use courage in our life on a daily basis."
                         Don M. Green, Wise, Virginia
              Executive Director, Napoleon Hill Foundation

"Mom, I feel very put to life by what you have written about me. Thank you so much for letting me be a part of this book. I truly appreciate it!"
                     Crystal Lutton, Lafayette, Colorado
            Cheri's Daughter, High School Junior, Vocalist

"Although Cheri and I have all of our wonderful history locked away in our collective memories, it is a pleasurable experience reading about it in her written words. It is truly a delight to read her paragraphs of our journey together."
                 Steven H. Lutton, Lafayette, Colorado
         Cheri's Husband, Co-Owner, Renegade Press, Inc.

"As I read the chapter about myself, I was struck by the wonderfully descriptive and simple nature of Cheri's writing. She was able to reveal things about myself that I often take for granted or just don't realize. I like this guy!"
                  Robert Troch, Brooklyn, New York
      Sports Trainer & Owner, Injury Free Athletics Institute

"Mom, I thought my chapter was great. You used really juicy words. It inspires me how much time you spend making your goals happen."
               Steven H. Lutton II, Lafayette, Colorado
         Cheri's Son, Fifth Grade Student, Football Player

"Cheri's writing is truly inspirational and comes from the heart. It made me take a good look at myself, realize what I

Critical Acclaim

have accomplished, and see my strengths again. Thank you, Cheri, for all your support and belief in me!"
Liz Mostov, New York, New York
Entrepreneur, Volunteer, Animal Lover

"When I read my draft, I was stunned. In a few sentences, Cheri has captured my innermost being. She sees the essence of others, as well as she knows herself. The result is inspiring and energizing. Like everyone she touches, I want to follow her example and achieve my own highest and best purpose. I invite everyone who reads this book to climb on board Cheri's celebration of humanity train. It is leaving the station and nothing is going to stop it!"
Steve Immer, Breckenridge, Colorado
Music & Sports Lover, Entrepreneur, Volunteer

"I am so grateful for Cheri's comments. When I read about myself, I wept and felt that I had been understood for whom I want to be. This portrayal in writing has lifted me closer in my own self-confidence. I am thrilled to see her work and know that others out there are trying to make a difference in uplifting people."
Dean Nixon, St. George, Utah
Emotional Growth Facilitator and Coach

"Cheri has captured the magical essence of my being and the parallel to Merlin was uncanny. I truly feel heard and seen far beyond what may appear obvious. I appreciate her for her clarity, wisdom, insight, and humor."
Patricia Krown, Boulder, Colorado
Life Coach and Therapist

"I feel honored to be mentioned in Cheri's book. She is one of the most gifted writers and friends that I know. She has a

Critical Acclaim

great heart for teenagers."
Scot Keranen, Portland, Oregon
Teen Mentor, Youth Mentoring Int'l. Foundation

"What a beautiful writer ...I feel like I'm having an out of body experience and reading about someone else. I am truly blessed by being in Cheri's life and having her in mine!"
Steve Barnhill, Denver, Colorado
Former Baseball Pro, President, Bridges Int'l, Inc.

"Cheri's writing has an almost mystical quality about it. I enjoyed her insights and feel flattered and honored to be included in such a powerful mission."
Renee Sisney, Longmont, Colorado
Director for Religious Education, St. John Catholic Church

MIRRORS of Love™

In Acts of COURAGE

Cheri Lutton

Foreword by Larry Wilson,
Founder, Wilson Learning Corporation

Afterword by Don Green,
Executive Director, Napoleon Hill Foundation

Word Alive Press
in collaboration with
CCQH
Winnipeg • Lafayette

Mirrors of Love – In Acts of Courage
Cheri Lutton

Word Alive Press, Inc.
131 Cordite Road
Winnipeg, Manitoba, Canada, R3W 1S1
In collaboration with
CCQH, Inc.
Lafayette, CO 80026 USA

Copyright © 2002 by Cheri Lutton
All rights reserved. Published 2002
Printed in the United States of America

Mirrors of Love and CCQH are U.S. registered trademarks pending.
This book or parts thereof, may not be
reproduced in any form without permission.
ccqh.com and/or mirrorsoflove.com
Published simultaneously in Canada.

Library of Congress Data
Lutton, Cheri.
Mirrors of Love – In Acts of Courage / Cheri Lutton
Foreword by Larry Wilson
Includes bibliographical references.
ISBN   0-9716449-3-4   (softcover)
1. Mirrors of Love – In Acts of Courage

Printed on acid-free paper
Edited by Stephen Immer and Amanda Okker
Cover and Graphic Design by Nikki Braun

These publishers have generously given permission to use excerpts from the following copyrighted works. Excerpts from CROSSING THE THRESHOLD OF HOPE by His Holiness Pope John Paul II, translated by Vittorio Messori, copyright © 1994 by Alfred A. Knopf, a division of Random House, Inc. Used by permission of Alfred A. Knopf, a division of Random House, Inc. From GIFT AND MYSTERY by Pope John Paul II, copyright © 1996 by Libreria Editrice Vaticana. Used by permission of Doubleday, a division of Random House, Inc. From HIS HOLINESS by Carl Bernstein and Marco Politi, copyright © 1996 by Carl Bernstein and Marco Politi. Used by permission of Doubleday, a division of Random House, Inc. From DARE TO WIN by Jack Canfield and Mark Victor Hansen, copyright © 1994 by Mark Victor Hansen & Jack Canfield. Used by permission of Berkeley Publishing Group, a division of Penguin Putnam Inc. Excerpted from ROMEO AND JULIET by William Shakespeare, edited by Louis B. Wright and Virginia A. LaMar, copyright © 1984 by the Folger Shakespeare Library. Reprinted by courtesy permission of Simon & Schuster. From MY AMERICAN JOURNEY by Colin Powell with Joseph E. Persico, copyright © 1995 by Colin L. Powell. Used by permission of Random House, Inc.

(Continued in Permissions Acknowledgment Section)

To My Loving Husband,

Steve

&

My Beautiful Children,

Crystal and Steven

To Mary, Our Lady of Roses

And,

To the brave who have

Dared to follow their Inner Light

CONTENTS

Lyrics xv
Foreword by Larry Wilson xvii
Preface xxi
Acknowledgments xxiii
Permissions Acknowledgments xxv
Chapter Overview xxvii

PART ONE *Courage in Spirit*

Courage in Spirit:
Know Thy Self and Gain Strength of Character 3

PROFILES

Jesus of Nazareth 17
Mary, Blessed Mother of Jesus 25
Pope John Paul II 31
Steve Barnhill 45
Mother Teresa 59
Crystal E. Lutton 65

Contents

PART TWO *Courage in Mind*

Courage in Mind:
All Things Are Possible to He Who Believes 79

PROFILES
President John F. Kennedy 91
Larry Wilson 103
Bob Proctor 119
Mark Victor Hansen 133
Steven H. Lutton II 145

PART THREE *Courage in Body*

Courage in Body:
Stay the Course with the End in Mind 155

PROFILES
Steven H. Lutton 167
Steve Siebold 179
Rachael Lampa 193
Robert Troch 205
Steve Immer 211

PART FOUR *Courage in Family*

Courage in Family:
Pray and Laugh Together, and Stay Together 221

PROFILES
First Lady Jacqueline Kennedy 231
Yvonne Kalench 239
Doc Moody 247
Renee Sisney 255
Melissa Montoya 265

PART FIVE Courage in Work

Courage in Work:
Live Today like There is No Tomorrow 273

PROFILES

Robert F. Kennedy 285
Dean Nixon 299
Anita Sanders 309
Secretary of State Colin Powell 315
Patricia Krown 333

PART SIX Courage in Society

Courage in Society:
Love Thy Neighbor as Thy Self 343

PROFILES

Scot Keranen 353
Grace, Princess of Monaco 361
Elizabeth Mostov 371
Diana, Princess of Wales 381
America's Finest in the Wake of Tragedy 395
Afterword by Don Green,
Executive Director, Napoleon Hill Foundation 411
Author's Comments 413
References 415
About the Author 423
About CCQH, Mirrors of Love 424
About MercyCorps 425
About Diana, The Work Continues 426
About The Princess Grace Foundations 427
About The Missionaries of Charity 428

"Mirrors of Love in Acts of Courage"

Vocals sung by Crystal Lutton /Lyrics written by Cheri Lutton/ Music by Rory Hoffman
Final music composed by Rory Hoffman and Depot Music Productions, Inc.
Produced & Distributed by Depot Music Productions, Inc. and CCQH, Inc.
"Mirrors of Love" and *Mirrors of Love – In Acts of Courage* © Cheri Lutton 2002
All publishing rights reserved. Mirrors of Love pending registered U.S. trademark.

What spurs a man to call the strength from within?
Reaching in his soul, beyond fears and sin
Living his passion in truth and loyalty
To push forth and find Joy and Harmony.

What drives his woman's heart to care 'til she aches?
Kissing tears away, mending tender breaks
Holding her vision for possibilities
To see through dark to bright realities.

Chorus:
Mirrors of Love,
Mirrors of Love,
Mirrors of Love
In Acts of Courage.

Bridge:
Closely watch these brave, so bold and so selfless
See reflections of the beauty they possess
A human rose in bloom, unfolding more each day
On God's grand path . . . He leads the Way!

Falsetto Double Chorus

Can their youth be shown to tap this golden might?
Seeking their best, soaring wondrous height
Reaching that place where action leads the way
For all to see . . . the Joy of Victory!

Mirrors of Love,
Mirrors of Love,
Mirrors of Love,
In Acts of Courage,
In Acts of Courage,
In . . . Acts . . . of . . . Courage.

FOREWORD

At some point in most people's lives, the two questions hit us right in the heart; Who am I? Why am I here? We could be faced with answering these tough questions very early in life, or, for some, in life's last few moments. Not that these questions were early or late; they've always been there, sitting on our shoulders, patiently waiting to be heard.

For some, the readiness to deal with life's queries occurs as an Awakening, a special time, a special place, a special happening that says, "You're ready, let the journey begin." For others, the questions seem to have always been there, hanging around like old shoes or old friends we wear or visit when the time is just right. Yet, I suspect for most, the state of denial is a favorite hiding place from the reality that these questions even exist. Or a clever way to avoid the uncomfortable possibility of our answers not being right, or fearful of our 'Being' just not being right.

Yet, whenever the student is ready, the right book seems to come along. And good news, Cheri Lutton's book has come along. As a gifted story teller, she also brings along interesting people whose stories hit us right in the heart as well as in the mind by including valuable clues, keys, insights, and wisdom to help us find our way on our own hero's journey.

I believe the purpose of a Foreword is to help the reader look forward to their experience of the book. So, with your

Foreword

permission, I'd like to coach you to have the best possible experience with Cheri's diverse list of guests.

For the last few years, I've been helping organizations establish cooperative learning groups to support the personal growth of the associates of the various entities. We call these BE IT groups, the acronym standing for Being Energized and Inspired Together. The purpose of the BE IT group is to help all members support, encourage and coach each other to enjoy the greatest success and fulfillment while playing in The Great Game of Life.

We've learned some things about learning and growing. First, personal growth is not accomplished by just having the answers to life's two big questions. That's just the beginning, as in, "Let the games begin."

From there, we've got to get in the game, participate as a full-out player, step up to life's problems, challenges, and obstacles. Then, take the biggest bite out of life as possible. In Cheri's words, we've got to rediscover our inner courage and our innate capacity to love.

Now, if you're up to that picture, then picture this. Your primary life coach is Cheri herself. In this book, she's going to bring you stories of fascinating people who, in a big way, have been there and done that. They're going to share life experiences directly with you. You're going to take a look at courage from all walks of life with both famous and private individuals. You'll see firsthand how courage knows no boundaries and how we can *all* tap into its infinitesimal resource of strength and stamina. You're going to view humanity from the positive side of the world through Cheri's heart and words. You'll get a tiny glimpse of the enormous potential within humanity just waiting to be noticed and allowed to grow.

Ask and receive this book as your window of discovery. Knock and find your very own BE IT group that will support,

Foreword

encourage, and coach you to find your own answers. How? Imagine yourself sitting with Cheri and her special guests in a tight circle. As each guest softly tells their story, the pain, the joy, the laughs, and the tears flow through the circle like an energy wheel spinning clockwise, then without warning, reverses polarity and goes the opposite direction. You're hearing and learning how they failed, and how they succeeded. What worked and what didn't work. How they found their courage and overcame their fears. How an ounce of love can defeat a pound of fear. How their inner beauty and capacity to love reflects upon us through their extraordinary acts of courage. As a member of the circle, an entire current of emotional energy and inspiration infects you. Their story becomes *your* story. Your story becomes *their* story. When you come to this book with an open mind and an open heart, be prepared. Be prepared to reconnect with the human race. Be prepared to wake up to a higher state of consciousness, awareness, alertness, and aliveness. Be prepared to look into this book as a mirror of love and courage. Please remember, though, that what you may have forgotten is your heroic self. Be prepared to come home. Enjoy the trip. So BE IT!

Larry Wilson
Founder, Wilson Learning Corporation
Best-selling author, *Play to Win*
Co-author, *The One Minute Sales Person*
International speaker, consultant

PREFACE

I hope that I can move you, as I have been moved, in the deepest sense of feelings . . . by the inner spirit that characterizes all the beautiful human beings that I have honored in the first of a multi-media series. They are honored for their touching acts of diverse bravery . . . through *Mirrors of Love*.

Nothing would delight me more in this tiny life of mine than to realize and witness a dream that I have of honoring people for their inner beauty and genius . . . and creating a positive movement toward celebrating the centered qualities of humanity.

For what more can I offer than to honor my fellow man? What individual does not like to be valued and recognized for his or her ordinary acts of goodness and inner beauty? Who does not enjoy the inner warmth that radiates with a bright glow once a human being's spiritual light has been ignited?

I offer to you the first flames of that igniting glow that I hope to build into a radiant illumination around the world. In *Mirrors of Love – In Acts of Courage*, I have etched a cross-section of literary portraits on various individuals—both celebrated and private—from all aspects of life who have illustrated their own unique acts of courage in their everyday lives. In surrounding our thoughts and heart in these acts, we create an experience that draws the spirit of our infinite goodness like a powerful magnet.

Preface

This project is, however, based on these assumptions:
1. All men and women are created equal as human beings.
2. All men and women are created in the image and likeness of God.
3. All men and women are imperfect and may freely choose evil or good.
4. Good and evil coexist in earthly life.
5. Evil is a natural expression of hate.
6. Goodness is a natural expression of love.
7. Love nourishes and stimulates growth.
8. Growth, expansion, and fuller expression are the essence of life.
9. Life is supported by lawful principles of absolute certainty and beauty that apply to all of us equally.
10. Beauty is beyond skin deep, and needs to be expressed and nourished to thrive in life.
11. Each of us is a purposeful part of the universal miracle of life.
12. Each of us possesses infinite resources of courage.

Once these assumptions are understood and trusted, it becomes easy to realize how I might desire to spur interest in the courageous acts of love that human beings illustrate in their daily lives. In fact, I feel honored to express myself in this literary and multi-media endeavor. I consider this work as a very purposeful instrument that I have been inspired to accomplish through my devotion and faith in God.

In our unwavering quest for excellence, we must savor the joys, which spring forth from our daily lives and admire ourselves for our blessings while being gentle with our errors. Only then, can we delight in our quest to honor the golden rule of compassion and embrace our neighbor in a sincere celebration of humanity.

ACKNOWLEDGMENTS

It is with heartfelt emotion that I express my gratitude to my husband, Steve, and children, Crystal and Steven, for their unwavering faith and support in me. I know that I am blessed to be surrounded by so much love and inner beauty from all three of them. My marriage only grows in love and joy as we share our visions with each other. Many a long night of writing and typing has kept me from my family, and I thank them for their patience and support.

Throughout this entire project, I have grown to rely on the good judgment of two of my close friends and business associates, Steve Immer and Robert Troch. Their belief in *Mirrors of Love* and CCQH, Inc. has kept me going during the valleys and fogs of this vision's arduous journey. As editors, Steve Immer and Amanda Okker have been instrumental in the integrity of this book. They pushed my envelope in the art of rewriting. I also thank publisher Jeremy Braun, graphic designer Nikki Braun, publicist Dan Smith, and the staff at Word Alive Press for their wisdom.

I thank the major publishers, photographers, libraries, and foundations that have either assisted or granted me permission to include their works in this book, especially Dan O'Neill – Mercy Corps, Don Green – The Napoleon Hill Foundation, Andrew Purkis – The Princess Diana Memorial Fund, Toby Boshak – The Princess Grace Foundations, the Sisters at The Missionaries of Charity, and staff at The JFK Library. Credit lines for these sources can be found on the copyright page and the Permissions Acknowledgments.

Acknowledgments

I thank the Ulmers, especially Kim, Jackie, Eric, Kersten, and Steph for their inspiration, their belief in my vision, and in me. As the owners of Depot Music Productions, Inc., they have been instrumental in distribution and production of the "Mirrors of Love" theme song and book. Thanks to Rory Hoffman for his musical genius. Also, to Chris and Ash for their initial assistance. I am so thankful to my daughter for her beautiful voice and partnership. I thank many friends and family for all their enthusiasm as I pioneered into authorship and purpose. Thank you Lorraine, Herb, Anita, Cheryl, Harry, Shannon, Scott, and children. Thanks also to Robin, Laura, Sam, Shari, Termah, Diane, Liz, Sue, Aunt Irene, Mary Lou, Bobbi, Jeanette, Maureen, Rachel, John, Susan, Judy, Kurt, Jeff, Al, Reed, and Ed. Thanks, Catherine, Philissa, and the supportive nurses with whom I rocked preemies during many a long night. Thanks, Ms. Gilpin and the fourth graders for continued support and comments. Thank you, Betsy, my maid of honor, and bridesmaids, Lynn, Debbie, Mary, and Bev, for your support of whom I've become today.

I thank Larry Wilson for all of his unique words of wisdom and gentle BE IT support. The friendship and mentorship that I have enjoyed throughout this experience has proven to be one of the best gifts of the whole project.

I thank every person that I asked to be a participant in this book for their honesty in revealing their thoughts and feelings—and their belief in me. I take them very seriously and consider it an honor to be their friend. Of course, I am grateful to those individuals who have passed on for the privilege of studying their lives and their courage. Most of all, I thank the Lord for allowing me to honor his Son and Blessed Mother Mary. She has truly guided me.

Finally, I thank *you* for sharing in my journey. I hope that I have touched your heart and made a difference in your life. You have made a difference in *mine*. Dreams do come true!

PERMISSIONS ACKNOWLEDGMENTS

The following credits are in acknowledgment of the generous support that has been received in granting permissions for valuable excerpts, lyrics, photographs, and other supportive documentation.

From WITNESS TO HOPE by George Weigel, copyright © 1999 by George Weigel. Reprinted by permission of HarperCollins Publishers Inc. on pp. 39. From THE NOBEL PEACE PRIZE 1979 – PRESENTATION SPEECH and MOTHER TERESA – NOBEL LECTURE, copyright © 1979 by The Nobel Foundation. Used with courtesy permission of The Nobel Foundation. From THINK AND GROW RICH by Napoleon Hill, copyright © 1963 by The Napoleon Hill Foundation. Used with courtesy permission of The Napoleon Hill Foundation. Submitted excerpts (pp. 1,5,6,16,237,238-9,246) from PROFILES IN COURAGE by John F. Kennedy, copyright © 1955,1956,1961 by John F. Kennedy. Copyright renewed © 1983,1984, 1989 by Jacqueline Kennedy Onassis. Foreword copyright © 1964 by Robert F. Kennedy. Reprinted by permission of HarperCollins Publishers Inc. on pp. 98-101. From WITH KENNEDY by Pierre Salinger. Used with courtesy permission of Random House, Inc. From YOU WERE BORN RICH by Bob Proctor, copyright © 1997 by LifeSuccess Productions. Used with courtesy permission of LifeSuccess Productions. From PLAY TO WIN by Larry Wilson and Hersch Wilson, copyright © 1998 Pecos River Change Management Group, a Division of Aon Consulting, Inc. Used with courtesy permission of Larry Wilson, Pecos River Change Management Group, a division of Aon Consulting, Inc. From Lyric of "The Sound of Music" by Richard Rodgers and Oscar Hammerstein II, copyright © 1959 by Richard Rodgers and Oscar Hammerstein II, copyright renewed. WILLIAMSON MUSIC owner of publication and allied

Permissions Acknowledgments

rights throughout the world. International copyright secured. All rights reserved. Reprinted by permission on pp. 136-7. From THINK AND GROW RICH WITH PEACE OF MIND by Napoleon Hill, copyright © 1967, 1995 by David Hill and The Napoleon Hill Foundation. Used with courtesy permission of The Napoleon Hill Foundation. From PERFECT VILLAINS, IMPERFECT HEROES, RFK'S WAR by Ronald Goldfarb, copyright © 1995 by Ronald Goldfarb. Used with courtesy permission of Ronald Goldfarb. From JACQUELINE KENNEDY: THE WHITE HOUSE YEARS by Mary Van Rensseler Thayer. Used with courtesy permission of Little Brown and Company. From AS WE REMEMBER HER: JACQUELINE KENNEDY ONASSIS: IN THE WORDS OF HER FRIENDS AND FAMILY by Carl S. Anthony, copyright © 1997 by Carl S. Anthony. Used with courtesy permission of HarperCollins Publishers Inc. From GRACE by Robert Lacey. Used with courtesy acknowledgment of Penguin Putnam Inc. From EARL SPENCER: TRIBUTE TO DIANA, PRINCESS OF WALES, copyright © 1997 by Earl Spencer. Reproduced by kind permission of Earl Spencer for the Althorp Charitable Trust. Excerpts from personal interviews and photographs used by kind permission of Steve Barnhill, Crystal Lutton, Larry Wilson, Bob Proctor, Mark Victor Hansen, Steven H. Lutton II, Steven H. Lutton, Steve Siebold, Rachael Lampa, Robert Troch, Steve Immer, Yvonne Kalench, Dr. Richard Moody, Renee Sisney, Melissa Montoya, Dean Nixon, Anita Sanders, Patricia Krown, Scot Keranen, and Elizabeth Mostov. Makk Serigraph "Nativity" and "Resurrection Sacred Art prints reprinted with courtesy permission of Bridges International, Ltd. "Jesus" and "Mary" illustrations reprinted with courtesy permission of Crystal E. Lutton. "Jesus of Gethsemane" reprinted with kind permission of Painet, Inc. Excerpts from web sites and logos used by courtesy permission of MercyCorps; The Diana, Princess of Wales Memorial Fund; and The Princess Grace Foundations. Denny Nauman photographs reprinted with kind permission of Denny Nauman. Associated Press photographs reprinted with kind permission of Associated Press. Photographs of Jacqueline Kennedy, John Kennedy, and Robert Kennedy reprinted with kind permission of the John F. Kennedy Library.

CHAPTER OVERVIEW

Celebrating the Centered Qualities of Humanity

Having immersed myself in the fine thoughts of these honorable people, I can honestly say that my life has become a spectacular experience of joy, emotional reward and spiritual awe in the glory of God. Join me now and delight in the words that are set forth to celebrate their acts of courage, which deserve to be cherished by all. As we are what we think, we will receive seeds of goodness for giving our time to positive reflection. I wish you the same joy as you experience these . . . Mirrors of Love.

PART ONE *Courage in Spirit*

CHAPTER ONE
Know Thy Self and Gain Strength of Character

"Ask and Ye shall receive. Seek and Ye shall find." These are the words of advice from Jesus according to Matthew 7:7. In our quest to find the meaning within our lives, we learn to listen to our inner voice and trust God's boundless love for us in our human journey. Let us explore the laws of the universe and take a walk in the garden of our inner character. Thereupon, we will create a wondrous vision for an expressed life filled with peace, joy, and harmony.

Chapter Overview

CHAPTER TWO
The Courage to Minister the Mystery of Life:
Jesus of Nazareth

Jesus exemplified a life of the purest integrity. He laid down a modeling path for all of us to be shown the way in our own daily lives. He did this so that we may walk with faith, courage, and serenity through our human journey of enlightenment toward eternal peace and salvation. All of us, Christians or otherwise, can take heart in the strength of character that Jesus demonstrated during his ministry. His short life on Earth has left us with much insight into how close we really are to God.

CHAPTER THREE
The Courage to Trust Her Destiny:
Mary, Blessed Mother of Jesus

Although Mary did not understand why or how she would be chosen to be the Mother of God's Son, she acted in harmony with her destiny. Mary's inner strength and unwavering trust in God's love reaffirms the beauty of purpose. Her life reflects the epitome of faith.

CHAPTER FOUR
The Courage to Walk His Talk of Catholicism:
Pope John Paul II

As I watched this little man get off the plane in his gifted hiking shoes after his visit to the Rocky Mountains of Colorado, I knew I was witnessing an historic moment. This would be a moment where love and law are woven together in this gentle hero of our time, Pope John Paul II. Any of us can benefit from the acts of spiritual grace that flow courageously from this wise Father of the Century.

Chapter Overview

CHAPTER FIVE
The Courage to Become a Player on God's Team:
Steve Barnhill

As the CEO and President of Bridges International, Steve Barnhill is one of the twenty-first century leaders who will bring about a bridge of mutual respect and understanding of the five traditional religions of the world. Steve shares with great candor his decision to move away from Corporate America and toward his mission for God.

CHAPTER SIX
The Courage to Embrace Humility in Leadership:
Mother Teresa

Mother Teresa exemplified a true, saintly life dedicated to purity. Yet, she was still a human being in modern society with all of the pressures of the world beckoning her attention. Mother Teresa, as petite as she was, moved mountains of indifference so that society would become more aware of the enormous need for compassion toward others. Mother Teresa helps us to understand that a focused thirst for God will guide us to his spiritual presence within us all.

CHAPTER SEVEN
The Courage to Trust the Inner Voice of God:
Crystal E. Lutton

My daughter, Crystal, at fifteen years of age, has shown remarkable strength and desire to push through fearful thoughts and peer pressure and find her own spiritual voice. I am honored to acknowledge her acts of bravery as the master of her own positive thoughts and actions.

Chapter Overview

PART TWO *Courage in Mind*

CHAPTER EIGHT
All Things are Possible to He Who Believes - Mark 9:23

As in the gardens of nature, we, too, sow what we reap, especially in the recesses of our thoughts. Thoughts are things and powerful ones at that, so we must take careful observation of the precious thoughts we allow into our gardens of human life. We are the masters of our soul and the makers of our destiny. We can set our imaginations onto a wondrous journey of our own positive creation. We will examine the ways that we can assure ourselves a garden of bountiful blossoms in acts of goodness. We will tap into the precious resources of the human mind, which will strengthen our resolve even in the face of adversity.

CHAPTER NINE
The Courage to Envision and Execute:
President John F. Kennedy

This is the daunting story of the Cuban Missile Crisis and the wise leadership that President Kennedy displayed in the thirteen days of unprecedented suspense. John F. Kennedy inspires the world and provokes thought on the irrational and somber possibilities of fear-based thinking without regard for humanity.

CHAPTER TEN
The Courage to Play to Win:
Larry Wilson

Larry Wilson is a world-renowned speaker, author, and founder of two management-consulting firms. Larry will catapult his audience and readers into a vivid state of adventure.

Chapter Overview

A pioneer of growth-based leadership, Larry is a man who has used his mind to master his dreams and turn them into awesome realities.

CHAPTER ELEVEN
The Courage to Think and Grow Rich:
Bob Proctor

Bob Proctor is a true gentleman, a scholar of modern times, and a mentor of mine in the Three Percent Club. I have been inspired and guided by his life, books, live programs, mentorship, personal advice, and living example of strength with style. Bob has shown enormous generosity in his willingness to help humanity in its quest for excellence. With wit and wisdom, Bob conquers mind over matter.

CHAPTER TWELVE
The Courage to Dare Beyond Belief:
Mark Victor Hansen

Mark Victor Hansen has risen to the top of the best-selling charts along with his partner, Jack Canfield in their phenomenal creation of the *Chicken Soup* book and merchandising series. Mark has touched my life in his inspirational messages through tapes and live mentorship in the Three Percent Club, a prosperity-building organization. Mark is a master at thinking outside the box and actualizing extraordinary dreams.

CHAPTER THIRTEEN
The Courage to Be Honest:
Steven H. Lutton II

My son, Steven, at eight years of age, has shown me his ability to step up to the task of accounting for his own daily thoughts expressed through his actions. It warms my heart to

Chapter Overview

watch him grow and become a brave, young boy of integrity. He is learning that small daily acts of goodness begin to shape the person we will become during our life's journey.

PART THREE *Courage in Body*

CHAPTER FOURTEEN
Stay the Course with the End in Mind

Our physical expressions are a manifestation of our spirit and thoughts in action. As we listen to our spiritual voice of God and learn to master our thoughts, we cultivate the garden of our heavenly life on earth. Our daily acts of purpose become the blossoms, leading to our achievements. Together, let us enjoy this dance of words as we observe the human spirit in its physical expression of valor.

CHAPTER FIFTEEN
The Courage to Resolve Life's Adversity:
Steven H. Lutton

My husband, Steve, has brought to my life an entire collection of courageous experiences. He lives each day with perseverance and a hardened resolve to achieve a desired accomplishment. Steve's gallant character is reflected in his ability to put intent into action with glimpses revealed through the story of his tumultuous ski accident.

CHAPTER SIXTEEN
The Courage to Go Pro Physically and Mentally:
Steve Siebold

A former tennis professional and championship player, Steve Siebold has coached many professionals toward achieving mental toughness in going for the gold in one's

Chapter Overview

life. Although I have never enjoyed watching Steve on the tennis court, his "eye of the tiger" approach to all of life's victories has been a not-to-be-missed experience.

CHAPTER SEVENTEEN
The Courage to Sing for God:
Rachael Lampa

As a young teen, Rachael Lampa has not only inspired me in her early success as a Christian vocal artist, she has indirectly given me encouragement in helping my own daughter in her gift of song. Rachael's life exemplifies her lovely mission to sing and live for God.

CHAPTER EIGHTEEN
The Courage to Inspire Fitness and Fun:
Robert Troch

A successful coach and entrepreneur in sports therapies, Robert Troch has become a close associate and friend of mine. He has brought lots of fun and insight into my life. Robert shares a portrayal of his focused stamina and his desire to enjoy life and touch others. As a fellow marathon runner, he knows how to stay the course and enjoy sweet success.

CHAPTER NINETEEN
The Courage to Be Real:
Steve Immer

A warmhearted friend, Steve Immer delightfully portrays the motto, "to thine own self be true." As a happy bachelor and a successful entrepreneur, Steve enjoys living and skiing in what he refers to as God's country in Breckenridge,

Chapter Overview

Colorado. Steve shares the joys of a lifestyle carved by a man who is driven to listen to his spirit of goodness, to think positively, and to become the person of his dreams.

PART FOUR *Courage in Family*

CHAPTER TWENTY
Pray and Laugh Together, and Stay Together

There is no stronger communal love than the bonds of unconditional love between husband and wife, parent and child. With God as our Heavenly Father, we can be guided through the pressures of life by our spiritual voice. We can learn to lean on our family values to build our thoughts and develop our inner character. We can trust in our family's love for us and model our strength of character in daily life.

CHAPTER TWENTY-ONE
The Courage to Walk through Darkness:
First Lady Jacqueline Kennedy

In 1963, the First Lady of America was called upon to lead her country and her family through the tragic loss of our President, her husband. I reminisce on her final walk of grace and strength during President John Kennedy's funeral, as well as her last days as our First Lady. Mrs. Kennedy's acts of bravery and her devotion to family life will continue to be a great source of inspiration throughout time.

CHAPTER TWENTY-TWO
The Courage to Love Unwaveringly:
Yvonne Kalench

Yvonne Kalench is a woman who honors the wedding vows "for better or worse, in sickness and in health, 'til

Chapter Overview

death do us part." As a mother of two young boys and the widow of a genuinely great human being, Yvonne brings to my life her quiet inspiration of love and loyalty. Yvonne shares insight and poignant memories of her late husband, John Kalench, a celebrated author and founder of the successful coaching business Millionaires in Motion.

CHAPTER TWENTY-THREE
The Courage to Model Unconditional Love:
Doc Moody

No family should be without Doc Moody in their lives. As Clinical Director for Sun Hawk Academy in St. George, Utah, Doc brought the light back in focus for our family during a dark period of stress. He also gave my daughter the tools to discern the path of goodness from the path of evil. His generosity and quiet, yet steadfast, example of the high road have always made me think of Saint Nicolas, Kris Kringle or Santa Claus. Doctor Richard Moody is well respected and admired for his work in the field of personal development and family counseling.

CHAPTER TWENTY-FOUR
The Courage to Model Respect and Value:
Renee Sisney

Renee Sisney was the director of youth ministry at our parish, Sacred Heart of Jesus in Boulder, Colorado. Yet, in my eyes, I see her as a humble saint of the heart who values the human spirit. Renee speaks to young and old alike with a sense of joy and compassion that re-ignites the sense of community that is so needed in modern life. Renee gives families the kindling sometimes needed at home to nourish the warm fires of family life and values.

Chapter Overview

CHAPTER TWENTY-FIVE
The Courage to Embrace a Christian Family Life:
Melissa Montoya

Melissa, affectionately known by loved ones as Missy, has made a conscious decision in her youth to follow Christ and live her spiritual faith through her family as a devoted wife and mother. Missy has successfully created a home business so that she can combine her work and family life into a more balanced mission and lifestyle. Melissa's Christian model of living is inspiring through her quiet and loving acts.

PART FIVE *Courage in Work*

CHAPTER TWENTY-SIX
Live Today Like There is No Tomorrow

Earl Nightingale describes success as the progressive realization of a worthy ideal. In his gentle, yet, wise voice I can still recall Earl's message in the *Lead the Field* audio program, "Do all that you can today, giving all that you have, and take heart in the satisfaction that you have given the day your best." We can discover the fun in our work once we are certain that our work is in harmony with our true purpose. It requires just as much effort to work in disharmony as it does to work in harmony with oneself . . . if not more.

CHAPTER TWENTY-SEVEN
The Courage to Care Regardless of Consequence:
Senator Robert F. Kennedy

Robert Francis Kennedy played many roles: son, brother, husband, father, uncle, friend, author, attorney general, senator, advocate, crusader, and more. In all of Kennedy's works, I am reminded of the constant flame within him. This flame illuminated his bold spirit and actions, leaving the world a better place for all.

CHAPTER TWENTY-EIGHT
The Courage to Push the Envelope:
Dean Nixon

Dean Nixon, a true family man, was the program facilitator of the behavioral growth seminars for youth and adults at Sun Hawk Academy in St. George, Utah. He has grown from his own struggles as a teen and has risen above limiting labels that would have caused many to crumble. Dean has struck our family's heartstrings and has moved me to become unstoppable in a quest for self-actualization. A delightful human being, Dean is a leader who can wear his heart on his sleeve and still get the job done.

CHAPTER TWENTY-NINE
The Courage to Honor Conviction:
Anita Sanders

Anita Sanders, my husband's sister and a hero of my heart, shares her moments of triumph and trepidation while serving in the Persian Gulf War. Her humble acts of loyalty illustrate her unwavering convictions. Anita is a devoted family woman who is also willing to make tremendous sacrifices in honor of her country.

CHAPTER THIRTY
The Courage to Protect Human Dignity and Freedom:
Secretary of State Colin Powell

As a family woman and an American citizen, I take pride in knowing that Colin Powell is the top diplomat in our

Chapter Overview

country, making a significant mark in our foreign policy. It is assuring to know that there are leaders evolving in the free world that can help us discern the high road from the low road in our quest for peace and freedom. This is a man of "courage under fire" who will shape our history and our future.

CHAPTER THIRTY-ONE
The Courage to Reach Out and Touch Others:
Patricia Krown

Patricia Krown, a life coach and therapist in Boulder, Colorado, has inspired me with her "live in Heaven on Earth" approach to her own daily choices. Patricia discovered her spiritual voice early in life and has a gift for helping others to find their voice. Patricia has grown firm in her spiritual nature and carries this strength in her quest to surround herself with like-minded playmates.

PART SIX *Courage in Society*

CHAPTER THIRTY-TWO
Love Thy Neighbor as Thyself

"No man is an island in of himself," it has been said and proven true over time. The worthiest of life's treasures are only available to us when we are willing to realize our universality and oneness with God. We can feel the emotions of joy, laughter, love, peace, and harmony only when we are humble enough to pay homage to humanity and all living creatures—great and small. With warmth and fun, let us walk together in our observation of this marvelous spectacle we call life and develop both our unity and uniqueness.

Chapter Overview

CHAPTER THIRTY-THREE
The Courage to Step Up to God's Calling:
Scot Keranen

Scot Keranen, a sixteen-year-old student from Oregon, has befriended me through our voluntary work together in the Youth Mentoring International Foundation (YMI). Scot inspired both my teen daughter and me in his warmhearted and genuine spirit. Scot shares his success in overcoming physical and social challenges and his leadership in promoting strong family life based on Christ's teachings.

CHAPTER THIRTY-FOUR
The Courage to Lead from the Heart:
Grace, Princess of Monaco

Grace Kelly was an icon in her Hollywood days and went on to become a real princess in Monaco. Throughout her life, she displayed a desire to please, be loved, and to love. With grace and style, she sought to become happy even with the pomp and protocol that she attracted in her life. Grace showed us just how much she cared through her boundless contributions to society.

CHAPTER THIRTY-FIVE
The Courage to Show Compassion for All:
Elizabeth Mostov

My dear friend, Liz, has lifted the hearts of many, including mine, with her laughter and her tears. Never afraid to show her true feelings, Liz models a life of tough love in the Big Apple. I see a determination in Liz that shows her zest and respect for life. Liz shares her love of service, especially her compassion toward animals, including her cats — Kiwi and Bonzai.

Chapter Overview

CHAPTER THIRTY-SIX
The Courage to Find Goodness in Everything:
Diana, Princess of Wales

Diana truly was the people's princess, for she searched for goodness and found it in her compassion for others. Princess Diana never lost her shyness in spite of unprecedented public adoration. Still, she found the inner strength to overcome her celebrity, using her beauty and allure to captivate the world in her quest to serve humanity.

CHAPTER THIRTY-SEVEN
The Courage to Face Evil and Fight for Good:
America's Finest in the Wake of Tragedy

There were so many diverse acts of courage displayed when evil and good crossed paths in recent American history. Oklahoma City, Columbine, and September 11 have only served to harden the resolve of the American spirit in our pursuit for world peace, liberty, and happiness. Journey with me through these events as we pay tribute to all of the heroes who have risen above terrorism, and helped us to heal and grow.

PART ONE
Courage In Spirit

Know Thy Self and Gain Strength of Character

Ask and Ye Shall Receive.
Seek and Ye Shall Find.
-Jesus of Nazareth
Matthew 7:7

CHAPTER ONE
Courage In Spirit

Know Thy Self and Gain Strength of Character

Ask and Ye Shall Receive. Seek and Ye Shall Find. Words of Jesus of Nazareth according to Matthew 7:7

These words affirm the message that Jesus indeed believed in the friendliness of the Universe. He did not say that only some might ask or seek. All human beings inherit this birthright. The only requirement is that we act upon our desires to ask or seek. We ask for what we want in order to receive it. We seek what we desire in order to find it. Yet, we must first go within to find out what we desire to receive or find. We listen to our Spirit or Divine inspiration from which our eternal light radiates. We take deep breaths, relax our muscles, our bodies, our minds, our hearts, our senses, and we trust and observe.

Will that mean sometimes going against the popular crowd's choices? Yes. We make courageous decisions when we are willing to listen to our spiritual essence, regardless of the outcome. All true heroes of life—whether they are of the spirit, mind, body, family, work, or society—have all shown this quality of courage. They have found their voice and are in deep harmony with their truer purpose. They become moved into purpose as passion drives their souls.

As we give ourselves permission to trust our inner spirit and receive our own spiritual power, we can unleash the untapped potential hidden deep from the noise of our earthly delights. This is courage in the making. The more you ask, the more you receive. The more you seek, the more you find. Our ability to choose—our gift of free will—sets the course for our muscles of courage. If we want to grow to our full human potential with complete confidence in our strength of character, we must first make a committed decision to choose to walk within and through our spiritual garden. What is a committed decision? It is a decision to act on our choice with one hundred percent intention to complete the desired good, regardless of the outcome.

Are we ready to commit to this decision? As Patricia Krown says, "Are we having fun, yet?" Will we feel frightened, dark, cold, or lonely at times? Perhaps. However, we will never be alone, for we will be letting go and letting God. We will be letting the divine side of our human nature lead us rather than continually following the ego side. How will we know the difference? Usually, if we are truly honest with ourselves, we will feel a calmness that transmits a sense of strength and certainty throughout our being. It may well raise our heartbeat and make us nervous, yet, it will feel right. If the inner voice we hear is in harmony with our purpose, we fall in love with the idea, and it is in service without violation to the lawful rights of others or the universe, then spirit has arrived.

We may also feel scared when our ego fights the unknown. Yet, we will feel very warm, enlightened, empowered, uplifted, loved, and understood as we overcome our emerging fears. We will experience and observe these qualities as we continue to gather the necessary tools and seeds of insight. We can then use these tools to transform ourselves into the fully realized human beings that we were created to become in our lives. We can develop our muscles of spiritual courage so that we become more defined in our daily actions. Our desire to stand up for our values, our purpose, and ourselves becomes harmoniously represented from within and displayed in our actions. We will have strength of character and integrity. We will have courage in spirit.

All of these blessings are available to us for the asking and seeking—forever. Now, let's go seek. As we walk together, imagine your own spiritual garden filled with all of the wondrous flowers and plants of genius, talent, and godlike qualities of goodness that are only found in you! In God's miraculous way, he finds repose as you reflect with gratitude, admiration, and respect on all that you are.

On our imaginary journey through our spiritual garden, we can delight in our awareness that the universe is friendly and cooperative with all of us in an absolute manner. Along the way, we will pass by tools or universal laws that will be as available to us as they are to Mother Nature. These laws operate with—or without—our conscious cooperation. We can choose to cooperate and use them in our service or we can become playthings for the universe of circumstance.

Let's walk our talk and enjoy the inner discoveries of universal empowerment that we can choose to embrace for our own expansion and growth. To add to our imaginative enjoyment, I shall take the luxury of creating a botanical walk through nature while we explore these lawful tools as we journey through the spiritual garden of life.

As we begin our walk, we will turn and look to our right. See the deep greenery of the ivy plants spreading their foliage profusely as ground cover. Once planted and nourished in the proper soil, this shade-loving perennial will multiply, year after year.

As gardening is an art, it is also a science. Now, let's take a look at these universal laws starting with the greatest from which all others are defined:

Energy is . . . it cannot be created or destroyed . . . and is always for expansion and greater expression.

This great law is simple. Note, it does not say that energy is not. That is the key. We are, so why not be the best that we can be? The natural flow of energy and life is to grow, to expand, and it is certainly much more fun! Can we use this tool to empower ourselves in the graceful acceptance of each moment? Always be aware that we live in the present—not in the past and not in the future. We cannot go back and we cannot go forward in the moment; but we can bridge the two in our willingness to be present and focused in our interface with the universe. The question is: can we take ownership of our power in the present and manifest into form our truest purpose?

We know from the science of astronomy that the universe is still expanding since the time of creation, approximately thirteen billion years ago. Galaxies have been photographed that are over ten billion light-years away. We are not seeing these distant galaxies as they exist today. Rather, we are seeing them as they existed ten billion years ago. Their light has had to travel ten billion years through time and space to reach us. What a vast universe God has created! Should we not be expanding, as well, to be in harmony with God's creation?

If so, we can expand in all aspects of our lives—spirit, mind, body, family, work, and society. By expanding our spiritual consciousness, our relationships, and our social awareness, our economic potential will automatically expand accordingly. Think of the expanding world population, which can create new markets in the global economy. For example, in the world of business, an innovative product initially sold in a local market often becomes a bestseller in an international market. This leads to more trade and a more productive world economy. The object created from the imagination does not have to be large to be effective and make a significant profit. Think of the enormous impact of such a modest looking device as the microchip.

"As a man thinketh in his heart, so is he" is so poetically defined in James Allen's *As A Man Thinketh*. His belief in the universal laws is clear in the following passage:

> "Every man is where he is by the law of his being; the thoughts which he has built into his character have brought him there, and in the arrangement of his life there is no element of chance; but all is the result of a law which cannot err."

Now, passing by the scent of the fresh blooms of the hyacinth bouquets of brilliant purple, white, blue, and pink flowers, we discover the first lawful tool:

Law of Perpetual Transmutation of Energy

Energy moves into physical form; therefore, the images we hold on the screens of our minds will eventually move into form as results—as achievements or crises.

How closely this resembles the seeds of the garden. Some seeds, of course, produce delicious fruits, tasty vegetables, and colorful flowers. Other seeds, sad to say, produce noxious weeds. However, even the weeds, which can be compared to the useless or counterproductive energy—or noise of our daily lives—are derived from some seeds of origin. Can we cultivate our desires for strength of character with seeds of discipline and self-control rather than seeds of doubt, criticism, or hesitancy? Which seeds will secure our bountiful fruits of goodness and plenty?

Our thoughts are not mere wisps of amorphous brain waves. Thoughts are real objects and the seeds of our future. Thoughts over time move into the physical realm. Whatever one thinks about matters, and eventually becomes matter, producing either positive or negative results. Positive thoughts produce positive results. Negative thoughts lead to negative results, especially when repeated over time and space. Whatever you feed, grows. Therefore, it would behoove us to continually check our thought patterns, to examine whether we are on a positive path towards greater fulfillment or a negative path towards decay and destruction.

As we leave this garden to meander down our path, let us make a curve to the right. There, we can stop to enjoy a drink of fresh, cool water and soak in the vibrant beauty of an array of red, peach, and yellow flowers in the rose garden. Fragrantly showing off their evolving petals, these roses are unique in their classic grandeur. "That which we call a rose, by any other name, would still smell as sweet," says Shakespeare's Juliet. This is so irresistibly romantic! It is no wonder that this is one of our favorite quotes.

Right beyond the rose garden is the second tool:

Law of Cause and Effect

Every cause has its effect; everything sown has its harvest. Energy is perpetually in motion. What we sow, we will also reap.

Our thoughts and actions always have effects, results, and consequences. Can we, therefore, tap into our inner resources of talent and wisdom to better serve our evolving purpose in this life? If we indeed begin to cultivate our spiritual garden and move into physical action toward the good that we desire, will we not reap the fruits of our harvest by law? With our desired effect in mind, can we take ownership of our causes to harmonize with our spiritual character? If every cause equals its effect, are we really hiding from the universe when we violate the rights of others in acts of disservice? If all acts are lawfully accountable, shall we not trust that our acts of goodness will always result in goodness for all? As so brilliantly questioned by Larry Wilson, in his philosophy and book *Play to Win*, can we begin to stop, challenge, and choose our life's decisions with the end in mind through trust in abundance rather than scarcity? How exciting.

O I do love the sprays of tulip plants that we are nearing in the foreground. The three tiers of circular beds parade a spectacular show of color in radiant hues and delicate fragrances. Isn't it interesting how tulip bulbs will multiply each year given the proper nutrients, temperature, and soil? Think about all that information in the bulb of a tulip. After all, we would never expect a rose from a tulip bulb. Yet, how does a tulip bulb attract all of the proper forces from the earth to create the shape, color, and scent of this romantic essence of beauty?

This brings us to the third tool:

Law of Vibration

Everything is energy, including our thoughts, and it vibrates in motion without rest. Conscious awareness of this vibration is called feeling.

Everything we do gives off vibrations, the nonverbal energy that permeates everything. As humans, we have various degrees of sensitivity to our vibrations, whereas animals sense our vibrations instinctively. Our pets know when we are happy, angry, or sad and react accordingly. We can learn a lot from our pets. The more aware we are of vibrations, the more feelings we have, the richer our emotional lives become, and the more sensitive we are to the needs of others.

Therein, if conscious awareness of our current state of vibration is 'feeling', would it not be in harmony with the law for us to master our thoughts? If our thoughts direct our vibrations, would not expanded or relaxed thoughts result in expanded or relaxed vibrations? If we are feeling tense, would it not be correct to presume that we are directing our thoughts on tense images? If we are feeling critical toward others, would it not be correct to suppose that we are thinking of others with critical thoughts? Can we cooperate with our spiritual nature on a daily basis to project the vibrations that are in harmony with our truest purpose?

O how do I love God's creations? Let me count the ways. This journey has led us onto a wondrous discovery of the serene nature of life. Behind us to the north, as we journey together, we will cast our eyes and other senses on a field of seeded produce. Do you like the taste of a freshly picked garden salad? Here we will soon enjoy tomatoes, lettuce, cucumbers, peppers, spinach, strawberries, garlic, and corn. They all have their particular seasonal periods for sowing and reaping. Some require cooler or moister conditions; some require hotter or drier conditions. All make for a delicacy to the taste. Off we go now to the fascinating fourth tool:

Law of Relativity

All laws are in harmony, related to and corresponding to each other. Therefore, as energy is, nothing is good, better, or best until it is compared to a form of reference.

There is always a reference in the universe. We refer to it as keeping it all in perspective. As the sun gazes through the skies to nourish and warm our planet, we can take comfort in the absoluteness of the universe to provide us constantly with all that we need and desire from which to measure and compare. Frequently, it is a natural landmark such as the sun or the North Star. Scientific inquiry can reveal others such as the equator or Arctic Circle. Many reference points are arbitrarily decided by world leaders to provide an orderly framework for human activity. These include zero longitude being at Greenwich, England, the modern calendar dated forward or backward from the approximate birth of Jesus of Nazareth, and time zones that are generally agreed upon at state, province or country borders. However, relationship and spiritual reference points are harder to define and may need to change over time as we are confronted with new knowledge. This requires an open mind and an understanding of reference points without necessarily becoming permanently attached to our perception of the relationship.

Indeed, can we also choose to keep our spirits flourishing by getting into the habit of always relating our situation to something better rather than something worse? In this frame of mind, might we not remain in a steady state of gratitude, continually drawing the good that we desire and deserve from God and the universe? Again, if energy just is, does it not—by law—follow that we have boundless opportunities to our avail, regardless of the relative state of life's appearance in form? Will not our spiritual nature always guide us in the direction that manifests our needs and fruits?

Now we come upon one of my favorite scents and flowers: the honeysuckle. Have you ever noticed the bumblebee as it sniffs the nectar from its favorite fragrances? The pollen it collects, while going after its desires, disseminates to create more abundance. Fruit trees depend on bumblebees to cross-pollinate the fruit blossoms for abundant crops. This cycle of life also manifests itself as we interact together in commerce. Many exchanges of goods and services begin with a primary benefit, but result in a secondary benefit, too. The United States exports farm produce to Europe and Japan for a profit, and imports electronic goods from those areas at low costs to consumers. Everyone benefits from this trade. Low price American wheat leads to low cost Japanese stereo gear. It is a win-win situation for all. This brings us to our fifth tool:

Law of Polarity

Everything just is and has an equal and opposite or complementary pole.

God created a world of wonderful opposites, the bright life-giving sun, and the cold reflective moon. He created vaporous atmosphere, fluid water, and solid earth, all of which interact in thousands of ways to bring life and diversity to our world. God created male and female, different, yet complementary. Everything in nature has an opposite, every action has an equal and opposite reaction. Imagine a full moon with one side brightened by the sun's light and the other side darkened without the sun's light. We see only one side at a time. Yet, could we actually separate the two from the whole? Will not someone, somewhere in the world be gaining a resource from each side at the same time, regardless of our perspective? If we choose to use this tool in our service, can we not uplift and expand our spiritual nature by always taking a position of courage in our appreciation for the whole? Must we dwell only on one side or another? Can we offer genuine appreciation for humanity and all living creatures, regardless of circumstances, so that others, too, may recognize their value to the whole? Can we use both sides of polarity, hot or cold, darkness or light, fear or trust, in serving humankind, the universe, and ourselves in our truer purpose?

Let us move on and take a closer indulgence at the perennial gardens of budding red, pink and white bleeding hearts. The shapes of the blossoms actually form a three-dimensional heart that shoots out from the center's top and dangles in the breeze in proud display. Alongside, we have the blue bells, which almost ring a song of splendor with their brilliant desire for attention. Dainty and yet very hardy, these shade-loving plants multiply and spread delicately with just the right tender loving care. Springing up on schedule, they are purposely next to the sixth tool:

Law of Rhythm

Energy is constantly in motion encompassing both swings of high and low, back and forth, to and from. This moving energy includes all human states of being.

As the sun sets, it will rise. As the perennials lay dormant, they will surely blossom in grand style in another season. The bears will hibernate and activate. The tide will rise and fall with the moon. We will sleep and we will play. We will feel lows and highs. As we observe this law, can we, perhaps, prepare ourselves to use it in our service? Might we observe our own down swings and be considerate of others and ourselves in these times? Can we bolster our resources and release our focused energy in harmony with our own natural swings? Can we also consider the rhythms in economic and social trends as forecasting insight in making wiser business decisions? If the law is universal, is it not universally applicable? Shall we be swept away by the tide or be prepared to ride out the wave through the passion of our truer purpose?

O this journey brings thirst! This is the thirst for both clear water and clear understanding. I do hear the babbling of a nearby brook. The tall trees cast a bit of shade and the breeze gently blows a bit of fresh air. Nearby, we can enjoy a fountain of fresh spring water from the mountains, and sit for a rest at a bench made for two. Lastly, our discovery brings us to a garden of purity with white calla lilies, and sweet lilies of the valley. This foliage stands tall with green stalks and white flowers peeking out, so graceful and poised in essence. Lest we forget our dainty friends in the herb garden—those airy, fernlike, and deliciously wholesome treats. The tarragon, parsley, chamomile, basil, mint, oregano, and many more tantalize our taste buds and soothe us with their bouquet of aromatic scents, healing our bodies in ways that Western man is just beginning to embrace and understand. Yet, always in due time, we must wait for all these planted seeds to germinate and parade their fashions for bountiful harvests of service to all.

This hails our attention to the final stop in our walk of discovery together through our own spiritual gardens to the seventh tool:

Law of Gender

Energy is and manifests itself in all things as masculine and feminine, resulting in the perpetuation of motion through regeneration. In due time, after an incubation period, all seeds of energy—including our ideas and goals —will manifest into form as physical results.

The universe is alive with masculine and feminine energy. Virtually all plants and animals reproduce sexually. The plant and animal kingdoms produce seeds, which lead to new life on a set time of germination. Likewise, our thoughts, plans, and goals germinate into physical form over time, but not on such a hard and fast schedule. No one knows the exact day that an idea will finally manifest itself, but the principle is the same.

Just as our plants will blossom, so too will our spiritual purpose. Therefore, is it not important for us to believe in our thoughts as vital instruments of energy? If we believe in and direct our thoughts to harmonize with our spiritual purpose, will we not be guided to our fullest actualization of self? Can we, thus, take ownership in shaping our circumstances in harmony with our character and worthy ideals? If organized thought linked with spiritual purpose is the only lawful way in which intelligent accomplishment in the universe will ever occur, then do we not have an obligation to ourselves—to control the weeds or useless thoughts and actions that may penetrate our minds? Will such weeds not just create chaos in our gardens of spiritual germination? Can we not count on our ideas to manifest and thereby prepare ourselves for the good of our truer purpose?

My friend, we are at the end of our spiritual and botanical journey together. I hope that you will visit often and take heart in the many examples of fine individuals in this book who have discovered, perhaps unwittingly, the secrets of the ages. In closing, I share with you the hero of your own life, a poetic stream of thought presented by James Allen in *As A Man Thinketh*:

> *You will be what you will to be,*
> *Let failure find its false content in that poor word,*
> *'environment',*

But spirit scorns it, and is free. It masters time,
it conquers space;
It cows that boastful trickster, Chance, and bids the tyrant
Circumstance.
Uncrown, and fill a servant's place. The human Will, that
force unseen,
The offspring of a deathless Soul,
can hew a way to any goal,
Though walls of granite intervene.
Be not impatient in delay,
But wait as one who understands;
When Spirit rises and commands,
The Universe is ready to obey. This is God's way.

Crystal Lutton

*Don't worry! I am Jesus.
Do not be afraid.*

—Jesus of Nazareth

Steve Skjold/Painet

*Jesus at Gethsemane
Praying for Strength*

CHAPTER TWO
Courage In Spirit

Jesus of Nazareth

The Courage to Minister the Mystery of Life

Don't worry! I am Jesus. Do not be afraid.
—Jesus of Nazareth according to Matthew 14:27

My Dear Lord, I am awestruck to understand how you chose me to create the eloquence in words that would describe your Beloved Son. I breathe deep, I close my eyes, I pray silently, and I release myself to you, O Lord, and open my heart to your voice.

Dear Jesus, as a Christian, I speak of you as my Savior, the One and Only Son of God. For those readers who are following other beliefs and traditions, I welcome you to read this prose in a spirit of love and acceptance for our differences. I practice the same tolerance when I read scriptures of other faiths. We are here together to celebrate the centered qualities of humanity to honor all the world's diversity and oneness in spiritual faith.

It has always enchanted me to imagine Bethlehem on the night of our Savior's birth. Imagine the splendor. See the radiance of the twinkling North Star. Envision the angels preparing the heavens for the earthly event; the animals in the lowly stable awaiting their guests and their infant leader. Imagine the Three Wise Men, the little drummer boy, and the sheep in pilgrimage through the sands in search of the Newborn King. Visualize in your mind Joseph, the faithful carpenter, protecting his beloved wife with Child ...the Child of God. Imagine the Innkeeper looking into the weary eyes of Joseph and Mary, while turning them away from the comfort of a night's sleep inside the Inn. If only this Innkeeper knew that the Son of God was about to bestow his ever-humble presence upon Earth. If only he knew that the Virgin Mary and her loyal husband, Saint Joseph, were beckoning his aid for the coming of the Messiah, the coming of the most celebrated birthday that will ever be known to humankind.

O to be one of those Wise Men and be blessed with the awareness about to behold humanity. These three fine prophets were in peaceful bliss in their quest to follow the Bright Star to the Holy Stable. What a Holy Night it was—bridging heaven and earth—for eternity! This is the night that Jesus, the Son of God, would arrive and begin his human journey. This infant would grow up to lead an exemplary life guided by the Ten Commandments proclaimed by Moses. Where Judaism brought the chosen people to follow the letter of the law, Jesus would soon personify the spirit of the law. I shudder to ponder at what the world would look like had we no gift of Jesus sent to us from Heaven through the Holy Family.

Jesus of Nazareth

Regardless of one's religious faith, we can all cast eyes upon the life of Jesus and the importance of a firmly convicted state of courage. Just like Mary, Joseph, and Jesus, we all have a truer purpose that resides in the deepest recesses of our hearts. An inner flame perpetually warms our every thought and gesture.

To study Jesus of Nazareth's life is to begin to glimpse the simplicity that is required for us to connect with our inner flame and hear the whispers echoing from our hearts. These whispers and warming flames will show us the way each day. Jesus lived out each passing day to the fullest and always had a calm resonance. Through Jesus' modeling of love, he gave us the hope and faith that true inner peace and harmony are available to us here on Earth. Once we discover it, we begin to grow our inner strength in facing these temptations squarely and we can stand firmly for our beliefs, our values, and our purposes.

To imagine Jesus as God is almost easier than to empathize with his manliness. Yet, he had his own visit with the temptations of evil—disguised through worry, anxiety, fear, and weariness. Jesus' fast in the desert for forty days and nights was no walk in the park. He exposed himself to a reflective state of sacrifice, surrendering himself to his calling and strengthening his free will to exercise choice. Jesus chose to love completely in the face of evil, standing eye to eye with the devil. We have the same choices. There is a silent surprise when one experiences victory in such adversity. The surprise lies within the silence. Our eternal flame grows deep within into a passionate torch with every triumph we hail in our own desert walk with evil or fear.

Just as Jesus triumphed through each test of his own beliefs, we, too, are made of the same stuff. Just as Jesus pursued his daily mission through a meek and humble spirit of service to his fellow man, we, too, can achieve our daily mission. There was an unstoppable boldness in Jesus' leadership—an unwavering faith in going about his father's business.

   I thank thee, O Lord, for these words inspired through my own passionate torch. I joyfully embrace your one and only Son. In my growing Roman Catholic faith, I pray for oneness in your presence and enjoy my quest to know and love your son, Jesus, and the Holy Family. I pray now for all those with me in these readings that they too will open their hearts ever so gently. I pray that each day they can listen to their inner voice and feel their eternal flame so that they may tap into their own true genius and callings. I pray that all humanity, regardless of religious beliefs, may study the life of Jesus and seek his Wisdom, Beauty, and Love.

   Lastly, I pray that we can nurture brotherly love and create a radiance from within that illuminates our earthly journey together. In closing, I humbly and gratefully quote Jesus from Matthew 5:3–10, 14–16:

> *"God blesses those people, who depend only on him.*
> *They belong to the Kingdom of Heaven!*
> *God blesses those people, who grieve,*
> *They will find comfort!*
> *God blesses those people, who are humble,*
> *The earth will belong to them!*
> *God bless those people who want to obey him*
> *more than eat or drink,*
> *They will be given what they want!*
> *God blesses those people, who are merciful,*
> *They will be treated with mercy!*
> *God blesses those people whose hearts are pure,*
> *They will see him!*
> *God blesses those people, who make peace,*

They will be called his children!
God blesses those people, who are treated badly
for doing right,
They belong to the kingdom of heaven!"

"You are like light for the whole world. A city built on top of a hill cannot be hidden, and no one would light a lamp and put it under a clay pot. A lamp is placed on a lamp stand, where it can give light to everyone in the house. Make your light shine so that others will see the good that you do and will praise your Father in Heaven. Amen."

◆ ◆ ◆

Crystal Lutton

I am the Lord's servant!
Let it happen as you have said.

—Mary,
Blessed Mother of Jesus

Nativity Scene by Makk Family

*Nativity Scene with
The Holy Family*

CHAPTER THREE
Courage In Spirit

Mary, Blessed Mother of Jesus

The Courage to Trust Her Destiny

**I am the Lord's servant!
Let it happen as you have said.
—Mary, Blessed Mother of Jesus**

Hail Mary, full of grace, the Lord is with thee. Blessed art thou, among women, and blessed is the fruit of thy womb, Jesus. Holy Mary, Mother of God, pray for us sinners, now and at the hour of our death, Amen.

O Mother of Jesus. Our courageous Mary, teach us in your shadow. May we beckon your grace to be a friend to us on Earth? We yearn to love you and hear your sweet whispers of guidance. May we have a hint of the courage that you exalted in your days on earth walking through your prophecy as the Virgin Mother?

What trepidation you must have felt as a teenage woman when you were visited by Michael the Archangel. You must have been bedazzled and overwhelmed by a visit from such an ethereal spirit as the greatest angel, representing our Heavenly Father. You must have been awestruck to be bestowed the honor of motherhood for our Lord's only Son. How could you have even pretended to live your life as a normal young woman, knowing from that moment onward, the role, and responsibility you would hold forever? Yet, you did just that—our sweet, yet brave model of womanhood. With so much inner strength, you took that next breath ...then, on your knees, you prayed to our Almighty for all the spiritual food you would need to set the holiest of examples for all women that would follow you.

What grace you portrayed! What silent gallantry you gave us in your exemplary life as you took Joseph in your confidence. The world in that moment mocked you, stoned you, and almost imprisoned you for what we know to be your Immaculate Conception. Yet, you overcame your fears and innocent resolve in return for quiet trust and faith that the way would always be shown.

How did you, beloved heroine, move through your daily footsteps and remain always so calm and certain about yourself, fully knowing that you—of all women on the earth—would be chosen for the role of roles? No words could be used to describe the magnificence of your chosen destiny. I want to fall on my knees just thinking of your awe-inspiring holiness and courage.

In the end, I shudder to retrace the events leading to your Son's crucifixion. Courage does not even begin to describe the quality you modeled for all women . . . for all mothers . . . for all parents . . . for all humans.

We love you, Mary, and pray that you will join us in our quest to know you better and to come even closer to knowing how to embody ourselves in heroism. I pray that you will bless all those in history who have reflected the trait of courage for the betterment of humanity. I pray dear Blessed Mother that you will read this lovingly and smile onto those wonderful human beings I have also honored in this book. Those brave human beings have so kindly touched my soul and added their goodness to me and certainly to the rest of the world. I pray that you will befriend us all and show us your lovely way, that we may each—in our own special way—make a difference in the hearts of our spouses . . . our children . . . our family . . . our friends . . . our community . . . our planet. Shower us, dear Mary, with your guiding grace and love in our quest to emulate your timeless faith and strength. Illuminate for us, Blessed Mother, the path in which we may follow your wondrous footprints of courage!

◆ ◆ ◆

AP/Broglio/Vatican

Brothers and sisters, don't be afraid to welcome Christ . . . and to accept his power.

—Pope John Paul II

AP

*Mother Teresa with
Pope John Paul II in Calcutta*

CHAPTER FOUR
Courage In Spirit

Pope John Paul II
The Courage to Walk His Talk of Catholicism

> **Brothers and sisters, don't be afraid to welcome Christ . . . and to accept his power.**
> **—Pope John Paul II**

I can still see his sneakers. I can still hear the roar of the U.S. army-green helicopters flying down, making small talk impossible. I can still feel my hair beginning to blow from the wind-gust created as the aircraft began to land in Denver. The country's finest law enforcement officials are at peak performance. After all, we have a very special guest in our presence—the 264th Bishop of Rome, successor to St. Peter—the first leader of the Roman Catholic Church, Vicar of Christ, the Supreme Pontiff John Paul II, commonly known to the world as . . . the pope.

I had hoped to receive a personal look from the vicar, but he stepped off the helicopter onto the opposite side of my view. All I saw were his sneakers and his white papal attire. Yes, sneakers! Pope John Paul II had just completed a trip to Saint Malo Retreat Center in the Rocky Mountains and had been presented with a thoughtful gift by one of the youth attending this '93 World Youth Day event—a pair of hiking shoes. Apparently, the papal leader had put them to good use as he kept his entourage hopping at the retreat as he pursued his enthusiasm for contemplative prayer hikes. Literally a mile high above sea level, the pope could elevate anyone in his presence much more than that with his own spiritual energy.

Now, at second glance, fate swings my way. His Holiness walks considerately around the aircraft to greet fans standing on the other side of the helicopter. He smiles and waves his arms above his head in a warm blessing. I blush. There were only a few of us tirelessly waiting for this brief glimpse, so when he waved and looked directly our way, it suddenly became very personal. How does he do it? I thought. How does he capture the full bloom of love in the earth and spread its fragrance so effortlessly? I suppose he would say that it is the grace of the Trinity at work—God, Son, and Holy Spirit. For even Pope John Paul II's own life is testimony to the grace of God in perpetual motion.

As I stand there behind the chain link fence with the other lucky onlookers, I am mesmerized by all the feelings that come over me. The mixture of tension and excitement that is depicted on the faces of the police and paramedics on standby reminds me of the awesome energy in our midst. Yet, there is more. This omnipresent icon had transcended religious dimensions in his global popularity in both ecclesiastical and secular walks. Even if you are not a Catholic, a Christian, or even a believer in God, it is hard not to feel the love that illuminates from His Eminence. There is a feeling of unspoken power that resonates during any event that surrounds this man of holiness. A mere smile from the pontifical leader could soften the hardest of hearts. A warm gaze from his pale blue eyes could capture the affection of anyone in his presence. A humble gesture with his hands could invite even his own would-be assassin to repent and connect through prayer. Now I am experiencing the grace of this fascinating and alluring figure of our times. Who is he . . . and how did he find his passion, purpose, and power?

As the Holy Father describes in *Gift and Mystery*, "Before I formed you in the womb I knew you, and before you were born I consecrated you; I appointed you a prophet to the nations" (Jer 1:5). Again, with inspirational words from the Bible, the pope speaks on purpose:

"So when on certain occasions—for example at Priestly Jubilees—we speak about the priesthood and give our witness, we must do so with great humility, knowing that God 'has called us with a holy calling, not in virtue of our works but in virtue of his own purpose and the grace which he gave us' (2Tim 1:9)."

". . . At its deepest level, every vocation to the priesthood is a great mystery; it is a gift, which infinitely transcends the individual. Every priest experiences this clearly throughout the course of his life. Faced with the greatness of the gift, we sense our own inadequacy. A vocation is a mystery of divine election. 'You did not choose me, but I chose you and appointed you that you should go and bear fruit and that your fruit should abide.' (Jn 15:16)."

So God's plan begins on May 18, 1920, Wadowice, Poland, as Karol Wojtyla is born as the son of Polish father and mother, Karol and Emilia. As all of us experience, the impact that the pope's family life had on his personal development was profound. Emilia raised her sons, Edmund and Karol, with great love, devotion, and joy—even though her health had been compromised during the pregnancies. Although she was saddened by her daughter's tragic death at an early age, Emilia was happy to mother her sons. She often told her friends that her Lolek (affectionate nickname for Karol) would become a great person.

Reading to her beloved Lolek, caring for his well being, and sitting with him in their courtyards as she managed her seamstress livelihood, Emilia delighted in her role as wife and mother. According to the pope himself, as shared in *His Holiness*, at the moment of his birth, his mother asked the midwife to open the window so that the first sounds her newborn son heard would be the singing in honor of Mary, Mother of God. The future pope began his life listening to hymns sung to Mary from the parish church directly across the street.

Emilia had attended a convent school as a girl and cultivated the deep love for God that nourished the Wojtyla family. Yet, sadly enough, Emilia's health would not permit her to realize her dreams to see her Lolek as Vicar of Christ. She died of inflammations to her heart and kidneys when Karol was eight years old and at school. His teacher and neighbor met him in the family courtyard to share the somber news with him. As Karol expresses, "Above all I am grateful to my father, who became a widower at an early age. I had not yet made my First Holy Communion when I lost my mother: I was barely nine years old. So I do not have a clear awareness of her contribution, which must have been great, to my religious training. After her death and, later, the death of my older brother, I was left alone with my father, a deeply religious man. Day after day I was able to observe the austere way in which he lived. By profession he was a soldier and, after my mother's death, his life became one of constant prayer. Sometimes I would wake up during the night and find my father on his knees, just as I would always see him

Pope John Paul II

kneeling in the parish church. We never spoke about a vocation to the priesthood, but his example was in a way my first seminary, a kind of domestic seminary."

Karol Wojtyla would again face the veil of death in an abrupt manner. On February 18, 1941, Karol's father died at home of a grave illness while Karol was out picking up some medicine for his dad. The pope's biographers write that his dad's death drove him deeper into mystical and philosophical reflection. At twenty, he had already lost all the people he loved. His friend Juliusz Kydrynski, described, "I'll never forget that night. I think it was extremely crucial in Karol's life."

So, does not courage fling its hand in the face of the dark? Does not our urge to rise and cast off our outdated shells take on a new force when we are laden with adversity?

In Karol, we witness the shape of times to come as we take this moment to empathize on the depths of his sorrow, fear, and loneliness. At twenty, he was alone . . . with God. Through his own private metamorphosis, he was able to recognize the Lord's hand on his evolution. He was able to benefit from the law of polarity or opposites. Spiritual courage would begin to shape and augment the character of one of the world's greatest leaders.

". . . In a way it [losing my father] was like being uprooted from the soil on which, up to that point, my humanity had grown. But it wasn't a purely negative process. Meanwhile, in fact, a light kept shining more brightly in my consciousness: *the Lord wants me to become a priest*. One day I saw this with great clarity: it was like an inner illumination bringing with it the joy and security of another vocation. And this awareness filled me with great inner peace."

Peace is such an elusive state of being, so connected to the full breath of relaxation and the illumination of knowledge and wisdom. This priest of peace and love would suffer through the scourge of world war, Nazism, Polish Occupation, Communism, Cold War, and, later on, many global atrocities of terrorism.

Pope John Paul II explains, "Certainly, in God's plan nothing happens by chance. All I can say is that the tragedy of the war had its effect on my gradual choice of a vocation. It helped me to understand in a new way the value and importance of a vocation. In the face of the spread of evil and the atrocities of the war, the meaning of the priesthood and its mission in the world became much clearer to me." He also affirms in *Gift and Mystery* that it was not mere chance that amid the overwhelming evil of the war, everything in his personal life was tending towards the good of his vocation.

Karol would take with him into his vocation the disciplines of art, literature, language, philosophy, nature, hiking, skiing, and theatre. Karol would continue to develop in the shadow of great thinkers, theologians and humanists. . . immortalizing their tributes as he embodied them in his own self-development. He would repay past heroes and canonize those blessed humans that were destined to martyrdom and sainthood—breaking all records for his extensive beatification of leaders from all occupations.

Karol's own armor never changed. "Prayer is the only weapon that works," he once replied to a friend during his labor days in the quarry plant of Solvay, Poland. For Karol, prayer and trust in God were the only way to combat evil and violence. They were his tools of courage to fight any onset of fear or temptation. As Vicar, he extolled that above all, one must have certitude and clarity about the truths to be believed and practiced. He felt that if one possesses insecurity, uncertainty, confusion, or contradiction, it would be impossible to build a strong faith.

His calmness and preparedness were clear and certain from the onset of his papal appointment in the new conclave. On the night of October 16, 1978, the Holy Spirit invested enormous strength in Cardinal Karol Wojtyla as the new apostolic successor in the Roman Catholic Church. With warmth, sincerity, and a sensitivity to timing and rapport, the new bridge builder (the translation for the Latin, pontifex) boldly connected to his audience in St. Peter's Square in their own Italian tongue:

"Praised be Jesus Christ! Dear Brothers and Sisters. . . . . . I was afraid to receive this nomination, but I did it in the spirit of obedience to our Lord Jesus Christ and in total confidence in his Mother, the most holy Madonna. I don't know if I can make myself clear in your . . . *our* Italian language. If I make a mistake, you will correct me. . . . . . . And so I present myself to you all, to confess our common faith, our hope, our trust in the Mother of Christ and of the Church, and also to start anew on this road of history and the Church, with the help of God and with the help of men."

From the beginning, Pope John Paul II defied traditions, stepping out as a fit man at home in hiking shoes with youth or with pen in hand. He would write his own bold and provocative speeches, and would continue to publish books, essays, and prose. He certainly broke uncharted waters and unexpected courses, as in the controversial *Love and Responsibility,* published earlier when he was a young Catholic disciple in his priesthood. It conveys a refreshingly candid perspective on the topics of love, sex, and marriage. Diplomatically, he skillfully tilts the tides of politics as he draws nations closer to the ecclesiastical gates of freedom and eternal love, just as his King of Kings taught in his own walk of humanity.

"Be not afraid! Open up, no, swing wide the gates to Christ. Open up to His saving power the confines of the state, open up economic and political systems, the vast empires of culture, civilization, and development," he addressed. This inaugural message and the Holy Father's presence struck a bold chord of welcomed hope and change. This was not going to be a pope of paper, but a pope of people —all people. For Pope John Paul II would truly open his heart to all of humanity. Like Christ, he continually shows respect and deep concern for the dignity of all humankind, regardless, of creed, culture, or race. Pioneering beyond the ecumenical spirit of Christian unity, the new pope moves into a spirit of universality amongst all of humankind. Five months into his pontifical mission, Pope John Paul II published his encyclical *The Redeemer of Man* and poses the following questions:

"Is progress really making life more humane? Is it being matched by an equally vigorous moral and spiritual development?" The pope described the human condition in the contemporary world as "far removed from the objective demands of the moral order; far from the demands of justice; and farther still from charity." He stressed, "even in time of peace, human life is condemned to suffering, as different forms of domination, totalitarianism, neocolonialism, and imperialism inevitably arise. . . . Man cannot live without love. Without love, he remains incomprehensible to himself. His life is devoid of meaning, unless love is revealed to him, unless he encounters love, unless he experiences it and makes it his own, unless he has a lively sense of participation in it."

Before God and the world's inhabitants, Pope John Paul II took an unprecedented and pivotal turn in stated defense of all religions and the rights of man. In his impervious nature, the papal leader would take his office and immediately command respect from everyone. The successor of Pope John XXIII and Pope Paul VI spoke in the name of all the nations whose rights had been violated and forgotten expressing, ". . . Freedom of religion for everyone and for all peoples must be respected by everyone everywhere." Solidarity with humanity and opposition to intolerance would soon become household concepts within the Holy See. Pope John Paul II encouraged the defense of persecuted neighbors as an act of charity. He felt that the international community had the same right and duty toward any nation that had been attacked—and as a last resort to defend the innocent nation by the force of arms.

No stranger to the political powers of covert intelligence and executive authorities, the Holy Father became a powerful instrument of diplomatic authority alongside U.S. President Ronald Reagan during the fall of Communism in the 1980's. They had a rare common understanding on the dangers of global leadership. Both leaders had experienced assassination attempts during their public lives and they both felt that their lives were spared in the name of the freedoms they pursued for the world. In that spirit, the two men worked quietly, but effectively to aid freedom movements in the communist states of eastern Europe, particularly with the labor organization solidarity within the pope's native Poland. The moral, financial and intelligence assistance that the pope and the president provided to this cause were vital to the victories they achieved for democracy. Ultimately, their united efforts freed millions of Europeans from communist rule.

The new millenium became the pope's jubilee era in which he vowed to bring humanity closer to God. The Holy Father ignited a flame of spiritual renewal throughout the world. All of these visions have directed the pope's eyes to great horizons and landscapes. . . attracting more and more of us deeper into our spiritual faiths.

He is a leader who reveals the grace of God through his own ministry of spiritual courage. This courage with which the vicar of Christ breathes his day is in part a testimony to his own surrender of self and also, of course, to the divine works of the Holy Spirit—the third in the Trinity of the Catholic church. Karol Wojtyla had been preparing all along and grew into his own greatness through his ordinary events of life, as well as through his turbulent times of deep, emotional strife. Yet, above all, Pope John Paul II, often times coined as the pope of surprises, quickly embraced his powerful instrument of faith in breaking through new horizons. The modern day pope learned how to maximize the power of the media and a personal audience. Even to this day, the eighty-two year old pontificate in his twenty-fourth year of leadership has never relented in his quest to appeal to the humanistic side of life. "Be not afraid!" consoles His Holiness. Such a man of humble beginnings certainly had many occasions to be afraid and have a heart broken by the trials of life and people. Yes, he, like all of us, has had to overcome his own trepidation, weaknesses, and undesirable circumstances. Yet, because he trusts and believes in the invisible leader of leaders, Karol can carry on boldly and "be not afraid."

On one of his missions, the pope described, "As a steward of God's mysteries, the priest is a special witness to the Invisible in the world. For he is a steward of invisible and priceless treasures belonging to the spiritual and supernatural order. As a steward of these treasures, the priest is always in special contact with the holiness of God. . . . God's majesty is the majesty of Holiness."

As I sit here writing these words on the edge of the torn day of September 11, 2001, I contemplate on this great leader's wisdom. His messages—both early on and those of recent days—ring like a resounding wake-up call. Even at the brink of disaster and the dawn of a new war on terrorism, the world can find enormous encouragement in the passion of Karol's purposeful life. In the pope's *Crossing the Threshold of Hope*, I have discovered new visions, new territories, and new evidence that assure us of the goodness in the divine order. I share with you some of his poignant and relevant thoughts.

"At the end of the second millennium, we need, perhaps more than ever, the words of the Risen Christ: 'Be not afraid!' Man who, even after the fall of Communism, has not stopped being afraid and who truly has many reasons for feeling this way, needs to hear these words. Nations need to hear them. ...Peoples and nations of the entire world need to hear these words. Their conscience needs to grow in the certainty that Someone exists who holds in His hands the destiny of this passing world; Someone who holds the keys to death and the netherworld; Someone who is the Alpha and the Omega of human history—be it the individual or collective history. And this Someone is Love—Love that became man, Love crucified and risen, Love unceasingly present among men. It is Eucharistic Love. It is the infinite source of communion. He alone can give the ultimate assurance when He says, 'Be not afraid!'

"You observe that contemporary man finds it hard to return to faith because he is afraid of the moral demands that faith makes upon him. And this, to a certain degree, is the truth. The Gospel is certainly demanding. We know that Christ never permitted His disciples and those who listened to Him to entertain any illusions about this. ...At the same time, however, He reveals that His demands never exceed man's abilities. If man accepts these demands with an attitude of faith, he will also find in the grace that God never fails to give him the necessary strength to meet those demands. The world is full of proof of the saving and redemptive power that the Gospels proclaim with even greater frequency than they recall demands of the moral life. How many people there are in the world whose daily lives attest to the possibility of living out the morality of the Gospel!

"To accept the Gospel's demands means to affirm all of our humanity, to see in it the beauty desired by God, while at the same time recognizing, in light of the power of God Himself, our weaknesses as according to Luke 18:27: 'What is impossible for men is possible for God.' . . . It is very important to cross the threshold of hope, not to stop before it, but to let oneself be led."

◆

Within the heart of each man, woman, and child lies the voice of God . . . through Love. Through our trust in ourselves as being created in the likeness of God, we can achieve God's desire for us to give of ourselves to others. We can become mirrors of love in our own noble acts of courage. Therefore, I say, thank you, O Holy Father, for your reflection of genuine love. For your love will be indelibly engraved on our hearts as your timeless imprint on humanity!

◆ ◆ ◆

Steve Barnhill with Bridges International Sacred Art by Makk Family

Courage is rising above yourself in such a way that you didn't think was even possible.

To live life on the edge . . . rather than in the safety of the middle.

—Steve Barnhill

*Steve Barnhill with Bridges
International Sacred Art
by Makk Family*

CHAPTER FIVE
Courage In Spirit

Steve Barnhill

The Courage to Become a Player on God's Team

> **Courage is rising above yourself in such a way that you didn't think was even possible. To live life on the edge . . . rather than in the safety of the middle.**
> **—Steve Barnhill**

Rising above the majestic Rocky Mountains, lies a place where the heavens and the earth become seamless. The golden sun casts its radiance down on a lovely alpine valley. The site almost appears surreal. As if on the wings of a dove, we set our senses for a vision of the horizon's edge . . . Bridges International. For on this landscape, the words, "Peace on Earth; Goodwill toward Men" ring true and the surroundings transform into a thriving sanctuary of commerce and artistic inspiration.

Courage in Spirit

As the pure white dove glides closer, we capture the vision of a lush setting of wooden bridges crossing ponds and streams while we hear the pleasant sounds of flowing waters. Botanical gardens spread hues of green, gold and brown with accents of red and blue. Truly, this is a place where both people and wildlife can rest their weary heads and take comfort in the serenity. This is a place where the birds and the angels can both sing their songs of sweet joy. Mirrors of love ...are seen from above. Still, as we sweep in closer, we capture the vision. On the wings of our sweet dove, we beseech the austere home of the Bridges Institute. O and what a remarkable sight! We see human beings from all different cultures and creed—White, Black, Oriental, Middle Eastern, Christians, Muslims, Jews, Hindus, Buddhists, and many others—young and old, famous and everyday—all coming together in the enchanting spirit of mutual respect and interest in their differences...and their oneness.

The stately entrance introduces the natural and open-aired architecture of the Institute. The massive doors into the circular atrium welcome visitors who desire to open their minds and hearts to a spiritual and artistic tour of five of the most noted religions on Earth, God's homeland for humanity: Christianity, Judaism, Islam, Buddhism, and Hinduism. Quietly we soak in the beauty of the many, unique differences in each religion as we pass through the five majestic arches. Each one leads us over a bridge into a breathtaking experience of religious education and cultural exchange. Beautiful wall hangings in vivid colors of gold, red, blue, green, white, and black catch our eye. Our senses soak in something new and we become someone greater giving back to somebody else. This cycle—something new making something greater for somebody else—expands our communion with the divine goodness of the universe in the likeness and loveliness of the Divine Creator, our all-loving God. O the beauty of it all!

Steve Barnhill

Suddenly, our eyes capture the rich textures evoked in the sacred art portrayed throughout the five bridges of Faith. We hear the sounds of symphonic harps and violins while cultural dances beckon us to move and connect with our brothers and sisters in celebration. We celebrate our distinct, yet communal, spirit of worship to the Almighty One. We glorify Him for the many gifts of splendor he has bestowed upon us through our humanity. We take in the creative prose as we glean the literary works presented by writers of all perspectives. We refresh in the tastes and scents of freshly, prepared foods and beverages that offer us—once more—an aperitif to a new way to the joie de vie, the joy of life.

"So," you ask, "Where exactly is this lovely institute of bridges?" At this writing, it exists only in the imagination of its founder and supporters. However, all imaginative seeds nurtured by God's love will eventually sprout into full-blown reality, as the laws of the Universe continue to unfold. With pride and great anticipation, I unveil to you the seeds of creation for Bridges International from the mind, heart, and spirit of the man behind its vision, a man that I have grown to admire deeply, the president of Bridges International, Steve Barnhill.

Initially, I met Steve through our parish's pastor, Father Bill Breslin. Father Bill suggested that I might enjoy meeting his friend, Steve Barnhill, once Father Bill became acquainted with my vision for *Mirrors of Love*. Again, I observed the Lord in motion in strange and marvelous ways as he shapes the world through his Divine Providence in all of its splendor and grandeur.

I met Steve over lunch at a cosmopolitan restaurant in downtown Denver. I knew within minutes of our conversation that Steve was a man on a mission. I knew that he was someone that I wanted to know and help in his quest. As a natural promoter, I also knew that I wanted to study with him and share my experience. After all, it is not every day that I stumble on a former, professional baseball player gone successful corporate executive who decides to leave it all for the opportunity to blaze a trail...for God.

Standing over six feet tall with hazel eyes and brown hair, Steve has an attractive, commanding presence. Just ask Darlene Garlutzo, the woman of his dreams, his loving wife and high school sweetheart. "I believe that I loved her all along," he confides, although they moved in different directions in their individual lives before they became united as man and wife.

Yet, by the time that Steve rekindled the flame in his heart for Darlene, he had been married three times. "Darlene has had such an impact of love on me that my life's journey has been forever transformed," Steve expressed openly to me with pride gleaming in his face.

So, on a beautiful fall day in Colorado, Steve revealed to me just how much his life had been transformed in the past few years. Starting with the dramatic events that led up to his life with Darlene, Steve shares a candid and humble tale of real life.

On an earlier path, Steve would have been easily recognized as the successful executive on the corporate ladder. Even earlier, Steve was recognized as a professional athlete in the minor leagues of baseball. However, the Steve Barnhill of today, the visionary for Bridges International, is a man of deeper purpose who is willing to risk being vulnerable and follow an uncharted path under the leadership of his new leader—the voice of God.

Born on June 2, 1948 in the same humble town in Missouri as Mark Twain, Steve credited his solid foundation in life back to his beginnings. "My parents were always very supportive and encouraging," Steve remarked tenderly. "Dad was a great salesman. I suppose that has helped me in my sales career," he chuckled. Steve was also blessed

Steve Barnhill

with considerable athletic skills, and he became an all-star baseball player, eventually signing a professional contract in the minor leagues with the San Francisco Giants. Unfortunately, his baseball career as an outfielder (1968-72) was cut short because of a knee injury after four seasons. Undaunted, he quickly shifted gears, diving full force into the business world. It was in the health supplements industry that Steve eventually discovered his own knack for sales. In 1980, Steve landed a lucrative position as the vice president for the well-known bodybuilder Joe Wieder.

"Cheri, I had the proverbial, Corporate America lifestyle. I'll be very honest with you, I am not proud of it," he began. He caught my curiosity and without any hesitations, Steve poured out his past—the good, the bad, and the ugly.

"I quickly learned how to master the money and power game. I moved from five figures into six figures and began to live the fast-paced, executive's lifestyle. I had moved from the Midwest to the southwest and finally, ended up in Los Angeles—not what I would call the city of angels. By now, I was in my third marriage and failing miserably as I had fallen prey to the temptations of an office affair. While I was living a life dominated by the flesh and material rewards, I began to feel a sense of emptiness growing inside of me. In fact, this feeling was beginning to take form as a bleeding ulcer," he confided. Steve looked down in a sobering pause for a moment. I could feel a shift in his life about to unfold in his very personal journey down memory lane.

"I can still recall the morning with vivid detail that changed my life forever," he continued. "It was actually a beautiful day in Southern California. I was about to begin another business trip, full of hotels, deals, dining, wine, and women. I was barely involved with my wife and, not surprisingly, the marriage simply vanished. We were living separate lives. I remember being in the shower and hanging my head down because I had a terrible feeling inside about beginning this cycle again. I was not at all happy and actually becoming very sick of my lifestyle. Apparently, my body was sick of it all, too. I started to cough and noticed that I was coughing up blood. I cleaned up and got scared as I looked at myself in the mirror. Who was this man and where was I heading in my life? The success of the corporate lifestyle that only represented money and power—day in and day out—was draining rather than rejuvenating my spirit. I began to realize that if we are all either growing or dying in life that I was on the wrong side of the cycle and . . . dying from the inside out," Steve revealed sincerely.

I interrupted with a question that I felt was appropriate. "Steve, I have to ask you, was your faith in God alive during all of this stress?" I queried. Steve chuckled as he replies, "Cheri, although my folks raised me with a good Lutheran foundation, the only praying that I was doing revolved around "Hail Marys" while watching Sunday football games. Seriously though, I believe I had lost my way and lost my connection with my own spiritual voice and with God." I recap, "Here you are, Steve, living in the fast lane preparing to ramp it all up again and you're in the shower spitting up blood. Let me ask you again, did you think then about talking to God?"

Steve's big hazel eyes widened as he looked directly at me and leaned forward as he whispered, "You bet I did." In fact, all of a sudden, that morning while I was shaving I felt an impulse to make a big decision. Rather than move in the original direction, I decided to make a defining telephone call to the president of the firm and tell him that I resigned at that moment. Then, I went for a walk around the lake within my condominium complex. Immediately, I started to feel better ...freer ...more alive. My stomach began to settle down and I felt more at ease with myself again. It was here that I began to pray again and look within for the voice of God. Now, I realize that the Holy Spirit had prompted me through the impulse that I felt to make the call. Once the decision was made to resign, everything else in my life began to fall into place, and new doors started to open for me."

"Did strange and marvelous things begin to happen?" I asked knowing all too well, how Divine Providence reveals itself in the tapestry of life. Steve smiled confidently, yet humbly and replied, "Oh, yes." Enter Darlene, the woman truly behind this man.

Steve continued, "I called my mother happily informing her that I'm coming back home to Colorado." Steve's parents had relocated from the Midwest to Colorado in his earlier days and his mom had survived his dad. "I packed up, cut my Los Angeles ties, and drove to Colorado. I felt great, golfed, relaxed, reflected, and rekindled an acquaintance with a woman for which I had a crush during high school. Her name was Darlene. Once we became serious, she made it clear to me that I would have to convert to Catholicism if our relationship was going to blossom into marriage. From there, a series of cathartic events led to my genuine retribution with my former wives, along with the proper annulments of those marriages. I sent letters of apologies to all of my previous wives and began to repair my relationship with my daughter. It's a process, but our relationship is growing as we get closer and closer," he confides to me. Steve's heart was revealed in his face now as we spoke further. Color and radiance illuminated his complexion as he expressed his affections for cherished loved ones.

"Along with this, my love for God emerged and began to grow very deeply and fervently. I am also pleased to say that Darlene and I were finally married in the Catholic Church on September 2, 1994," he highlighted. Then, with a sly grin on his face, he remarked, "I might add that upon Darlene's insistence, our engagement period turned into a period of old-fashioned sexual abstinence. Considering my past patterns, I guess Darlene knew just what God needed of me," Steve concluded sheepishly.

The inner strength and self-discipline that was required of Steve during this time steeled himself, strengthening the love that he had felt for his wife, his daughter and new stepdaughters, and for his new CEO, Jesus Christ. Personally, I was touched by the humility that I could sense from this man's powerful persona. Still an attractive, well-built man of corporate savvy, I am certain that Steve could contract a successful business negotiation without even trying. So, how did he become the CEO and president of such a spiritually driven vision such as Bridges International?

"Two people have influenced this turning point in my life: Monsignor Robert Hoffman and Father Bill Breslin. I met both of them as I was studying to become a Catholic," he shared. He continues, "I'll never forget Monsignor's insight to me during my R.C.I.A. classes [Rite of Christian Initiation of Adults]. He called me over to look at the portraits of all of the popes displayed in the corridor. As we walked together, he said to me, 'Steve, you know you were good when you were in sports and you always wanted to be on the best team, right?' 'Sure', I replied. Monsignor Hoffman retorted as he placed his arm on my shoulder, 'Welcome to the best team of them all . . . God's team. Are we clear now, Steve?' I replied affirmatively, 'Very'. I never looked back after that, Cheri," Steve remarked with utmost certainty.

"Beyond firming up my Catholic faith, Father Bill woke me up to my mission and passion to serve on God's team. The opportunity to impact society with positive images of sacred art and an education into other religions presented itself and stirred the passion within my soul to make a difference to others. I realized that my gifts in business and other areas would come to the table now in following my love to serve God and my fellow man. Bridges International became my new mission and passion," he said with a big smile and a sparkle in his eyes.

I anxiously asked him more questions about the vision and objectives of the Bridges Institute. Bringing the good

Steve Barnhill

news of Christianity, Judaism, Hinduism, Islam, and Buddhism to the forefront of secular America, especially post September 11, seemed more important than ever.

"The for-profit mission for Bridges International is to re-acquaint the marketplace with sacred art, commissioned by some of the best artists in the world. I am pleased to say that three breathtaking paintings are already available for the public. On the non-profit side, we will create the Institute. Of course, the vision here is to embrace the five traditional religions of the world and develop an atmosphere for mutual respect and understanding for our unique differences and common bonds. 'Ask and ye shall receive—seek and ye shall find,' commands the Bible. It is all coming to pass and now it is time for me to use the talents that I received from God and pay him back by dedicating my life to Him," Steve remarked with clarity in his voice.

"You see, Cheri, for a long time I chose the easy life—what many perceive as the good life. It was ego-driven, material, and empty. Once I chose the life that God designed for me, the void was filled immediately with meaning, passion, and purpose. Now, I want to serve the Lord and make a difference within humanity. I believe that I have been called upon to pioneer Bridges International and it will be my legacy to mankind. I consider it an honor and a privilege to do my best to fulfill this vision," Steve concluded.

In closing, I asked Steve what advice he would offer to Corporate America. Steve replied, "For starters, Corporate America needs to change their thinking from me to us. If they can focus on a win/win cooperative strategy rather than a win/lose competitive strategy, then everyone ultimately wins. I believe that is how our forefathers originally set up the democratic process of capitalism. Somehow, we've gotten away from the genuine ideals that really work! Secondly, they [Corporate Americans] need to pray."

Courage in Spirit

I asked Steve his thoughts on facing fears and overcoming challenges and . . . on courage. He responded, "When I keep allowing myself to put this adventure of life in God's hands and pray daily for the strength to glorify Him, then my focus shifts and He leads me. Sure, I'm on the edge most days, yet I always see the vision within reach. I have the faith now and absolutely nothing can stop me."

Indeed, nothing can stop a man on a mission who is guided by the Light of God, the Son, and the Holy Spirit. Steve Barnhill's conviction was glowing throughout his being. I felt a surge of contagious enthusiasm rush within me as I listened to his fascinating tale of truth and discovery. Certainly, Steve's mission will be profoundly useful and yet, no easy task to accomplish in these confusing times. Yet, with the wings of the Holy Spirit leading the way, I am confident that the vision for our tomorrows will become today's new realities.

O I do see that light blazing radiantly within the hearts of the Barnhill family. I am ever thankful to the Lord, Father Bill, and my parish Sacred Heart of Jesus, for guiding the light of Love and Truth upon me so that I may share this gracious family with you. God bless you, Steve, and God bless this beautiful planet Earth, the homeland for God's children. See you all on the wings of the doves flying toward Bridges International!

◆ ◆ ◆

Steve Barnhill

The Five Traditional Religions of the World

Buddhism was founded in India about 500 BC by a teacher called Buddha and has been a dominant force in most of Asia with about 350 million followers. Buddha (originally Siddhartha Gautama) preached that existence was a continuing cycle of death and rebirth. He said that people could break out of the cycle by eliminating any attachment to worldly things, gaining a state of peace and happiness, coined *nirvana*.

Christianity was founded about 30 AD and based on Christ's life and teachings with almost 2 billion followers and denominations established as Roman Catholic, Protestant, or Eastern Orthodox. Christians believe there is one God who sent His only son, Jesus, into the world as the Savior. Christianity teaches that humanity can achieve salvation through Jesus and his model of a virtuous life. Faith in a peaceful eternity, Heaven, derives from the Christian belief that Jesus resurrected and conquered death.

Hinduism dates back to prehistoric times with roots and cultural influence in India with over 750 million followers. Hinduism has basic beliefs about divinities such as life after death and personal conduct that are part of one universal spirit called Brahman. Hindus worship both living and dead men as saints such as yogis (men who practice yoga) or gurus (spiritual teachers), along with certain animals.

Islam was founded by the Prophet Muhammad after 600 AD and has over 1.1 billion followers called Muslims, originating in the Middle East. The central concept is *Tawhid*, the oneness of God. Muslims believe that children are born without sin and can lead themselves to salvation based on their life's actions once God has shown them the way through the revealed books of God's messengers.

Judaism is the oldest religion, founded during the time of Abraham with over 15 million followers named Jews. Both Christianity and Islam developed from Judaism, teaching the belief in one God. The basic laws and teachings of Judaism come from the Torah, the first five books of the Hebrew Bible, which is what Christians call the Old Testament. Judaism teaches that a person serves God by studying and practicing the scriptures. Jews, like Christians, believe that all people are created in the image of God and deserve to be treated with dignity and respect. Jews still await a Messiah or Messianic Age here on Earth.

AP/Lepri/Vatican

Jesus will use you to accomplish great things on the condition that you believe much more in his love than in your weakness. Only then, His hand will be free with you.

—Mother Teresa

*Mother Teresa with
Princess Diana at Missionaries
of Charity, New York*

CHAPTER SIX
Courage In Spirit

Mother Teresa

The Courage to Embrace Humility in Leadership

> Jesus will use you to accomplish great things
> on the condition that you believe much more in
> his love than in your weakness. Only then,
> His hand will be free with you.
> —Mother Teresa

In your grand shadow, our Mother of the Poor, Teresa, I bow in honor of your unquenchable thirst, your unbridled determination, your fierce desire to extend your purpose far beyond the imagination's limits.

The world stood speechless in 1998 as we absorbed the realities of your death. We were already stunned and grief-stricken by the disastrous tragedy that occurred that week with Princess Diana. Our hearts were ripped apart and raw with anguish. Hearing that you were intending to be at Princess Diana's funeral drove the feeling that our Blessed Mother, Mary, would indeed embody your presence with the comfort that we all craved in those hours of sadness.

Then the tiny footsteps stopped walking on earth. Our precious Mother Teresa had also passed from our physical experiences. We no longer had a little woman in our daily glimpse as she stoically moved mountains for the poor and rich alike. No more did we have her physical inspiration. No small loss that in one-week's time, the modern world lost two women who epitomized timeless courage in its finest valor.

Mother Teresa, you always spoke to us in such gentle yet certain words. Your undying mission to reach the poorest of poor ignited your spirit and the universe. Your exemplary acts to seek fulfillment in your quest called for every ounce of your strength. To remain steadfast and calm in the face of calamity and adversity had to require an unquestionable level of belief in your self, your purpose and, above all, your Creator. Through your stamina and calming reproach, we learned to lift our hearts from our own imprisonment and begin to believe in the good that we must share with our own weak, our own poor. We must embrace your living message and continue in your footsteps to believe in our own capacity to spread our desires for a better world. In this journey, we shall hold the hand of those calling us for help. Thank you dear Mother Teresa, Mother of the Poor, our mother of truest abundance —of Hope, Joy and Love.

Mother Teresa, you lived tirelessly in your desire to reach the poorest of poor. However, we see that your crusade does not end with the poor in health or monetary wealth. It only begins there and must carry on even in those individuals with heavy pocketbooks such as we have seen in the white-collar crime of corporations. Your model of courage and compassion is duly needed in today's world for the poor in spirit who

Mother Teresa

cry for renewal in their heart, mind, and soul. It begins within each of us in our own capacity to give and receive infinite love . . . especially when we are tired or afraid.

How did you, O Mother of Hearts, break through the doubts and fears that must have teased you as you were a young woman? How did you develop your inner voice calling you to rise and stand tall in the face of poverty-stricken India? How did you grow the whispers of your brave heartedness into triumphant roars of saintly heroism? How did you deny the distractions of anxiety and fatigue from penetrating your indomitable bravado?

Mother Teresa, when you were just a young girl in Yugoslavia, you not only listened to your inner voice to become a Catholic nun, you also heard and responded to a calling . . . to help the poor. Moreover, you continued to receive the Spirit within, when you felt an urge to establish a new order of nuns in India that would serve . . . the poorest of the poor. Even as a youth, you exemplified the miraculous power that is available to all of us when we simply let go and let God.

Persevering gracefully with your vision to begin the Order of the Missionaries of Charity in 1947 to nourish the neediest, you attracted both compliment and attack from the world around in politics, religion, entertainment, and all other lifestyles. Mother Teresa, you once said, "In these twenty years of work among the people, I have come more and more to realize that it is being unwanted that is the worst disease that any human being can ever experience." Certainly, you have made many, many people feel wanted in the courage of your compassion.

In being awarded the Nobel Peace Prize in 1979, Mother Teresa, you replied, "I accept the prize in the name of the poor. The prize is the recognition of the poor world. Jesus said, 'I am hungry, I am naked, I am homeless.' By serving the poor, I am serving Him." By your model of strength, we are able to witness the joy that you experience in your love for humanity—an experience that is available to everyone—because you see Christ within every human being. You see the radiating joy of love even in the faces of the hungriest of children who have been satisfied with the tiniest portions of rice. I have seen that joy reflected in your face, Mother Teresa, as you cradle the face of your neighbor in your loving hands. You have shown the world that all individuals are deserving of respect and recognition, regardless of their stature in life. In your Nobel Lecture, you reminded us to love until it hurts, to meet each other with a smile. You reminded us, ". . . I believe that love begins at home, and if we can create a home for the poor – I think that more and more love will spread. And we will be able through this understanding love to bring peace, be the good news to the poor. The poor in our own family first, in our country, and in the world."

In 1972, the President of the Republic of India said of you, "Mother Teresa is one of those liberated souls who have transcended all barriers presented by race, religion, and nationality. In our present-day troubled world, incessantly plagued by conflict and hatred, the life that is lived and the work that is carried out by people like Mother Teresa bring new hope for the future of mankind." No words could be more true, even thirty years later, when the world continues to struggle with the conflicts of evil versus good, outer versus inner beauty, pleasure over happiness, and personality before character. Your spirit of drive continues to nourish our soul, and invite more of us to realize that the path to truth is within us all through love.

O Mother of the truly rich, how you showed us the way to courage in your pious acts of thoughtfulness. Your grand shadow is ever so present and our lives are fuller, our hearts warmer, and our spirits higher . . . because of your vision.

◆ ◆ ◆

Denny Nauman

Courage is having the willpower to do something out of your comfort zone . . . to grow and overcome the fears inside of us.

—Crystal E. Lutton

Denny Nauman

Crystal E. Lutton
"Mirrors of Love"

CHAPTER SEVEN
Courage In Spirit

Crystal Elizabeth Lutton

The Courage To Trust the Inner Voice of God

> **Courage is having the willpower to do something out of your comfort zone . . . to grow and overcome the fears inside of us.**
> **—Crystal E. Lutton**

"Hi, girls and boys. My name is Mrs. Lutton and I am substituting for Crystal this morning. Crystal is snowboarding today at Copper Mountain with her dad," I announced to the first grade children attending religious education after Sunday morning Mass at Sacred Heart of Jesus Church in Boulder, Colorado.

I looked around the room for a moment at all the big eyes staring at me, awaiting signs of their approval of me. From the far right side, I caught the attention of a well-dressed boy with brown hair who raised his hand and rather shyly stood while he announced, "I have a Christmas present for you to give to Crystal from me, Mrs. Lutton." "Well, thank you," I replied and asked, "And what is your name?" He walked up to me, handed me the nicely wrapped gift, smiled, and replied, "My name is Sam and I gave her a present last year, too. She's really nice." I am beaming with pride now as I continued this conversation expressing, "I am sure she'll really appreciate this gift, Sam." All at once, two girls in the front row raised their hands as if their life depended on being heard. "Yes?" I queried. The first little girl stood quite emphatically and exclaimed, "I like Crystal, too. She's been my teacher for two years." Then the other young student jumped up to stand, abruptly adding with a big smile, "I hope Crystal has fun snowboarding ...she's pretty." I glanced around the room and noticed other heads bobbing in agreement. I realized that I had quite an act to follow and suddenly I came to a peaceful discovery. Try as I may, I could not fill the shoes of my sixteen-year-old daughter in the hearts of these young fans. Crystal Elizabeth Lutton had become a charismatic young leader. . . for God.

Children flocked around Crystal—no small secret to me. A beautiful young lady—inside and out—with her golden brown hair, strong 5'2" stature, and pure complexion, Crystal radiates her playful zest for life and love. With her warm heart, pretty smile, and genuine love for honesty and innocence, it is no surprise that my teenage daughter would capture the admiration of anyone, least of all, children.

"They're so cute, Mom!" Crystal remarked as we casually strolled arm-in-arm along with my nine-year-old son, Steven, to our car on another Sunday morning after their bible classes. Looking up at the spectacular view of the rugged Flatirons of Boulder (foothills actually named because of their flat iron shapes) serving as a backdrop to the picturesque valley, I admired the dramatic steeple of our

Crystal E. Lutton

church in the foreground. With all of this natural beauty, I could not help but marvel at the rich memories that I have savored throughout the years here with Crystal.

From her Baptism, Communion, and now Confirmation, Crystal's life has become fundamentally woven into the fabric of God's home. My husband, Steve, and I even have the memory of her five-year-old presence in our wedding here. I can still see the brown horse and white carriage out in front of church on that gorgeous sunny June day with the blue and gold balloons flying up and around the green leaves of the oak trees. I can still hear the laughter of the family and friends celebrating in front of church and see them waving to greet us with big smiles of joy as we step into the carriage, now as husband and wife. I can still feel the rings carried by our young ring bearer, our niece Krystal. I can still smell the fragrance of flowers from our little flower girl, our daughter, Crystal. Both of these young girls were dressed like princesses in gold satin gowns with royal blue sashes and flower wreaths crowning their golden locks. As they stepped up and into the tall carriage, they would join us for a romantic and memorable ride of new beginnings around the charming town of Boulder. The memory of this beautiful scene lingers on as clear as ever for me. Crystal and I earned that day together.

As a single mother never married, I had the privilege and responsibility of raising Crystal on my own for her first four years. I had been engaged to a man who was not right for me, but instead from that relationship, I became pregnant and received the blessing of my daughter. Although I had help from family and friends, ultimately, Crystal and I only had each other. It was fun, but it was tough. I had to be a responsible mother, fill the role of father, and maintain a full-time career. Yet, amidst it all, I felt that it deepened my beliefs that dreams do come true. I had wished for a daughter in my life, just like Crystal. It was worth the wait then—

for what she and I consider her true dad—to eventually come into our lives.

Steve chose to adopt Crystal soon after our marriage and prove to her that his commitment to her as a dad was just as real and forever as his promise to me in our marriage vows. Crystal was certainly meant to be a Lutton and the bond that has grown between all of us is immeasurable. So began a chapter that would shape our daughter's character into the woman that God designed within her heart. God's voice would remain strong within Crystal, and her courage would carry her to great heights.

"My life isn't mine. Everything that I have is from God. What he asks of me is to live my life as Christ would live in this day . . . to learn how to listen to his voice," Crystal shared with me reflectively one day as I probed her for deeper insight to share in this book. "Listening to my inner voice, the voice of God within me has helped me to stay away from peer pressure. My faith has helped me to make better choices and be more aware of the path that I am on and to follow it one way. I am stronger about not straying onto other paths," Crystal continued while we were enjoying a pleasant conversation in the sunshine of our backyard last summer. We spoke of friends and mentors that she admires. "I look up to my friend Laura [Peverley] for her quiet leadership, her individuality and her strong faith in Christ," added Crystal with a look of radiance in her face. She always lights up at the sounds of her friends' names. This comes, as no surprise to me since one of the first words that Crystal ever uttered was, "Hi!" Crystal has always loved people and it has been consistently noted by all of her teachers during school conferences. Crystal remarked about another friend, "I also look up to Melissa [Montoya] as my big sister. I respect how she has kept herself real throughout high school without the need for popular and superficial acceptance." She giggled as she added, "Oh, John [Solis] is a great mentor, too. I really admire his leadership qualities and sense of self-confidence." I smiled in gratitude for the great friends that Crystal has attracted in her life. She added more seriously, "Of course, you and Dad are my mentors. You give us our family life, our values. You are involved with our lives and are willing to be a friend to Steven and myself. Yet, you set the rules, so I know my limits." Certainly, this is not the typical conversation that one would expect from a teenager living in twenty-first century America. It was not always this pleasant either.

When Crystal was thirteen, she was struggling with choices, her attitude, and was not—shall I say nicely—as appreciative of our parental guidance. We tried our best, but nothing was going right. In fact, everything we said or did was moving us in the wrong direction. If you are a parent, you get the picture. If you are not, trust me, times were tough. We did not feel that Crystal was associating with friends that had similar values to ours and she did not understand or agree with us. Finally, after much prayer, careful deliberation, research, and anguish, Steve and I felt that Crystal would benefit from the guidance of professional leaders in personal development. We decided to enroll her in an academy in Utah that specialized in outdoor education as the key to understanding the natural consequences for one's actions. Sun Hawk Academy had a reputation for being very effective in opening up teenagers who may not necessarily be involved in any issues other than behavioral struggles and poor-choice-patterns. Although it was a tremendously tough decision for us as parents, we felt that a summer and fall program at Sun Hawk would provide Crystal with priceless experiences for life. We believed that she would gain tools in a safe environment that she could use in finding the courage to listen to her own wisdom and counsel in choosing the right path.

We prayed that our hunches were true. We missed our daughter. Steven missed his sister. Yet, as parents we knew that we had to sacrifice our own lifestyle in order to provide Crystal a unique time in her young life. Crystal was clearly troubled and acting out in behaviors that would only cause harm to her, us, and potentially others. She had closed the three of us out. It was our family's worst crisis. These were the toughest times we had ever lived as parents and as human beings. We had to let go and let God. We prayed more and we waited more. . . .

"Mom, I really appreciate you, Dad, and Steven—and I love to pray! God has been so good to me and I feel so close to him now. I love my friends and family at Sun Hawk Academy, especially Doc, Dean, Joji, and Melissa who cared enough about me to be honest with me and help me work through my stuff. Sun Hawk will always be closely tucked in my heart. Mom, they are really doing great things for teenagers. I am so glad that you and Dad loved me enough to help me," Crystal expressed with exuberance during that summer.

I have treasured these words from our brave daughter since she began to open herself up to us again. I found out that when children shut out their parents, it is a cue for parents to step out of their comfort zones and take risks of growth, which will eventually re-earn children's respect for their parents and vice versa. It was not enough for us to express our love for Crystal. We needed to show her through our actions. That action did not require enabling, but it did require some tough love and large extensions of our own courage, our commitment to truth, our faith in goodness, our willingness to grow, our ability to forgive and most of all, our love and belief in God.

Through the grace of God and our genuine interest for freedom embraced with responsibility, we recognized a critical opportunity proactively rather than reactively. Even so, parenthood in today's society remains an awesome challenge with all of the temptations of freedom without responsibility. As parents, we are not an island. Our children need us, and we need them. Together, as a close-knit family unit, we can move mountains . . . as long as we believe in the power of unconditional love to conquer evil. Through our daily actions, we, the adults, can show our children the way of goodness and fun, the way of God, the way of Heaven on Earth.

Today, Crystal is like a young attractive flower blossoming with the fragrant essence of joy, hope, and vitality in the air. Her roots are firmly grounded in a clear vision of the true character that she desires to nurture and yield. Although there may be bumps, forks, and windy turns each day, Crystal has the strength of her convictions to guide her life's journey.

"My gift is singing, Mom," Crystal expressed sincerely one day and added, "I've gotten so many signs from God. My singing has touched others. I love to sing and I want to inspire other kids to find God, especially those that don't know God at all. Besides, it's fun!"

Crystal sings regularly at sporting events at her school, Holy Family Catholic High School, and she is involved in their choir and theatre department. Crystal has become serious about her academic interests. She is a leader at our parish youth group and sings in their newly formed choir. Together, Crystal and I have written many songs and hope to launch her singing career with her own vocals on the theme song and CD for this book. I know that Crystal's divine heart has led her to sing beautiful songs of praise and glory for the world. My whole being shivers with emotion and clarity as I listen to her sing so beautifully of her passions of life. As her mom, I feel a great sense of joy and pride.

What truly moves me when I watch my daughter go through her day now is her desire to grow . . . to learn . . . to reach out . . . and to sharpen her sense of who she is and own her values. Closer yet, I really admire Crystal's courage to search for her spiritual voice. She yearns for God, and, as parents, this fills us with joy! As Crystal so eloquently states in one of her school papers:

"A lot of times we get caught up with temptation in the world and believe that true happiness comes from all the things you can physically touch, taste, feel or hear. We tend to only believe it if someone else experiences it also. What I personally think is that Jesus wants us to know that we just need to look inside ourselves and ask for God. He doesn't just come to you because you are his. He loves you and with that love, he gave us free will. He wants us to come to him first. He doesn't want to prove himself to get our love in return; He wants us to have Faith.

"Just like with our relationships with family, friends and boyfriends or girlfriends, we're happiest with each other when the other person believes in us for who we are. So God wants to be loved for the love he gives to us and wants us to know him because we believe!"

As I gaze admiringly into Crystal's big brown eyes, I see the delicate beauty and passion of her spirit glimmering from within her. I see the mirror of mirrors—a mother's cherished reflection of all that she prides and fears. Most of all, I see that she has received the best gift of all—her inner voice. I feel privileged to say that Crystal gave me the best proof of her inner voice—and the best gift a daughter could ever give to her mom—words of kindness and love written expressly for me. I share a few with you now.

"Mother, all you do is heartfelt and is truly an act of love for others that shows tremendous integrity and compassion. You will make someone's day when this book is done—*everyday*! Like our Father says, 'Do nothing out of self-ambition or

vain conceit, but in humility, consider others as better than yourself and look for the interests of others instead of your own.' Mom, you are putting in so much of your time and interests to praise others and that is what God is seeing and asking. You are giving him the answers, and I can see Jesus coming out through you. God is on your side. I thank the Lord each night for such a blessing of a family and for all the support and love that I receive from you, Dad, and Steven. I know that I am not always worthy of all this, yet, I know that our God is a righteous God. He knows when we open our eyes, follow our visions, and listen to our hearts that we will learn to appreciate all of our blessings and become truly worthy of the promises of Christ. He gives us all this graciously because he wants us to live our lives in purity and true holiness. I love you, Mom, and I thank you for all that you've done for me!"
—Your loving daughter, Crystal

May you enjoy the fruits of His message of Love and Joy all your days, my precious daughter, through your gifts of heart and song, Crystallina, you are a dream come true!

◆ ◆ ◆

PART TWO
Courage In Mind

All Things are Possible to He Who Believes.
—*Mark 9:23*

The ideals which have lighted my way, and time after time have given me new courage to face life cheerfully, have been Kindness, Beauty, and Truth.
—*Albert Einstein*

CHAPTER EIGHT
Courage In Mind

*All Things Are Possible
to He Who Believes.
—Mark 9:23*

**The ideals which have lighted my way, and time after time have given me new courage to face life cheerfully, have been Kindness, Beauty, and Truth.
—Albert Einstein**

Who among us could debate the intellectual genius of the acclaimed Albert Einstein, who laid the foundation for the understanding of our own forces of energy? Yet, even the brilliant, legendary Einstein summed up the qualities of daily life as simply as Kindness, Beauty, and Truth.

Why, then, do we find that so many consider this act of mastering one's thoughts so complicated? Unless we embrace the gentleness of our own true nature to love, to think, to be, will we ever really be able to discover our own heroism . . . our own valor . . . our own victories?

"To be or not to be—that is the question," so poetically wrote the great English playwright, William Shakespeare. Whether it is in our play, love, or work, do we not rely on our being present to participate? Being present, we engage our thoughts in the moment at hand. We are then able to fully receive the environment that we choose with 100% of our senses. We are ready to transcend this experience from our spirit and mind through physical action into bodily form. Yet, so many times, do we feel as if we are missing out? Do we reach out and grab each challenge with a proactive zest for growth, or do we stand by and react afterwards? Do we shape our circumstances or do circumstances shape us? Do we do what we say and think what we do? Do we think at all? One of my favorite mentors and one of the greatest thinkers of our age, Bob Proctor, believes that some would rather die than think. Imagine.

Thinking means wondering about and formulating an image of an organized idea. This calls for a mind that is free to be creative. Creativity relies on a calm and relaxed atmosphere with a certain balance of positive tension. Once the mood is set in motion, the new idea ignites and begins to create sparks of interest, enthusiasm, and focused concentration within us. Negative tension, however, accompanies worry, anxiety, and fear. This negative tension, if left unchecked or unresolved, often leads to serious breakdowns—mentally, physically, and spiritually. If we believe in an all-knowing and all-loving Supreme Being, are these non-trusting emotions really supporting this affirmation?

Steve Siebold, a professional tennis player and mental toughness coach, has pointed out to me that intelligent studies have shown—when we feel dumb, we act dumber. Such negative tension can not harmoniously co-exist in a relaxed, positive mind that is thinking creatively. Critical thinking, on the other hand, occurs daily in stressful environments as Ernest Hemingway coined it "grace under pressure." Many courageous leaders from heads of state, church, and business to the scores of heroes in law, order, and everyday life have been able to handle this pressure when it arises. Even then, there are moments of extraordinary events—as witnessed by all of us . . . all too often in the past decade—which bring out feats of supreme valor and honor.

More often, however, we are faced with the ordinary moments of life in which we could freely choose to think extraordinarily, and do so in a relaxed manner. Yet, we often hold back and follow the crowd. Why? Why are so few willing to stand apart from the masses? This hesitance can happen to us as business executives, employees, parishioners, students, teachers, citizens, performers, parents, youth.

The list goes on and on. We remain ordinary in the ordinary moments rather than thinking boldly and bravely in moving our extraordinary selves through to magnificent dimensions. Ultimately, if we choose the path of courage, we can fulfill our dreams with purposeful lives of daily significance!

What exactly happens to us? Perhaps it is in the explanation that we really do not think. There is an expression, which is used to explain this phenomena that says that we become immobilized by fear. We become like deer in the headlights. For some, it is the fear of making a mistake that holds them back. Yet, if we do not make mistakes, how will we know when we are not? For others, it is the fear of having more problems, which limits their creative stretch. This reminds me of a funny tale which was told by someone who told someone, etc.

A businessman named Joe Dense is distraught and overwhelmed by his worries and stress. He walks out of a Chicago hotel and sees a well-known entrepreneur Bill who he admires greatly and knows well. They go out for a cocktail and dinner at Pizzeria Due off Rush Street. Joe confides in Bill about his dilemma, "I can't tolerate my life anymore. I just want to go someplace where I won't have any problems at all." Bill responds with a consoling smile, "Well, it sounds like you will need to go somewhere else, if you don't want anymore problems in your life. If you'd like, I can show you just such a place tomorrow morning. Meet me in front of the Fairmont at 8:00 AM sharp and I can take you there in a cab." Joe is ecstatic. "Great. I can't wait to see it!" he replies.

They meet in the morning as planned and get into a cab and go west on the highway. Joe remains puzzled, yet excited that, at last, he may find the answer to his prayers. A fresh start or maybe a new romance, he thinks to himself.

After about half an hour, they get out somewhere in the suburbs and Bill pays the cab. They walk a bit. All of a sudden, they come upon a sight that completely stuns Joe. "Bill, this is a cemetery!" Bill nods and retorts, "Precisely, where else would you expect to be rid of problems? Life, by nature, represents problems to solve constantly. How do you think I became so successful in my career at building Microsoft if I didn't have any problems to solve? I thrive on them."

Other people have the overwhelming preoccupation with planning or worrying about the past, which deters them from investing time in creative thought or daydreaming. To some, it may seem to be child's play and accurately so, as most children are always thinking and starting their conversations with the question, "Why?" Unfortunately, we adults somehow get the impression that we have graduated from our questions of life.

In essence, we are not really empowering ourselves to be present. The past is just a memory and the future is just a promise, while the present is truly a gift. Our call-to-arms is to seize the moment. Harnessing the experiences that we receive from our senses, we can fully engage our attention on the subject that we choose to experience and focus upon . . . now. We command silence of our thoughts on everything else.

Do we lack courage? If we allow harmful noises such as self-criticism, worry, or self-doubt to take charge of our minds, then, indeed, we are not accessing our courage in mind. Thinking requires self-awareness, self-discipline, and, above all, self-trust and honesty. It demands courage and the ability to squarely face the fears that occur at any given moment. It requires a conscious decision to manage the thoughts that we choose to embrace or reject because we have direct control over our emotions as well as our thoughts.

If we listen and trust our spirit, we will be well equipped to choose appropriate emotions and thoughts. We choose these thoughts so that we can move toward the good that we desire. In our pursuit, we naturally expand in fulfillment of our truest purpose. This is the law. This courage lies quietly within us all. It is available upon request.

Contrarily, people often wander aimlessly through daily experiences in an unconscious mental state, like a ship without a rudder in an ocean of circumstances. This can be compared to the spiritual garden in the law of cause and effect. When we don't cultivate our thoughts with self-nourishment toward our purpose, then idle weeds of thought of a useless or even harmful nature, can enter our minds. Just as in our floral gardens, left unattended, the precious garden of our mind will harvest weeds of negativity. This can perpetuate the self-debilitating chatter of irrational fears and/or inherited beliefs. These limiting beliefs or myths have a finite box around them. That box tends to prevent one from pondering about thoughts outside the box as if there were a "no trespassing" sign that inhibited any notion of mental adventure. Some will go through their life and never question any of these limiting beliefs or paradigms. They are simply accepted as fact without any conscious examination because that is just the way it has always been.

The result is a surrender of our power to be in charge of our own journey. What we gain is comfort to some extent in the known—until, of course, life changes it anyway. What we lose is our true sense of becoming all that we are fully capable of being . . . and giving to the world.

With courage and creativity, we can consciously organize our thoughts to serve us throughout our day. We can call on our senses to keep us in harmony with the environment as we engage in the moment. Notice a child as he or she interacts playfully with his or her environment. There is an intensity and wholehearted participation in the moment's experience. As they run through the sprinkler in laughter, there is a visible sense of bold and brave curiosity. Kids have the delightful capacity for quick, sharp, mental decision to go for it, regardless of the outcome! So, how can we take this spirit of adventure to conquer the untapped frontiers within our minds? We can seek a helping hand from an expert, if need be, which is a courageous act of honesty within itself. We can also reclaim our God-given intellectual resources. What are they? Are we educated about these resources in our school years?

Many rely totally on the tools that we call our senses as critical determinants for arriving at their decisions. This can be akin to a motorboat left at sea to steer only by the course of waves and weather conditions. The external stimuli will influence the boat, but the navigator will be useless in charting his own desired course. He will be reacting frivolously to every whim of nature, bouncing and colliding in random chaos with the sea's will in charge.

Now, add a few resources of the mind, and the navigator can empower himself to chart his course to the destination of his dreams, making the boat an instrument to fulfill his or her purpose. With respect for the powers of nature, he or she can leverage his knowledge to work in harmony with the environment. In our mind's sea, we navigate our heart's desires, our visions and dreams, our truest purpose. We conquer the unknown conditions of our wildest storms.

What exactly are all these forgotten resources? This is the stuff that has made great the earth since the beginning of time. Heroes of humanity have left their imprints in time using these innate treasures given to man as a birthright by the Creator. These gifts are: Imagination, Memory, Reason, Perception, Will, and Intuition. Let us journey together to tap into these precious jewels to reveal their amazing powers!

IMAGINATION

Our imagination is the workshop of our dreams. This is the place that fosters our seeds of creative imagery.
Great leaders create great visions. Take heed of leaders such as: Jesus of Nazareth, Mother Teresa, Michelangelo, Ghandi, the Wright Brothers, Thomas Edison, Walt Disney, Louis Pasteur, Albert Einstein, Bill Gates, Martin Luther King, Presidents John Kennedy and Abraham Lincoln, Mozart, Monet, Shakespeare, Hemingway, Van Gogh, Spielberg, Oprah, Balanchine, J.K. Rowling, Colin Powell, President George W. and First Lady Laura Bush and on and on. These heroes built their visions making their own dreams come true. These visions first appeared in their imaginative minds and then eventually in the physical world for all of us to enjoy. The never-ending cycle of life's desire grows and expands upon its own purpose. We dream our painting and then paint our dream through imagination.

We must first realize that we think in visual images on the screen of our minds. Let's expound on this theory. What happens when I say to you, "I just saw a blue-eyed, blonde-haired beautiful lady driving a red convertible." What happened? Didn't you 'see' the woman in a particularly colored open-top automobile in your mind's eye? Now, I say to you, "I just saw a white elephant driving a black Porsche convertible." Well, now what happened? Is it a remarkable sight? What fun we could have in our minds, if we would just tap into our imagination. Isn't this what God intended for us? Isn't this what children do? They love to play with words and make funny situations in their minds. How creative! Just think of someone at the office that says something rude to you. Do you allow their words of negativity to affect you by reacting and repeating something equally rude to them? Try mental humor inside your mind and just let their rudeness pass right by you into the wind. You might even be able to see this office person as a nice angel trying to disguise himself as rude. Get so hilarious that you find yourself audibly laughing every time this happens.

I am certain this is what great comedians like Robin Williams and Jim Carey do to retain their self-empowerment. This is the power of imagination. The only limitation on this immense power is that we can only imagine one thought at a time, although we can change images at the speed of light. When I say, "There is a red Mercedes convertible speeding down the highway with Elvis Presley driving it," can you simultaneously see in your mind if I say to you, "Now how about a black truck driven by Marilyn Monroe?" Well? Quite a sight! Your imagination shifted mental pictures instantly from Elvis to Marilyn. You did astonishing work at all this in just a few seconds. All I did was string a combination of letters in front of your eyes.

The exciting treasure about our dream shop is that we can choose amazingly wonderful jewels of thought and let go of the junk of useless thought. We can s-t-r-e-t-c-h our creative mind to imagine the life and the good that we were intended to attract to us from the universe. Yes, attract, for all things in form are first created in the mind. Jesus of Nazareth said it well; "Our Father already knoweth what we desire." Then, what is it that we must do to seek and find? Perhaps, make our vision clear? Is that so much to ask of us? Maybe childhood was meant for us as adults to learn to play and create so that we can sharpen our imagination rather than toss it aside as child's play? Van Gogh said, "I dream my painting and then, I paint my dream." What a marvelous lifestyle!

MEMORY

So, what did I say? Please do not tell me you forgot already! Actually, I find this resource elusive to describe yet, so incredibly powerful to possess. It is often taken for granted until eventually—without use—it withers away.

The computer was invented from this place. As art imitates life, so, too, life imitates art. The storage house of all the events of our lives are within our memory. We can create interesting associations with words so that our memory can file pertinent data in our lives. Our memory muscles are like any other in our body. They require use to become sharper! Rather than clutter our creative minds with trivial data, we can command our memory to store meaningful information while we use our creative energy to relax, to envision our hearts' delights and to enjoy the moment through our senses! Lots of worry is generated by the fear that we will forget important stuff if we don't keep it on the front screen of our minds all day. Ironically, we often forget to use our memory as an instrument for daily life. So, now what? Forgive yourself, put your memory back in motion, forget about worry, and be happy!

REASON

This is the lawyer's love! Our ability to reason could probably cause world peace in a heartbeat, if we simply used it every day. Do you think that reason is being used when Joe Anxious beeps his horn at John Early whose car is in front of his while in a traffic jam that has nothing to do with either of them? Will the sound of Joe's horn suddenly cause the universe to wake up and instantly erase the cause of the traffic jam and allow, at least, Joe to swiftly drive away to his destination? Alternatively, will it simply cause more insensitivity and tension? When we reason with circumstances, we reclaim our lives and become self-empowered to stop, challenge, and choose our response. We begin to lighten our burdens because most fears are irrational or unreasonable. Fear disappears in the face of reason. The calm and wise leaders of life have learned to astutely make use of their innate ability to reason. Pour Quoi or Pour Quoi Pas? Why or Why not?

PERCEPTION

It is the treasure (or curse) that so cleverly reveals who sees the world as either half-full or half-empty. Which one are you? Of course, we know that they both exist. So what? What good is dwelling on defeat, negativity, weaknesses, or faults of humans? Please don't bore me with the mundane in life. No, I shall not spend my last day of life in pity for what I could not accomplish today. Forgive me, but I am not in the least bit impressed with the faults of my neighbors and I am certainly not interested in dwelling on my own! What did Thumper say in Disney's *Bambi?* "If you can't say anything nice, don't say nuffin' — —."

Yes! My time is oh so precious and I yearn to hear one more tale of the beauty that exists within your soul. I will never tire of the feeling I experience when love bids her presence to stir my heart with your innermost beauty. For the beauty is as real as the beast, yet, I have come to accept my fate as a person eternally blinded by goodness and love. Indeed, it takes deep courage to perceive the positive in the negative and believe in the unbelievable. I thank God for the eternal optimists determined to achieve the impossible.

WILL

I will, I do. They are both the same—a decision of conscious commitment to act in a certain way in order to fulfill our truest purpose. Will is the driving force that moves thoughts into things. What is the will of the human spirit? It is the concentration of energy directed toward a certain ideal. We fall in love with an idea and we set in motion the desire to fulfill our dreams and transform them into realities. A strong will that is tempered with a desire to serve humanity can create a heavenly paradise on earth. Contrarily, a strong will tempted to serve only self can also create hell on earth. We, the stewards of the earth must strive to lead by example. Ideally, our will to serve others results in the sheer joy of our truest purpose! Use it wisely or lose it to the whims of fanciful bystanders who will mind your will for you. Keep your will closely in touch with your heart and you will have all that you ever dreamed possible in life.

INTUITION

"How did you know where I was, Mom?" asks my son after I find him in the sports department of the store. "I had a hunch," I say with a grin on my face as I give my son a big hug. Intuition is speaking to me through my feelings. Intuition is God's way of communicating with us. Its significance as a higher power cannot be overstated. Sharpen your intuitive sense and you cannot go wrong. Like any muscle, our intuitive sense can become more useful with practice. Exercising your intuition by following it and testing it will provide you with the confidence to rely upon it when reason is inadequate or does not feel as comfortable. Actually, if you think about times when you used your intuition in a sudden occasion, the logic of reason is probably standing just around the corner to explain the intuitive feeling. Being in touch with these feelings and vibrations that your subconscious generates will allow you to respond in a natural manner. Intuition is sometimes referred to as spirit and it is closely related to the magic of courage. In times of fright or flight, the amazing grace of our intuition miraculously shows up.

Women are generally known to be more intuitive, which is not surprising because women are generally more in touch with their feelings. Yet, intuitive skills can be developed and sharpened just like a golf swing or tennis stroke. Men can take heed from this cue and practice, practice, practice. Nothing is more sexy and attractive to a woman than a man who is in touch with his feelings and the feelings of others. Whomever you are, if you spend some quiet moments each day getting in touch with this special gift, you will be amazed at the rewards that will bless your world. Trust your intuitive feelings as if your life depended on them . . . it does.

I leave you with a three-point guide for making wise decisions:
1. Will this choice move me toward the progressive realization of my worthy ideal?
2. Will this choice be in harmony with my values?
3. Will this choice violate the rights of any others?

As long as the answers are yes, yes, and no—and you feel excited about the prospect of the decision—then go for it!

Go now and observe as you discover these six treasures within the fine individuals in this book. "Whatever the mind of man can conceive and believe, it can achieve."
—Napoleon Hill, *Think and Grow Rich.*

John F. Kennedy Library/Inaugural Address

. . . Ask not what your country can do for you; ask what you can do for your country.

—President John F. Kennedy

John F. Kennedy Library

President Kennedy with the First Family on Vacation

CHAPTER NINE
Courage In Mind

President John F. Kennedy
The Courage to Envision and Execute

> ... Ask not what your country can do for you;
> ask what you can do for your country.
> —President John F. Kennedy

Dawn breaks with intensity in the air on October 22, 1962. The world will tremble by dusk as the most powerful leader of the free world speaks on global television with grim, yet calm resolution. His message will become one of the greatest hallmarks of political leadership ever witnessed on the face of this planet.

Ladies and Gentlemen, the President of the United States of America, John Fitzgerald Kennedy:

"Good evening, my fellow citizens: This government, as promised, has maintained the closest surveillance of the Soviet military buildup on the island of Cuba. Within the past week, unmistakable evidence has established the fact that a series of offensive missile sites is now in preparation on that imprisoned island. The purpose of these bases can be none other than to provide a nuclear strike capability against the Western Hemisphere.

"The new weaponry on Cuba includes (some 64) medium range ballistic missiles capable of carrying a nuclear warhead for a distance of more than 1,000 miles. Each of these missiles, in short, is capable of striking Washington, D.C., the Panama Canal, Cape Canaveral, Mexico City, or any other city in the southeastern part of the United States, in Central America, or in the Caribbean area. . . .

"The urgent transformation of Cuba into an important strategic base. . . constitutes an explicit threat to the peace and security of all the Americas . . . This secret, swift, and extraordinary buildup of Communist missiles. . . is a deliberately provocative and unjustified change in the status quo which cannot be accepted by this country, if our courage and our commitments are ever to be trusted again by either friend or foe."

President John F. Kennedy (JFK) announced "a street quarantine on all offensive military equipment under shipment to Cuba" and more intense aerial surveillance of Cuba. "Should these offensive military preparations continue, thus increasing the threat to the hemisphere, further action will be justified. I have directed the Armed Forces to prepare for any eventualities. . . .

"It shall be the policy of this nation to regard any nuclear missile launched from Cuba against any nation in the Western Hemisphere as an attack by the Soviet Union on the United States, requiring a full retaliatory response upon the Soviet Union. I offer you, Mr. Kruschev, abandon this course of

President John F. Kennedy

world domination and join in an historic effort to end the perilous arms race and to transform the history of man.

"The path we have chosen for the present is full of hazards, as all paths are, but it is the one most consistent with our character and courage as a nation and our commitments around the world. The cost of freedom is always high, but Americans have always paid it. And one path we shall never choose, and that is the path of surrender and submission.

"Our goal is not the victory of might, but the vindication of right; not peace at the expense of freedom, but both peace *and* freedom, here in this hemisphere, and, we hope, around the world. God willing, that goal will be achieved."

The address was over and the Cuban Missile Crisis would perilously shake the world and test the president's character for a total of thirteen days. ". . . I never knew him to be more in command of himself or of events. And I can never forget his courage, his smile, and his optimism that this crisis too, would pass," remarked Press Secretary Pierre Salinger.

In spite of the tremendous consternation surrounding such an expose of covert operations, John F. Kennedy maintained a state of composure, poise, wit, and wisdom throughout the dark days of autumn 1962. Even immediately before Kennedy's historic televised address to the American public, he kept vigil with Prime Minister Milton Obate of Uganda during a long-standing appointment for a respectable forty-five minutes. The President displayed remarkable courtesy and coolness under fire in his genuine consideration for others in the midst of this crisis.

Kennedy kept his wit in the face of the enormous stress that challenged him and remarked, "I guess this is the week I earn my salary." The president was clearly a man of great awareness about himself and the critical position he held in those hours of life's destiny in-the-making.

Courage in Mind

In 1959, Cuban revolutionary Fidel Castro had led a successful overthrow of the capitalist but corrupt government of the island nation just ninety miles off the Florida coast. Castro swiftly transformed the island into a repressive communist dictatorship. He invited the leading communist state, the Soviet Union, into close partnership, much to the concern of the United States. In the early 1960's, America was watching Cuba very closely, and for good reason. High-altitude photographs taken from American spy planes revealed rapid Russian installation of the many mid-range missile sites in Cuba with excavations for even larger missiles. These larger missiles, when in place, could reach virtually every corner of the U.S., southeastern Canada, all of Mexico and Central America, and much of South America. JFK remarked to a colleague that the Soviets were feverishly building enough launching sites to fire a single volley of missiles capable of killing eighty million Americans.

The youngest elected President in United States history was confronted with any President's greatest fear—the possible destruction of his country. It was a moment that defined his courage and exemplary leadership.

U.S. Attorney General Robert F. Kennedy, described his brother poignantly in *A Question of Character* comparing this current state to earlier times of personal strain and hurt. He remarked that JFK's hands went up to his face, covering his mouth while he opened and closed his fist. His face seemed drawn, his eyes pained, almost gray. . . . The younger brother noted how he thought of when his older brother was ill and almost died; when he lost his child; when they learned that their oldest brother had been killed.

Yet, through the maze of intense confusion, tension, and anxiety, President Kennedy remained calm and focused. Always open, JFK freely encouraged debate, discussion, argument, evidence, opinion, candor, diplomacy, strategy,

President John F. Kennedy

criticism, and compliment among his advisors. In return, the president received loyal and loving support from his wife, children, family, friends, and supporters.

In the end, however, President Kennedy knew how to make a decision alone. He held himself totally accountable for his actions. John Fitzgerald Kennedy would draw from all that he had ever become in his young life and from all that his parents had instilled in him. He would draw from all that he had enjoyed and suffered physically and emotionally with his siblings and schoolmates. He would portray the same heroic instincts that we saw in the U.S. Navy in World War II on PT-109.

He would require the strength he drew from the essence of his wife, Jackie, and his children, Caroline and John—all so sacred to him now more than ever. He drew from his beliefs in God and his Roman Catholic faith. Kennedy grew stronger, as well, from all the storms and rainbows he had experienced in his political decision-making life. He gained from his own insight into courage illustrated so candidly in his Pulitzer Prize winning *Profiles in Courage*. Kennedy had the wisdom to respect that every action causes an equal and opposite reaction—the law of cause and effect. The Russians were fully capable of launching a deadly nuclear intercontinental ballistic missile attack on the United States, which would kill millions of innocent citizens. America would then be set up to defensively respond in return. Ultimately, atomic blasts would be triggered worldwide and the subsequent radiation fallout would eventually destroy life on earth as we know and cherish it.

Emotions were escalating on both sides. Some of Kennedy's own generals had recommended immediate air attacks on the Cuban missile sites rather than a blockade. He wisely rejected that counsel, but would the Russian Premier be able to do the same? Would both sides come to a peaceful decision or would the Cold War suddenly become the Armageddon?

Courage in Mind

On October 28, 1962, a glimmer of light from the dark storm began to emerge by way of a fax from Premier Nikita Kruschev. The Communist leader fortuitously revealed words of concession. A rainbow had brilliantly appeared through a diplomatic meeting of the minds. The Nuclear Arms Crisis had finally ended in a remarkably peaceful manner. The Russians agreed to remove their missile bases from Cuba. Moreover, good was achieved in creating a climate for discussion toward nuclear disarmament and peaceful discourse toward a more global economy—and more valuably—improved human relations.

The decisive mind of John Kennedy brought the world closer to a state of peace and prosperity. No doubt, President Kennedy gave the ideal of courage considerable thought. He was well prepared to assume the responsibilities of leadership during his political career. From the echoes of his own *Profiles in Courage*, I bring you, ladies and gentlemen, the thirty-fifth President of the United States of America:

"This is a book about that most admirable of human virtues—courage. . . . And these are the stories of the pressures experienced by eight United States Senators and the grace with which they endured them—the risks to their careers, the unpopularity of their courses, the defamation of their characters, and sometimes, but sadly only sometimes, the vindication of their reputations and their principles.

"A nation which has forgotten the quality of courage which in the past has been brought to public life is not as likely to insist upon or reward that quality in its chosen leaders today—and in fact we have forgotten. . . . We do not remember—and possibly we do not care.

". . . Some of my colleagues who are criticized today for lack of forthright principles—or who are looked upon with scornful eyes as compromising 'politicians'—are simply

President John F. Kennedy

engaged in the fine art of conciliating, balancing and interpreting the forces and factions of public opinion, an art essential to keeping our nation united and enabling our Government to function. Their consciences may direct them from time to time to take a more rigid stand for principle—but their intellects tell them that a fair or poor bill is better than no bill at all, and that only through the give-and-take of compromise will any bill receive the successive approval of the Senate, the House, the President and the nation.

"But the question is how we will compromise and with whom. For it is easy to seize upon unnecessary concessions, not as means of legitimately resolving conflicts but as methods of 'going along.'

". . . It is difficult to accept the narrow view of the role of the United States Senator—a view that assumes the people of Massachusetts sent me to Washington to serve merely as a seismograph to record shifts in popular opinion. I reject this view not because I lack faith in the 'wisdom of the people,' but because this concept of democracy actually puts too little faith in the people. Those who would deny the obligation of the representative to be bound by every impulse of the electorate—regardless of the conclusions his own deliberations direct—do trust in the wisdom of the people. They have faith in their ultimate sense of justice, faith in their ability to honor courage and respect judgment, and faith that in the long run they will act unselfishly for the good of the nation. It is that kind of faith on which democracy is based, not simply the often frustrated hope that public opinion will at all times under all circumstances promptly identify itself with the public interest.

"The voters selected us, in short, because they had confidence in our judgment and our ability to exercise that judgment from a position where we could determine what were their own best interests, as a part of the nation's interests. This may mean that we must on occasion lead, inform, correct, and sometimes even ignore constituent opinion, if we are to exercise fully that judgment for which we were elected. But acting without selfish motive or private bias, those who follow the dictates of an intelligent conscience are not aristocrats, demagogues, eccentrics, or callous politicians insensitive to the feelings of the public. They expect—and not without considerable trepidation—their constituents to be the final judges of the wisdom of their courses; but they have faith that those constituents—today, tomorrow, or even in another generation—will at least respect the principles that motivated their independent stand.

". . . This has been a book about courage and politics. Politics furnished the situations, courage provided the theme. Courage, the universal virtue, is comprehended by us all—but these portraits of courage do not dispel the mysteries of politics.

". . . It was not because they [the Senators] 'loved the public better than themselves.' On the contrary it was precisely because they did *love themselves*—because each one's need to maintain his own respect for himself was more important to him than his popularity with others— because his desire to win or maintain a reputation for integrity and courage was stronger than his desire to maintain his office—because his conscience, his personal standard of ethics, his integrity or morality, call it what you will—was stronger than the pressures of public disapproval—because his faith that *his* course was the best one, and would ultimately be vindicated, outweighed his fear of public reprisal.

". . . It is when the politician loves neither the public good nor himself, or when his love for himself is limited and is satisfied by the trappings of office, that the public interest is badly served. And it is when his regard for himself is so high that his own self-respect demands he follow the path of courage and conscience that all benefit.

President John F. Kennedy

". . . We, the people, are the boss, and we will get the kind of political leadership, be it good or bad, that we demand and deserve.

". . . The courage of life is often a less dramatic spectacle than the courage of a final moment; but it is no less a magnificent mixture of triumph and tragedy. A man does what he must—in spite of personal consequences, in spite of obstacles and dangers and pressures—and that is the basis of all human morality.

". . . In whatever arena of life one may meet the challenge of courage, whatever may be the sacrifices he faces if he follows his conscience—the loss of his friends, his fortune, his contentment, even the esteem of his fellow men—each man must decide for himself the course he will follow. The stories of past courage can define that ingredient—they can teach, they can offer hope, they can provide inspiration. But they cannot supply courage itself. For this each man must look into his own soul."

—*John Fitzgerald Kennedy, 1917–1963*

◆ ◆ ◆

Courage is an internal resource we are given as a gift to get us through the fears and adversities of our lives. We just have to tap into it and access it. The soul mate of courage is creativity.

—Larry Wilson

Larry Wilson

CHAPTER TEN
Courage In Mind

Larry Wilson
The Courage to Play to Win

> **Courage is an internal resource we are given as a gift to get us through the fears and adversities of our lives. We just have to tap into it and access it. The soul mate of courage is creativity.**
> **—Larry Wilson**

I hung up the telephone and stared out the turret of windows at the tall locust trees from my upper level sitting area. The views of the Colorado Front Range were spectacular. This romantic castle of mine called home had set the scene for what was to be . . . an incredible day.

I noticed the white puffy cumulus clouds moving slowly toward me in the bluest-of-blue morning skies. The majestic snow-capped mountain peaks soared high and proud as a backdrop to my reverie. For I had just enjoyed an exhilarating conversation with an intriguing visionary and entrepreneur . . . Larry Wilson.

In fact, for a moment or two, I felt as if I had been swept away by an ethereal magic carpet and flown right up to one of those clouds to visit with one of the wisest souls in the universe. I felt as if the Highest Authority purposefully attracted Larry into my world. As always, universal laws were in motion.

Larry is one of those delightful human beings who can catapult an experience into an event. Just to hear him speak can move even the most sluggish person into thinking, "Wow. I like that. I want to think and act like that for the rest of my life, and I'm going to start right now."

Larry has been described accurately as being a "leader in a permanent whitewater world of change." He is certainly an adventure guide, a pied piper for an exciting life journey —physically, and more significantly, mentally. As one of the pioneers in the evolution of growth-based leadership, Larry has struck a gold mine of wealth from his own inner genius. He has a marvelous and refreshing way of thinking, and we are blessed to be able to enjoy his candid wit, leadership, and generous appetite for service.

Larry's sincere desire to share his passions of the mind has given the world an unprecedented opportunity to grab a new key and unlock the door to all the inherent treasures of human potential. He is a best-selling author, an insightful and entertaining international speaker, a leading consultant in business management, and the successful founder of five companies that have all evoked the philosophy of self-empowerment for which Larry is so popular. He currently leads Larry Wilson and Associates, a top firm in the field of management training and self-empowerment.

If you are a CEO or have any business acumen whatsoever, you would be serving yourself and your company a coup of paramount importance by contacting Larry Wilson

Larry Wilson

and Associates. Trust me. There are no better mentors. His work is the best. It's that simple. His philosophy, his quest, his presence impeccably conveys a modern day genre of nobility and chivalry, yet with a perceptive understanding of profitable leadership. For those outside the business arena, Larry's wisdom speaks straight to the core of humanity. From his most recent best-selling book *Play to Win*, he states, "I face my dragons every day. I find my courage to chase them away. I don't have to be who I've always been. I learn and grow. That's how I win."

His colleague Ken Blanchard, also a world renowned speaker, entrepreneur, and author speaks for all who have seen Larry in action:

"In 1979, I heard a young and dynamic speaker talk to an audience of business leaders from the Young President's Organization (YPO). The 'ABC's of Personal Power' was an intense and entertaining hour on how to play to win—to go for it—in work and in life. It was a powerful speech and the audience was held spellbound not only by the passion of the speaker but also by the potency of his ideas. The speaker was Larry Wilson.

"Larry and I have since shared the speaker's platform all over the world. He continues to be a powerful, dynamic, and wise presence in the dais. I admire him principally because his life's work has been to help individuals grasp the significance of their lives and to use their courage and creativity to face challenges, handle adversity, and grow as individuals.

"It has been in the last fifteen years that Larry's message has really caught fire. He has the ability to look straight into the eyes and souls of people—from CEO's of some of our largest institutions to people who have spent their working lives on factory floors. He often asks them the same questions.

What is your life about? How are you making the world a better place? What will your legacy be?

". . . Look around! The companies we work for are reinventing themselves as we move from the industrial era to something else. In the very same way, we need to re-invent ourselves. . . . To be continually successful in the new era will require us, whether we are employees or entrepreneurs, to use all of our creativity, intellectual ability, and courage. We will each need to play to win—to go as far as we can using everything we have in order to thrive. In this paradoxical time of great opportunity and no job security, it is the people who understand and grasp this (concept) that have a shot at being successful and fulfilled!"

Larry describes his own synchronicity and how he began his march to success after an inspirational encounter with a wise and formidable man, Dr. Abraham Maslow:

"The journey to this book [*Play To Win*] began in 1960 on a brilliant autumn day in Minnesota. I was thirty years old then, an ex-schoolteacher and a successful life insurance agent. I was successful enough that I had been asked by Federated Insurance of Owatonna, Minnesota, to create a course to train their agents.

"Although I had instantly answered yes, I had no idea at all what the course should be about. I only knew that I didn't want it to have anything to do with how selling and business were conducted at that time. Business was a low-trust, adversarial world then, and I was completely open to new ideas.

"On that autumn day, I found myself wandering the University of Minnesota campus with two of my kids tagging along. There was football in the air and the excitement of a university coming back to life after a sleepy Minnesota August. We walked past the university bookstore. Outside, they were having a sidewalk sale, dumping books at a dollar each to make room for new inventory.

"Purely by accident, I picked up a book in the psychology section and opened it to an article titled, of all things, The Hierarchy of Relative Prepotency, by Abraham Maslow. A grabber of a title. (And, no, I had no idea what it meant.) But as I scanned it, I saw that Maslow was writing about human potential and what would become his famous pyramid of needs. Something inside me said this was important stuff. I bought the book, went home, read the article five times, and made a decision.

"The next morning, I took a leap of faith and called Maslow at Brandeis University. I told him I was an insurance agent and asked if I could visit him for a day. Maslow being Maslow, he said, 'Of course.' Back then, Maslow was emerging as the third force in psychology— Freud being the first force and the behaviorist school the second. Maslow represented an island of humanism in a sea of behaviorists at most all universities. The humanists essentially rejected the behaviorists' claims that there was nothing to human psychology but behavior, nothing but 'stimulus-response.' The humanists knew there was more to us than just responding to stimuli, we weren't simply Pavlov's dogs.

"Abraham Maslow was clearly the most outspoken and well respected thinker of the humanist school, so I was nervous when I arrived for our meeting. How much time could a man in his position have for a young insurance agent? But Dr. Maslow was open, kind, and gracious. We met for a whole day. I remember thinking all the while that he was treating me like a peer, instead like some salesman from the very distant (and obscure) Midwest. We talked about people and about his pyramid of needs. Because we were both fathers, we talked about our kids and raising children in the wild sixties.

"And then the conversation took a turn that affected the rest of my life. Maslow talked about Eupsychia. He used the term *eupsychia* to mean 'the good mind,' in much the same sense that *euphoria* means 'the good feeling.' Eupsychia was his imagined island of a thousand people who were all self-actualized. *Self-actualized* was his term for that relatively rare group of people who were motivated to discover their true selves and answer their deepest questions about meaning and purpose. Self-actualized people were those who had met their physical survival and status needs, they were now motivated to grow, to serve, and to reach their full potential.

"Close to the end of our conversation, Maslow asked—I thought rhetorically—what I thought living on that island would be like. He leaned forward, pointed at me, and said, 'Why don't you go find out?' Although I probably could not have articulated it this way at the moment, finding eupsychia—'the good mind'—and helping others discover it became my life's mission.

"A few years later—after having designed a very successful sales training course—I launched Wilson Learning Corporation. I almost named it Eupsychia—with Maslow's blessing—but I couldn't spell it and no one else could pronounce it.

"Our purpose statement was 'helping others become as much as they can be.' We became the second-largest training company in the country and based much of our work on Maslow's theories and fellow psychologist Carl Rogers' work in counseling.

" . . . This book [*Play To Win*] is in large part a result of what we—[the staff at Larry's next company, Pecos River in Santa Fe, New Mexico]—have learned from helping well over 500,000 people and countless organizations on that journey. To Abraham Maslow, Viktor Frankl, Albert Ellis, Kurt Hahn, and Maxie Maultsby—and others—we owe a great debt. They are the artists; we, the copyists."

Larry Wilson

Maslow, the father of humanistic thinking, made an enormous impression on Larry. Maslow created the acclaimed concept of the "hierarchy of needs" of which self-actualization stands as the pinnacle. As Maslow describes in *The Farthest Reaches of Human Nature*, "Self-actualized people are devoted to working at something, which is very precise to them—a calling or vocation in the old sense. They are working at something which fate has called them to somehow and which they love, so that the work-joy dichotomy in them disappears."

Larry's visionary leadership and style are captured succinctly in *Play to Win,* which comes to life from the first page. His writing transcends beyond the basics with a mythical element of eloquence, genius, and imagery blended into his own spirit of passion and boldness. His insight into the journey of the human mind is riveting. I remember listening to Larry speak at a large venue. I was suddenly intrigued as I heard his philosophy favoring growth and abundance over fear and scarcity. His charm, wit, and charismatic personality added to his highly informative presentation, yet, there was more. While most corporate speakers clearly focus first on profit, this luminary sets the priority straight on principle. Naturally, profit would follow a man of such integrity anyway.

I recall feeling as though suddenly a door within my inner being was beginning to open wide. Up until then, I had become very disenchanted with the scarcity mentality in corporate America, society, and other professional industries. As an eternal optimist, I have always felt as if we, human beings, are suppressing vast inner resources because of our materialistic enthusiasm for outer resources. God has endowed each of us to think and create independently. All we need from leadership is a mirror and a glimpse of the vision and path. However, ego-based politics from a survivalist's perspective can cause us to use fear, control, and authoritarian tactics instead of encouraging productivity, education, and creativity. Self-centered leaders want the swift spontaneity of butterflies in conditions more fitting of caterpillars. Such negative thinking did not make any sense to me, and so I began to search for a new path.

Larry's message began to strike a chord of resonance that sent a surge of excitement filled with hope and clarity through every fiber of my being. I cannot describe the emotion, yet, I am sure you have experienced such an awakening of your own as if a strong ray of hope is cast into your heart's desire to find that which you seek. I also discovered that hope is the initial key that opens my heart and restores my spirit of well being. Once my emotions are unleashed and free to flow, then the second key of clarity is able to open my mind and show me the way. Hope in the heart and clarity in the mind frees energy to move on. These qualities expand human visions away from feeling or thinking that our goals are impossible and on to believing that they are very doable.

My own opportunity to speak candidly and personally with Larry Wilson came to fruition in a cosmic manner. I was listening to a prerecorded audiotape of a live interview between Larry and Bob Proctor, a mentor of mine. They were talking about the excitement of an adventurous life.

All of a sudden, I felt propelled to contact Larry myself. I looked in the book that Larry co-authored and called the resource number only to be greeted by a pleasant woman who informed me that he was no longer there. She cordially acknowledged me for my sincere enthusiasm and rewarded me with an alternative number. I called, left a message as I smiled, and wondered about Larry's journey these days. Then, I promptly moved on to my day's agenda. A few hours later, the telephone rang. When I answered, I heard to my astonishment, "Hi. This is Larry Wilson—you called?" I grinned. The universe had responded perfectly. Larry had

Larry Wilson

shown me the way. He had been bold in seeking out Dr. Maslow, and I was following suit in seeking our Mr. Larry Wilson. I re-learned a great lesson, "Seek and Ye Shall Find."

Our initial telephone call was short as Larry was on his way to a Caribbean vacation with his family. This true-to-heart guy seemed to be having fun just being himself and getting paid handsomely for it all. Some things just go right. We would reconvene our acquaintance the next month by telephone. I share with you excerpts of that conversation.

Larry had just finished a morning tennis match and was just as warm and gracious as ever. He conveyed a genuine interest in my quest for celebrating the centered qualities of humanity and was very willing to mentor my desire to make a difference.

Happily married to his endearing wife, Elizabeth, I quickly recognized the pride in Larry's voice as he shared with me his family lineage: six—now grown—children, and eleven grandchildren. "Do you know there really are no children or grandchildren, Cheri?" Larry rhetorically added as we meandered into a commonly held interest. I agreed with a slight awareness on the direction he was going with this thought. Larry continued, "We are each born as an individual, a one-of-a-kind soul . . . with a purpose . . . uniquely different and not to be compared . . . all of us born lovable and special with our own God-given gifts and talents."

We subtly moved our conversation into parenting. He continued, "As parents, we are the caretakers of the gift of spirit while on a human journey called life." I sat back and got comfortable as I allowed my mind to be swept away by this man of metaphor. Larry continued in a storytelling tone, "Ideally, we can create a garden in which each individual child can bloom . . . a kindergarten! This is a German word, which means garden for children to bloom. Each of us is a unique flower designed to bloom and express our true nature, our true self, to our fullest potential. We need guidance and loving support as we grow through our life's journey. As parents, leaders, teachers, or employers, we can fulfill this role of fostering self-discovery. Yet, we can also cripple this growth through intimidation when we set out to control or induce individuals to do what we might think is right for them, the situation, or us. Fear is useful in survival responses, however, growth requires courage and creativity to overcome irrational fears. Most fears are irrational and just in our minds. We just need to think about what we are thinking about to prove it," he marveled.

At that moment, I remembered one of my favorite phrases of his—stop, challenge, and choose—and I asked him to expand. I could sense in his enthusiasm that this was one of his favorites as he replied, "Anytime we find ourselves reacting to an event that leaves us feeling anxious and powerless, it's probably because we're thinking irrational thoughts. We gave away our power, and our inner spirit is causing us to notice the conflict through the feelings that we call anxiety. Through these suggestions, we can remain self-empowered and self-confident. By first stopping, we intervene in our thinking process, or we call a time out with ourselves. Then, secondly, by challenging our interpretation of the event, we can ask ourselves just what is the irrational source of the fear that we have made up in our minds and compare that to an objectively real choice based on external reality. Or, we can decide what other interpretations would help us respond in a more optimal fashion. Thirdly, we can choose to try out the new response, which may in fact, be to choose not to respond at all. Choosing well is our birthright—the source of our own inner power," Larry explains.

I asked Larry about his perspective on arriving at one's own purpose. He paused and then graciously shared his thoughts. "Cheri, for all of us, this journey is the adventure of our life, simultaneously scary, yet filled with wonderment. Truly, this plan is far beyond comprehension. Yet, as

Larry Wilson

humans, we want to understand and explain everything. This is where we draw on our courage and creativity. We go as far as we can—with all that we have. Christ, for example, was a servant-based leader who exemplified the model for living to be who you are while coming from a place of love and faith," he explained. "Larry, this leap of faith is difficult for most of us to accept, would you agree?" I asked. He chuckled as he continued, "Oh yes, this is where we stumble and fight our purpose. For me, I guess I was on to my purpose of helping others become as much as they can be all along—as a teacher, as an insurance agent. I was helping others plan their future. Then, as a facilitator, I was still serving in the same manner. All these events served to continually prepare me to re-invent myself along the way until I finally recognized it after my visit with Maslow."

Larry's reference to reinventing ourselves echoed the words of other great thinkers and further aroused my curiosity. I began to imagine a treasure hunt where we were searching for clues to the secret of a golden life, transforming our illusions effortlessly—just like a magic genie. Larry led the way as he continued in a storytelling whisper.

"Through what I call a series of synchronistic coincidences in our lives, we all can step forward and go places in our minds and spirits that we have never gone beyond or before. Then, we can move into the physical level of participation with this renewed sense of purpose and begin playing to win!" he exclaimed. "Play to win?" I mused. "Yes. Play to win this great game called life! This is where I get passionate and excited," he added as if I couldn't feel it already. "What I love to do best is build a trusting rapport so that I can help people create a soil, which integrates mind, spirit, and body. Ideally, this soil would provide the seeds for their own gifted, self-empowered, and purposeful lives—that's the fun of it all."

I knew in that moment that I was enjoying the company of a unique individual that still believes in chivalry and nobility. Larry's style of communicating clearly portrays his knack for romantic prose in his usage of epic metaphors. He is very effective in conveying his messages on the triumphs of the hero. Larry continued, "We are all on a hero's journey with increasingly complex challenges ahead of us. Just like Gulliver, we have self-imposed threads we need to break loose; just like Dorothy in the Wizard of Oz, we have wizards and witches to overcome; just like the Fiddler on the Roof, we have the delicate balance of playing the fiddler and staying on the roof. Sometimes, we think we can't stand it. And I say, yes, you can. You're standing in it right now."

"But what of the inevitable fall after we stand?" I ask. Larry responded, "Let's face it. Life is a series of falls that don't stop until we're dead. Once we can get over our fear of dying and falling, we can get into the adventure of it all. The problem is not the falling—that's how we learn—it's when we avoid the falls and miss the learning process altogether. We want to avoid being uncomfortable, and we need to do just the opposite—get comfortable—being uncomfortable. We are always going to be fallible human beings—all of us. Sometimes, we just forget that fact about ourselves and others."

"How do we forget?" I asked. Larry laughs in a compassionate tone. "We can actually slip into a hypnotic trance through life and miss the whole point. Our ego takes over, we begin hiding our mistakes, and we become so overwhelmed with stress that we think we cannot access our inner strength . . . and we lose touch with our true spirit. That's when the universe gently or boldly nudges us with wake-up calls," he chuckled.

I noticed a crescendo in his voice as he builds his final image in a whispering storytelling fashion. "Cheri, the paradox is that we can slip into our own spiritual perfection. Our journey is really to discover that delicate balance. There exists a tennis player in me who, every once in

Larry Wilson

awhile, hits a perfect shot with tremendous ease. This being the integration of my true nature—in the moment just being while not trying to be. Then comes along my ego, or false self, that lures me to think about the past or future—to worry. Suddenly, my perfect spirit, or true self, begins to fade away...."

Larry's story reminds me of a movie I had just seen directed by Robert Redford, "The Legend of Bagger Vance." In this film, perfection is beautifully portrayed through a professional golfer who is the underdog determined to win a tough tournament. He also understands this delicate balance and journey to which Larry has so exquisitely dedicated his life's purpose. In legendary style, Larry chooses to jump into the great game of life, never losing sight of the boy within who dares . . . to dream . . . play his dream . . . and win!

We thank you, Lord, for your reflection mirrored in the love and courage we experience through Larry.

◆ ◆ ◆

Courage is facing and conquering our fears as we are acting on our thoughts. For there is no courage without fear. It is a very real part of our lives.

—Bob Proctor

Bob Proctor

CHAPTER ELEVEN
Courage In Mind

Bob Proctor

The Courage to Think and Grow Rich

> **Courage is facing and conquering our fears as we are acting on our thoughts. For there is no courage without fear. It is a very real part of our lives.**
> **—Bob Proctor**

The air is damp and cool. The sounds of slow, dripping water are all that I can hear in the deep core of this very dark cave. I can almost taste the mustiness in the air along with the grit of the rough stone covering the tunnel of shimmering black rock. I can barely see in front of me as I walk slowly through the deep caverns of this silver mine.

I look back and faintly see the glimmer of sun casting light upon the opening. We begin advancing into the bowels of

121

the mine, and shouts from ahead advise us not to step foot off the wooden plank . . . or risk the chill of the muddy waters trickling underneath. That must be what I am feeling as my socks begin to dampen and grow cold against my feet. I stumble and lose my bearing. Suddenly it is pitch black, and I haven't a clue where to step next, nor how I would ever get out of here. I may never see the light of day again, I think to myself. Then, as I move through a slight fright while directing myself with my hand stretched out in front of me, I feel something warm, and I screech, "Who are you?"

"It's me, Mom, Steven . . . you're son?" whispers Steven. Moments later, I hear the flicker of a match, and suddenly, the light of a candle vaguely illuminates us. The tour guide breaks the silence, and, simultaneously, we are reconnected with the third-grade field trip participants here for a glimpse of the past. "Thank you for joining us today, boys and girls, moms and dads, and teachers. Welcome to this old silver mine of Silver Plume," greets the guide. She leads the crowd while describing the conditions for the miners. The guide catches my undivided attention as she explains that these miners (whose photographs were hanging along the cavern wall) had been hired to trade ten hours of their days, Mondays through Fridays, to search for silver in return for $3.00 per day—no silver included!

She really gets me thinking. Here precious human beings with infinite reservoirs of untapped brilliance hidden within were trading their lives for $3.00 per day in dark, damp, and gloomy conditions to mine precious stones. Perhaps, they enjoyed it. I don't know. I hope so. After all, I have always appreciated the beauty of silver, its fine luster, and its usefulness on our tableware. However, I have never experienced the finer emotions of peace, love, and joy through the company of mere stones. No, indeed, this is reserved for the companionship of the many living creatures of the earth. I can think of none more precious than that which exists in the treasures of the human spirit.

Bob Proctor

As I allowed my imagination to linger on this journey throughout the coming week, I could not help but hear the words of my friend and mentor Bob Proctor. Words of wisdom in my mind's ear were asking over and over, "What are you willing to trade your life for? After all, success in life is the progressive realization of a worthy ideal . . . an idea we fall in love with. That is what we live for and what we would be willing to die for—at all costs." I can still see and hear Bob reminding his audience, "As the sand in the hourglass of our individual lives continues to slip away for each of us, none of us is privy to the knowledge of how much sand we may have left."

As one of the profound thinkers of the modern world, Bob Proctor is probably in this very moment, one of the most successful and yet happiest entrepreneurs on the planet. As an internationally acclaimed speaker for his company Life Success Productions, Inc., Bob is the epitome of a true gentleman and a scholar—the Fred Astaire of presentational thought. I define this as a new genre of education that combines philosophy, science, theology, economics, and entrepreneurism with inspiration and self-actualization in a performing art form. Bob will enthrall, intrigue, and jolt one's entire being and catapult actions to take place within a person's life that may actually cause you to run the other way and wonder, What happened to my life? As Bob would reply, "Wake up and get rocking because if you're not at the edge, you're taking up too much space!"

A paradox of sorts, Bob is not a gregarious person open to simple conversation if seated next to you on an airplane. In fact, I would venture to say that Bob might even appear unfriendly as an airplane companion—polite, yet reserved. Oh yes, this airtime is Bob's time. This is the time that he dedicates to expansion and prosperity by creating infinite streams of ideas and incomes that are flowing through the universe by the time his flight has landed. For, while some are snoozing or idly passing away their airtime, Bob transcends into the genie of his mind and builds castles of wealth that have been known to create fortunes for anyone who is ready to make the decision.

If you consider yourself a successful businessperson who has created a multi-million dollar income and lifestyle, and you have not heard of Bob Proctor, the co-founder of the prosperity-building Three Percent Club, then let me be candid in saying that you have not really hit the pinnacle of your growth. Whether you are Bill Gates or Donald Trump, you would still be wiser for your time if you considered taking into your life—this most unique individual.

It is in this truth that I discover the mystery in Bob's turning point in life. During a candid conversation, I asked Bob what propelled him on that eventful day of social change to leave the Canadian fire hall and his buddies over forty years ago. What moved him to act on his idea to leave a secure job in Toronto and go out into the unknown—in the face of mocking laughs and ridicule from his steadfast peers? Bob paused as he calmly shared with me, "Cheri, I've often thought about that very question. I'd have to say. . . unknown to me at the time . . . it was my urge to express my uniqueness as a human being and move into the right direction to follow it."

This urge to express our uniqueness, our truest purpose, in the face of what Bob has coined our "terror barrier" is quite simply life in its ever-present state of expansion and fuller expression. When we surrender to the urge, then courage and creativity become our inherent allies. For this internationally known speaker, consultant, entrepreneur, and visionary, the decision to cross the line from scarcity to prosperity consciousness included a huge leap of faith.

As Bob tells the story, "I was making $4,000 per year, and I owed five. Never making ends meet in a deadbeat job, I was not thinking much about self-actualization. In fact, I wasn't thinking much at all, and I was not a happy person. That was when a good friend of mine Ray Stanford stirred and woke me up. He introduced me to Earl Nightingale's The Strangest Secret book and audio program. After that, marvelous new ideas began to rush into my consciousness, and I began to attract the good that I desired within my life."

As Bob describes from a quotation by Louis Brandeis, "There is a spark of idealism within every human being that can be fanned into flame and will bring forth extraordinary results."

Bob repeatedly read this book and listened to Earl's instructions on the corresponding long-playing record. The program inspired him tremendously. Bob followed Earl's instructions and wrote down his dreams as goals with the specific income that he desired and the dates by which he expected them to arrive into his life. He wrote his goals on a pocket-sized card, read them aloud daily, and passionately believed that he was already in possession of his dreams. This began the process of turning Bob's fantasy into a theory, and eventually into reality.

To see Bob now—forty or so years later—as a successful businessman who can now command more income in one minute than he previously made in one year, one might say, "Well, it's easy for someone like him to become so successful. He's so gifted, so talented, so lucky, and so fearless." Oh, no, my friend. I am laughing as I write, because just as Bob teaches in all of his works—so are you! As far as fearless, as Bob stated in his earlier definition of courage, "Fear is a very real part of our lives." It is in the facing and conquering of our fears, through the mastery of our thoughts that we, too, can show our courage to succeed.

I am certain that when Bob's fire hall buddies found his goal card and began mocking him for thinking he could dream himself into a fortune, he was shaking in his pants with terror and embarrassment. Just like any of us, we want to be honored, liked, and accepted, but, more importantly, we long for recognition of who we really are. Sometimes though, our ego-driven physical being and our five senses are so compelling that our truer spiritual self can never get a word in edgewise. That is the decisive moment for change. Bob embraced his moment wholeheartedly—never looking back. Bob decided to leap away from the comforts and security of the known, and plunge forward into the risky journey of the unknown . . . to become all that he was designed to be in life, enjoying every minute along the way. Bob chose the path of true success—the progressive realization of a worthy ideal. "Cheri, it is in the doing that I get my enjoyment and reward," Bob confided. "To attract the images of the good that I desire and feel the beauty of God's presence in all that surrounds me is heaven on earth."

In Bob's book You Were Born Rich, in the chapter on the Image-Maker, he elaborates that, "The knowledge of image-making eliminates competition from your life by moving you from the competitive plane to the creative plane. You will soon understand, therefore, that in truth, the only competition you will ever have is with your own ignorance." More poignantly, we get a true glimpse of the genuine sincerity of his mission to share with others in the following passage:

"This idea [of image-making] truly excites me. To be more accurate, I should probably say sharing this idea with you excites me, because I know how it can improve every aspect of your life. I honestly love watching people grow or unfold as new ideas register in their consciousness."

I deeply felt this purity of heart within Bob when I first met him. Even from an audience of well over 10,000 people attending one of Bob's prosperity seminars, I recall a sudden flutter within my heart. I knew instinctively that in

Bob Proctor

some capacity, this man would have a profound impact on my life. At that time, I did not really understand the how or what; I simply knew it to be truth. I knew that strange and marvelous things would begin to happen in my life because when the student is ready, the teacher appears. I was ready.

Bob Proctor, in all of his uniqueness, has transcended into an extraordinary phenomenon; yet, he does it in the same manner as depicted by the Nazarene—in pure, bold and humble fashion. Through adversity and a reverent fascination for truth, Bob has risen from a life of lack, limitation, and physical turmoil to a life of self-actualization, true leadership, and abundance beyond his wildest predictions. He combines all of this with the joys of a beautiful marriage of twenty-three years to his beloved wife, Linda. Together, they enjoy their fruits of happiness with a heartwarming family of three children, nine grandchildren—and two very important members of the family, Ginger and Miss Honey, beloved Pomeranians. Socially, they attract an ever-growing circle of like-minded friends and dynamic business associates.

During our most recent conversation, I asked Bob to share with me his thoughts on marriage, youth, and God, particularly, with respect to courage. I could practically see Bob's smile through the international telephone lines during that dialog. Bob shared about marriage that, "Linda has been a tremendous influence on my life, and I'd like to think that I have also been one for her. We enjoy life, we have fun, and I admire her positive attitudes toward everything. We respect each other as individuals and as best friends." It was so nice for me to hear the ring of love and friendship that one sees in the two of them together.

We shifted our conversation to young adults and how we as their parental role models can influence their potential.

Bob replied, "As parents, we need to respect our children. They are extensions of us, and yet, they are their own unique persons. Our school systems are also a reflection of us, as parents. If we want change, we need to change within ourselves, and then through the systems."

Bob founded the Youth Mentoring International organization that mentors in a style unparalleled to any other program for teens. Through the teens—and the innate powers of each mind called imagination, will, reason, memory, intuition, and perception—Bob connects these young people to their birthright of genius and self-empowerment. Bob has the utmost respect for each youth as a unique individual, which is apparent in the electricity that draws so many young adults to his side. Whether it is with one or one thousand people, Bob is fully present and engaged with everyone.

Bob shared, "Cheri, my vision for YMI is to spread it globally and inspire teens to mentor other teens." I watched Bob inspire my own daughter as she became more involved in YMI participation. Even more significantly, Bob touched her heart by his genuine interest in her. As a parent, I appreciated Bob's acts of kindness when he offered his time by calling our home to share his compassion, words, and support during our times of family strife.

Then I asked, "How does God impact you, Bob?" He paused over the telephone. There is a brief silence. The kind of silence one expects when one is asked about something that is rather obvious to them. Then, he chimed, "Why, I see God in everything. The sound of God evolves through the law of vibration." In You Were Born Rich, he quotes the Bible saying, "It is the Power that do'eth the work." I share a special excerpt:

"The first step in the creative process is to relax and see yourself already in possession of the good that you desire. The second step is to—Let Go and Let God. In working with Spirit, [God, Divine Intelligence, or whatever name you prefer to use] it helps to focus on the truth that Spirit is in all places at all times. Since this is so, it follows that you possess the godlike ability to tap into positive thoughts anytime you wish and anywhere you choose. Moreover, once you become aware of your kinship with the creative power, that you are in truth a child of spirit, you cannot possibly be anything other than positive, forceful, radiant, and self-reliant in your dealings with the world. Once this happens, all the forces in the universe will come together to help you reach your goal or the manifestation of your Image. Finally, gaining the understanding that you are a vital part of the great creative force of the universe—and are a living part of eternal spirit—will ultimately transform the results that you are achieving in your life, every day.

"Another thing you should know about Spirit is that it is a power, which is forever flowing into and through you (we also call this power "thought"). But as Spirit or thought flows into you, you choose the image you will then form with it. Experiment for yourself—sit back, relax, and then become fully aware of this great creative capacity. You can actually form one image or picture, after another, on the screen of your mind (images of things which already exist physically, like your car, your home, your place of business, or images of things that do not yet exist—such as your short-term and long-term goals).

"But the point I want to impress upon you now, is that although Spirit is the very essence of your being, it will never move into form or into an image, without your assistance. . . . You must always build the image and know in your heart the image will materialize. You must come to look upon God as being a great unseen force which inhabits every fiber of your being, and you must also understand that the instant you form the image in your mind God will go to work in God's Perfect Way and move you into an entirely new vibration (i.e. you will begin to feel differently). So always remember, the new feeling coming over you is really God at work, and although you may sometimes express your elation by saying you feel enthusiastic, remember that the word Enthusiasm is just a derivation from the early Greek—"en theos"—meaning in God.

"Your enthusiastic attitude will, in turn, cause your actions to change, and you will start behaving differently. Moreover, not only will you begin to act differently yourself, but because of the new vibration you are in, you will begin to gravitate toward, and to attract to you, other like-minded people. Strange and wonderful things will begin to happen to you and with such regularity that you will be at a loss to explain or even to comprehend what is going on—so don't even make the attempt. Just understand it is God's Way, or the Way of the Creative Force, and accept the good as it comes and expect more of the same in the future. . . . For as long as you continue to hold the image in your mind of the good you desire, you will always be rewarded. Just have faith that what should happen, must happen, and in the right time, it will happen. . . . and guard this faith zealously!"

I hope that you felt close to your spirit in listening to the sounds of Bob's essence. O the quality of truth is so omnipresent. Like the mirror image in the calm of still waters, truth is reflected through the spoken or written word, and, in that moment there exists, amongst all of us the golden opportunity to connect spiritually as One. This is the highest resonance of harmony in the state of awareness that we all hold as our aspiration . . . world peace. This is the quiet place in our hearts where all differences melt. This is where forgiveness comes easy, and elation begins to permeate and soothe every fiber of our being. We experience the calm joy of surrender. We long to reach out and love one another. We relax in the serenity of the moment and let our hearts open unconditionally to the blissful nature of this experience. We keep going. Feel It. You deserve it. All of the jaded-ness that we have carried into our lives vanishes into the wind. We close our eyes, smile with our minds, relax our bodies completely, and become filled with marvelous visions. We soar to new heights that penetrate the clouds with effortless wings of confidence. We let go, and with great awe and an ever so deep faith, we let God. We become filled with our gloriously perfect spirit . . . expanding us ever so quietly into the miraculous beings we—each one of us—were designed to become! It is in moments of life, like these, where we, humans, have the chance to turn the tides of our lives. Cry, perhaps, and reach deep down inside your heart and. . . begin anew to decide, "What are you willing to trade your life for?"

As I reflect on the privilege of writing these words from my heart to yours through Bob, tears fill my eyes. If I were to pass on tonight, I would have accomplished my truest purpose in this mission of self-expression, and I cannot think of a more loving purpose than to honor my fellow friends in the sea of humanity.

Thank you, Bob for your light of God upon us.

◆ ◆ ◆

Courage is having a braveness of heart. Feeling the fear and doing it anyway. Laughing at your fear and letting it disappear.

—Mark Victor Hansen

Mark Victor Hansen

CHAPTER TWELVE
Courage In Mind

Mark Victor Hansen

The Courage to Dare Beyond Belief

**Courage is having a braveness of heart.
Feeling the fear and doing it anyway.
Laughing at your fear and letting it disappear.
—Mark Victor Hansen**

How do I capture the beam of love that radiates from the brave heart of this man's soul? How do I share with you the essence of goodness that unfolds with every vision that he manifests? How do I etch the profile of a delightful human being that has dared to face his own fears, look adversity squarely in the eye, transcend all barriers, and move into a realm of life that resembles Heaven itself? How do I keep his wave upon the sand or catch his cloud and pin it down? How do I pass this moonbeam to your hand?

Courage in Mind

I do it from my heart's melody as God moves my spirit in gratitude. I take a deep breath and pray in silent appreciation for the wisdom, I have recognized within myself though the reflection of Mark Victor Hansen, internationally acclaimed speaker, author, motivator, coach, visionary, humanitarian, and generous soul. Mark has nurtured my heart, expanded my intellectual awareness, and exalted my spirit, affirming to me that my dreams are, indeed, my realities-in-the-making. As a skilled mentor, Mark has helped me to realize that the person I was as a young girl—with big imaginative dreams—is the same person that God designed me to be—now and forever.

The co-creator of the *Chicken Soup for the Soul* book series and co-founder of the Three Percent Club, resembles a contemporary King Arthur who leaves a legacy of unprecedented contribution to humanity.

When I think of Mark, I reflect on the awesome beauty in all that is, was, and ever will be here in life. The song, "Sound of Music" by Richard Rodgers & Oscar Hammerstein II rings the joy of the moment in honoring the essence of Mark's genuine desire to bring Heaven within all human spirits:

> "The hills are alive
> With the sound of music.
> With songs they have sung
> For a thousand years.
> The hills fill my heart
> With the sound of music -
> My heart wants to sing
> Every song it hears.
>
> My heart wants to beat
> Like the wings
> Of the birds that rise
> From the lake to the trees.
> My heart wants to sigh
> Like a chime that flies

Mark Victor Hansen

> From a church on a breeze,
> To laugh like a brook
> When it trips and falls
> Over stones in its way,
> To sing through the night
> Like a lark who is learning to pray –
>
> I go to the hills
> When my heart is lonely,
> I know I will hear
> What I've heard before.
> My heart will be blessed
> With the sound of music.
> And I'll sing once more."

Certainly, God's will is in action as he works his benevolent ways through this man who dares to win, illustrating through his life that when the Lord closes a door, somewhere he opens a window.

The first time I met Mark, he was a guest speaker for a large audience of 10,000 enthusiastic entrepreneurs. His visionary and entertaining style of speaking captured the entire audience. Standing tall at 6'4" with his blonde hair and captivating blue eyes, Mark put us all in motion within moments. We were instructed to write our own one-hundred-one goals for life in just twenty minutes! At first, it sounded ridiculous and impossible, but Mark had done the same thing himself years earlier, and knew we could do it too. Mark shared with everyone how he and his *Chicken Soup* partner and friend Jack Canfield had produced their publishing brainchild on post-it notes in similar fashion. Mark impassioned us in his belief that we, too, could achieve our wildest dreams. Mark and Jack proved it so. It is quite incredulous to fathom the boundless opportunities already proven by what Time magazine has coined the "publishing phenomena of the decade." Collectively, the

Chicken Soup series has sold—last count—eighty million copies in the series, making it one of the most successful publishing franchises in America today.

I decided to follow the personal leadership of this master motivator, especially, because he was so highly recognized by another true mentor of mine, Bob Proctor. As all things occur on purpose, opportunities led these two great humanitarians and prosperity-conscious leaders together to create their celebrated Three Percent Club, designed to assemble a network of like-minded wealth creators. Statistics reveal that three-percent of the world's population own ninety-seven-percent of financial wealth. Mark and Bob are driven to create one million new millionaires within the next decade and direct this new economic abundance toward acts of goodness on earth.

Isn't this concept refreshing in a society where surface beauty and personalities tend to dominate media and public attention? In a society where internal beauty and exceptional character traits are clamoring to be called upon, yet rarely recognized, it is clearly progressive to work with such honorable leaders in this new millenium. Fortunately, I even gained enormous insight into my own purpose in life through my Three Percent Club membership. In listening repeatedly to Mark's audiotape program *How to Think Bigger Than You Have Ever Thought You Could Think*, I discovered my passion.

Day upon day, I would drive up the rugged hills of Colorado on Interstate 70 through the Rocky Mountain canyons up toward the spectacular snow-capped peaks in Summit County's ski country, where I was conducting business in sales and marketing for a large corporation. It was fun, but it represented someone else's mission and not mine. I was seeking something deeper in my life.

Tirelessly praying to God, I would ask for guidance to my own mission and visions to make a difference in serving humanity. I desired a lifestyle of income-generating abundance that would cultivate my purpose, nourish my human growth and development, serve my Lord, and keep me close to home with my loving husband, daughter, and son. I desired (like all of us) to contribute my ideas to society well beyond my physical presence in legendary manner. While driving, I would either listen to Napoleon Hill's *Think and Grow Rich*; Bob Proctor's remake of Earl Nightingale's *Lead the Field* or Mark's *Think Bigger* audio programs. One night on the way down the mountain back home, suddenly it came to me, listening to Mark's voice. I had always enjoyed writing and now I realized that I wanted to write about people. I wanted to honor their own inner beauty as reflected through their acts of goodness. I wanted to honor and celebrate the centered qualities of humanity while encouraging the awareness of character development, especially for our youth. I also wanted to create a positive movement toward this effort through the arts and media with the collective talents of others. From that moment forward, I became as focused on my desire as if I were preparing to give birth to a new child. I could not get enough of Mark's coaching. I became an avid student of his philosophy through tapes, videos, books, live discussions on the telephone, and in person at Three Percent Club summits.

As I listened to this fun-loving leader's effervescent voice, I felt like he was speaking one-on-one with me. Mark's dynamic message also conveyed a deep sense of genuine love for humanity and an unquenchable thirst for service to God and the universe. Sometimes, I even noticed myself answering his questions and talking to him aloud while driving. It made for an amusing scene when an adjacent driver caught me in the act, staring at me in bewilderment. So what, do it anyway! I thought to myself. That is the joy of Mark's leadership. He can inspire one to be utterly outrageous, spontaneous, and—human. That is his hallmark of bravado. He has the courage to open himself up to the world with humility, and share the trials alongside the triumphs.

I have watched Mark during our summits in a sobering weep as he allows himself to speak in candor and chagrin on heartfelt testimonies about his life. Ever so gracefully, he glides naturally into the next moment with total self-awareness and a fondness for the connection that he ignites with his audience. In so doing, Mark can make you feel like you are indeed a very important person who holds a valued place in his heart. Conversely, because of his deep faith in humanity and the immutable laws of the universe, he also trusts that you, too, care about him.

Even in my work on the sketch of this busy man, I am astonished at his transparent and sincere persona. One Friday evening, I walked into my home office to turn off the lights only to discover a fax from Mark. He had replied to questions that I had asked him regarding his thoughts on courage with handwritten notes. That night he got me going on my project into the late hours because I knew that this publishing magnate believed in me. I realized just how committed he was to mentorship. A few days later, I received a priority package from the *Chicken Soup* Office with his *Dare to Win* book that included Mark's handwritten notes of encouragement and other documents with insight to his perspectives.

In spite of his full schedule, I truly feel Mark genuinely cares to be as hands-on as humanly reasonable in his desires to mentor those who ask of him. Why not ask? After all, he and Jack produced the audio program *The Aladdin Factor* that teaches the benefits gained by those who dare to ask for what they want. Asking is perfectly healthy, the Bible tells us so. In fact, allow me to ask you, Would you like to catapult your success immediately? If so, I highly encourage you to visit both chickensoup.com and threepercentclub.com. Be prepared, however, for a completely new and exciting life!

Mark Victor Hansen

More poignantly, I would like to share some tender tales in Mark Victor Hansen's life that have so beautifully portrayed his brave-hearted deeds, which imbue his fine character. After all, can we relate to this icon? Has he ever had a bleak day? Can we identify with him as having any real problems? Let's see.

Today, Mark creates an idyllic lifestyle with his loving wife, Patty, and his two daughters, Liz and Melanie, that includes one week's vacation per month, a California estate, and a second home in Hawaii. As he says, quoting Jesus, "The kingdom is within so I decorate actively inside." Here lies the key to his winning attitude of gratitude and courage. How could this happy Christian be anywhere but in the kingdom of Heaven? How did he get there?

Beyond Christ, Mark attributes his auspicious enlightenment to Buckminster Fuller and Cavett Robert, both successful entrepreneurs. To anyone interested in becoming a person of stronger character—a bolder, braver person of integrity—Mark advises, "Get a mentor who has been there and will help you along your own path of greatness."

Buckminster Fuller indirectly transformed Mark's life through an unforeseen financial disaster. Mark was only twenty-six years old, yet he was successfully building his career in the construction of geodesic domes. Dr. Fuller had invented the popular domes, which were petrochemical triangles linked together to form living units. Suddenly, Mark's business crashed as the 1974 Middle Eastern Oil Embargo prohibited the purchase of the required products. Almost overnight, Mark was forced into bankruptcy due to the escalating costs related to the embargo.

Instantly, Mark went from the top to the very bottom of his career ladder. He still recalls the sober tone of the judge that declared him bankrupt. In fact, Mark actually had to borrow a book from the library called *How to Go Bankrupt by Yourself* to handle the case. Mark described this period of his life as his lowest of lows and said that he began to feel physically ill as tears, nausea, and earaches began to show up daily. "I felt rejected and dejected, personally and professionally. I climbed deep within a shell while sleeping nearly around the clock. I remember a diet of peanut butter and a lifestyle of escapist behavior. I was afraid that everybody knew that I was bankrupt, and I felt like a total failure at the time," Mark reminisced candidly.

With his self-esteem completely shattered, he was "at the bottom," as he says. Yet, ironically, this all-time crisis was the pivotal act that became his greatest opportunity in disguise. He learned to live the principles that he suggests in *Dare to Win*. One of the basics that Mark realized from this experience is that there was always a way to solve every problem no matter how bleak things looked and felt . . . and giving up was not one of them. Furthermore, he felt that things could not get any worse. In fact, from hereon, everything simply had to improve. Ironically, Mark realized that it was at the point of his bankruptcy when everything became a potential possibility toward future success. The world's endless opportunities become more visible to the open-minded person.

From that experience, Mark moved up all over again while applying and living by the principles he now teaches to all. He burned his bridges behind him and, therefore, felt that he had to succeed. The rest is history for as one idea lead to another, Mark eventually partnered with his friend Jack Canfield to launch the *Chicken Soup* book and merchandising series.

Although hard for us to imagine such a successful entrepreneur in this predicament, I believe he provides hopeful inspiration for all of us to rise above our adversities and even use our God-given sense of humor to laugh at ourselves from time to time. Moreover, as I read over many of Mark's books, I can't help but marvel at the harmony we share in our mutual desire to encourage acts of love and true character within humanity. His book *Miracles of Tithing* speaks eloquent volumes to his qualities.

What did I discover on Mark's brave-heartedness in romance? Mark feels a love that lasts a lifetime is generated by a belief that it will last a lifetime. He believes that when you find the perfect other for you, there will be no question and no doubt because you will know, and know that you know that you know.

In describing his own love, Mark expressed how his wife, Patty opened his heart in a magnificent, yet subtle way. "I was both startled and amazed. I had been to India in 1968 and had sat at the feet of a guru expecting what is called *shaktipat*—the experience of having one's heart opened. Yet, I had never understood what I saw other students learning. Now, suddenly, I felt my heart opening. I received the knowledge. Patty opened my heart, which in thirty-one years had never felt anything like it. I felt it again when my babies, Elizabeth Day and later, Melanie Dawn, were born. I gave each daughter their inaugural birthing bath in the labor room. The feeling was like a laser light of love that synchronized our two hearts."

Still, I cannot speak on this man's brave character without emphasizing the power within his awakening spirit — his inner voice. Mark admitted that his initial experiences with church were negative and unfulfilling. However, shortly after he went bankrupt, he was invited to hear Dr. Norman Vincent Peale at the Marble Collegiate Church in Manhattan. Mark felt uplifted and began to notice a spiritual void within himself that he desired to nurture immediately. He then went with friends to see Reverend Ike in Washington Heights, New York. Mark described, "We were three white men visiting a predominately black church for the first time. We were loved, hugged, kissed, and welcomed. No one knew or cared that I had gone bankrupt just days before. There was a feeling that everyone was growing and knowing spiritually. When Reverend Ike talked, he ignited my spiritual spark plug. He provided me with exciting new insights into spiritual teaching. I discovered that my bankruptcy had put my mind, soul, and spirit in bondage. I wanted to be free spiritually and economically. He said, 'God is rich. He created the Universe and all that's in it. God is infinite. You have God in you, so you have infinite creative possibilities within you.' Wow! I could feel the spirit moving within me (and it is a *felt* experience). My spiritual side was being awakened for the first time, and I was on my way toward becoming a spiritual person," expressed Mark in *Dare to Win*.

The nature of our own spiritual experience of humanity draws us toward serving others. For it is through our desire to love, serve, and give of ourselves that we receive universal feelings of joy, rapture, vibrancy, and value. In this very moment, as you and I celebrate Mark Victor Hansen, we are connected in that spiritual feeling of joy in our oneness with God and each other. For we, too, embrace the goodness that we recognize in the mirrors of love reflected in Mark's acts of courage. Just as in the joyous words of Rodgers and Hammerstein II's, "Climb Ev'ry Mountain," we are exalted and uplifted by each other in our quest to find our dream.

We honor you, Mark, and your immeasurable value to humanity.

◆ ◆ ◆

Courage is how much you believe in yourself... and how brave you are.

—Steven H. Lutton II

Steven Lutton on Easter Sunday

CHAPTER THIRTEEN
Courage In Mind

Steven H. Lutton II
The Courage to Be Honest

> **Courage is how much you believe in yourself... and how brave you are.**
> —Steven H. Lutton II

A mother's heart warms at the sights and sounds of her children. The tender hug in the morning cheers on the start of a new dawn. The sleepy kisses after a bedtime story promise sweet dreams and a good night's sleep. These tiny moments create a mother-child bond that not even an earthquake could ever quiver apart.

The silly laughter and creative make-believe that my son invites me to embrace reminds me of the essence of God's design which many of us, as adults, have forgotten or tossed out as child's play. The ability to dream of worlds beyond by expressing our imagination, free of inhibitions and fears, is a gift to be cherished forever.

These times are the stuff that life is made of and I thank God every morning that my son, Steven, reawakens me with these beautiful experiences. In the silence of our children, may we as adults find the way to our destinies . . . our hearts' delights.

My son, born April 8 1992, is only eight years old as I write this chapter. Yet, Steven inspires me with more lessons of human valor in his tiny life than I can even recall from any adult. Fears within a young mind are quieted in a child who is still blessed with purity and candor of thought. In other words, my son is still willing to talk openly with me about his fears, face them, and realize a solution that will "poof" them away.

I am especially proud of his genuine sense of concern for others. I can vividly recall an event this past summer in our neighborhood. We live in the country with majestic views of the Rocky Mountains of Boulder, Colorado, backdrop to the open space of farmlands and grazing horses right across the way from us. Our residential block is quiet and friendly and our neighbors have a caring sense of watchfulness for our small community. Those of us who have children all know to guide them with tender loving attention.

My son was disturbed because he felt that his young friend had been mistakenly faulted for participating with other boys in some mischief. Steven had been there, so he knew the truth. I could see that he was somewhat troubled by it all. "Mom, I really think I should say something," he confided and so we walked over to Steven's good friend Sam's home. My son bravely and politely spoke up for Sam to his friend's mother. Steven's only concern was to make sure that truth was known, regardless of the consequences.

There have been many instances where I have watched him quietly decide to take the path of courage over popular acceptance. I have seen tears well up in his eyes, and pallor come over his face in these seemingly innocent incidents of boyhood life. It is tough at any age to face fear and take the high road. Yet, these are the building blocks of a young boy's framework toward manhood. It is not a moment too early to inspire leadership within a child's heart.

In such a sweet face with the blue Paul Newman eyes of loyalty and the soft brown hair of a young prince, I see the beginnings of a man who someday could become the leader of the free world. I want my son to dream big and stand tall in the face of any adversity that crosses his path. I want my son to be proud of his American heritage. I want him to enjoy true freedom, yet respect the awesome responsibility it carries. Most of all, I want Steven to cherish his right to become all that he dares to dream . . . all that he believes . . . and all that God has created for him.

When I reflect on my son, I can assuredly affirm that even at ten years old, he has the makings of a great leader. I can rest in the comfort that the qualities he possesses are developing the foundations for his values and character. I share with you proven tales of Steven's courage from earlier days.

Once upon a day off during third grade, Steven expressed openly to me "Mom, I feel like a leader today," "How so, my son?" I offered curiously. "Well, yesterday in school, Mrs. Burns forgot to write my name on the blackboard for not handing in my homework on time. My friend noticed and said to me, 'Steven, you're lucky, you won't have to miss out on five minutes of free time, because Mrs. Burns forgot to write your name, and you didn't bring in your homework today.'

"Mom, I thought about it, and I got up and told Mrs. Burns," Steven continued, "My name belongs on the board, and I need to miss five minutes of free time. I'm sorry I didn't finish all of my homework on time, but I will bring it in on Monday." Mrs. Burns openly replied, "Thank you, Steven, for reminding me and for being so honest."

Steven and I went outside that morning and measured the circumference of trees, which was the rest of his homework project. Later, he confided to me that he felt so good about doing his homework, and showing his friends how he wants to be honest, even though it can be tough. For the rest of the day, my son was on top of the world because as he expressed, "I felt like I made a difference."

On the subject of leaders, I recently asked Steven whom he admired. He smiled and giggled as he responded, "Well, you and Dad, of course, Mom. I also look up to Crystal (his sister) and John [Solis]—he's cool! I really like my music teacher Mrs. Watson—she's so nice and makes everything fun. Actually, all of my teachers have been good leaders, Mom." Steven's grin gets bigger as he tops off his list exclaiming, "And, I've always admired my good friends—Sam [Garrett], Daniel [Johs], and Tyler [Slade]."

I cast my vote for Steven as a leader without bias. Yet, regardless of his future calling, I love him unconditionally and respect his brave and tender spirit. I feel a sense of serenity within my heart knowing that my part is complete in offering him God's design for life.

My heartfelt prayers go out for all mothers of the world who have offered their sons the Lord's way, and, yet, whose sons have reflected chaos and evil in their lives. Continue, O Lord, to watch over our children. Bless our own good intentions as parents. Grace us with the understanding and faith that . . . with each new day's awakening, we can all become grateful for our lives and another golden opportunity for self-discovery and growth. Please help us to offer forgiveness and goodness through unconditional love, which we vow to express in our modeling examples of your way. Lastly, give us the parental strength to trust and accept when we just need to let go and let God.

"Mom?" whispered my little hero as I drove him to his football practice—now a year and many American

Steven H. Lutton II

tragedies later. "I love you," he added, looking at me in the car with his big blue eyes and innocent smile. "I love you too, son," I replied, smiling as I admired the smallest player on the team with the biggest heart in the world.

O yes, my son, I love you very, very much. God bless you, Steven . . . and all of our world's children!

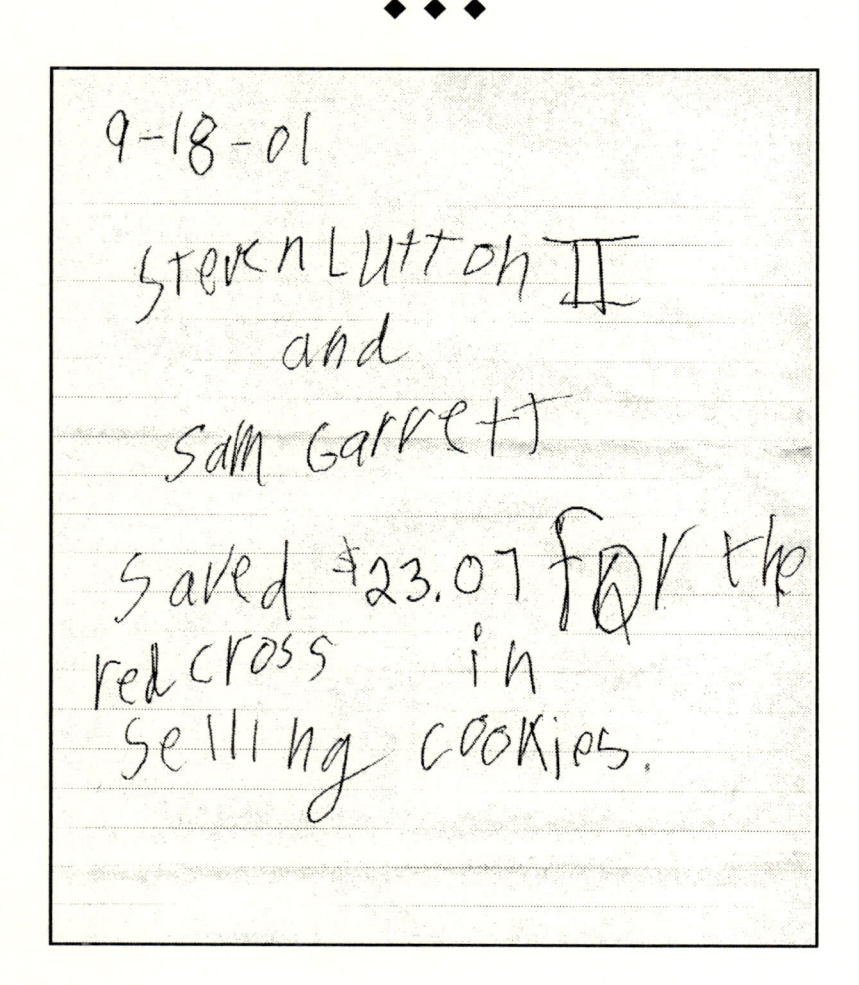

◆ ◆ ◆

> 9-18-01
>
> Sreven Lutton II
> and
> Sam Garrett
>
> Saved $23.07 for the
> red cross   in
> selling cookies.

PART THREE
Courage In Body

Stay the Course with the End in Mind

Day to day, individuals with courage will either elect to conquer the ordinary or be required to conquer the extraordinary. Either way, nature's forces will move on and new heroes will be standing tall in a world that is made better for all.

CHAPTER FOURTEEN
Courage In Body

Stay the Course with the End in Mind

Day to day, individuals with courage will either elect to conquer the ordinary or be required to conquer the extraordinary. Either way, nature's forces will move on and new heroes will be standing tall in a world that is made better for all.

What triggers a runner to continue toward the finish line of a marathon when he or she hits the wall of the 21st mile with a fatigue that screams for comfort? Is it the fear of defeat or the dream of victory that sends the body back into gear with a second wind? Join me as we take a run together while I share with you, my experience as a marathon runner. . . .

With salty sweat running down the sides of my cheeks, shoulders, and lower back, I grabbed a cup of water at the next water station. I quenched my thirst and poured the rest

Courage in Body

on top of my head to cool down my overheated 5'2" slender body. Rechecking my breathing pattern, I knew how important oxygenation is as fuel for the last five miles. My calf muscles tightened with the sensation of two lead balloons. My legs remained in motion only by command of a will now driven by the sheer grit and determination . . . to finish what I began. I stumbled as my right ankle buckled inward and I fell onto the asphalt street. My hands were stinging as I landed on pebbles that burned my palms. I looked up to the blur of legs ahead of me. I must get up, I thought. Now I can't see clearly through the salty sweat clouding my vision as it dripped down my forehead, through my brows, and onto my eyelashes. I knew that I had to get up or I would lose my momentum entirely. Yet, I had lost my speed, wind, and pace. For a moment, I thought of the overwhelming task ahead and I could not fathom finishing. I knew, however, that if I allowed this thought to remain, I would be doomed to failure. No, I said to myself, I must only think of the moment at hand and that—there is no other option. I must finish.

Blood was now dripping from my hands onto my face as I wiped the sweat, again, from my eyelids. I must get it back, I thought. I must continue. I must finish what I began. Panic began tempting me. Doubt was seducing me. Comfort was beckoning me to quit—as the heat of the sun on a mid-morning August day—began to bake the 15,000 athletes, running through the city of Denver. Delirium crossed my mind and I began to lose my focus. I took deeper breaths and shifted my focus. I was beginning to reclaim my mental power and relaxed back into a state of expectant confidence. I became a very determined marathon runner who began to get it back. I called upon all of the resources that lie deep within each fiber of my being. With the passion and conviction of my spirit, I called upon the will of my mind to ignite my body into total action.

Soon I captured a vision. The decision started to take over. I could see myself finishing in my mind's eye, and I smiled away the grimace expressed from my aches. Yes. I will. I can and I am, I began to affirm mentally. I will no longer give the pain in my muscles one more second of thoughtful energy, I silently announced. A new rush of blood now reinvigorated my circulation. New sources of oxygen began to replenish my lungs and a surge of fresh energy suddenly unleashed from my head to toes. I seized the moment and refused to succumb to any distractions. My attention was now laser-focused on victory and I screamed affirmations of joy aloud as I threw my arms into the air, turning around the last corner before the home stretch. I no longer cared whether I looked strange. We all did anyway. Now, in total command of my body, I would not permit any thought of aches and pains to penetrate my will. In fact, I felt great! The second wind brought relief to my muscles and I was now in rare form as I smiled and waved to the onlookers, cheering me on from the streets. My hair was blowing back with the breeze as I raced nearer to my destination.

I savored this last moment and . . . grabbed the victory that I had already received in my mind and spirit. Yes! Mission accomplished. I cross the 26-mile finish line. I was ecstatic, exhausted, and ready to accept the feelings that accompany such a win. I became the master of my fate, conquering my personal best in long-distance running. I realized in that moment that courage knows no barriers or boundaries.

The commitment to endure lingers in every human being that has ever been dedicated to any physical accomplishment. It may be a decisive commitment to start a nutritional diet, which nourishes our physiologic needs with fresh sources of energy. Or, the decision may be to commit one-hundred-percent to action toward a new career that is more in alignment with our truest purpose. Regardless, the launch

Courage in Body

of a new lifestyle can invigorate the soul to soaring heights. In each circumstance, we arrive at a committed decision in our daily lives with a call to action. We manifest our spiritual purpose through our mental images. We express our intentions in concert with our senses as an experience of physical activity. Eventually, this image takes form as our goal, ideal, or accomplishment. Then, voila! Our truest purpose comes to form for all to enjoy.

Yet, can we really move beyond any of these stepping stones without a respect for the miracle of our bodies? After all, isn't this our unique residence throughout our entire lives? Can we expect our physiological processes to perform optimally if we do not provide our physical beings with an appropriate and balanced diet? Truly, all one has to do is seek, and bountiful resources of delicious foods throughout the lands can be enjoyed for life. My husband, Steve, invests tender loving care every fall into growing herbs, fruits, and vegetables from seedlings in our home's grow-light room. Steve then transplants these carefully germinated plants outside, and into the sunniest area of our lush acreage. Throughout the spring and summer, he enthusiastically nurtures these plants to blooming life for our family to enjoy a continuous supply of fresh garden salads and seasonings. Whether or not you are married to such a gifted gardener, or enjoying the services of local resources, there are plenty of opportunities for anyone to reap the benefits of healthy nutritional choices in great foods, pure water, and delicious treats.

The world is a garden filled with a myriad of choices, the black, the white, and the gray. Just examine the ill-defined temptations of today that wittingly entice us toward unhealthy recreational pleasures. Can we really make clear decisions about the ingestion of alcohol, drugs, and tobacco without receiving any information on their short and long-term side effects? Would our teenage sons and daughters be so quick to experiment with any of these substances if they were given objective data on their crippling consequences? Ignorance is a liability that we must, as advanced nations, be ambitious to eliminate. Intelligent decisions by intelligent human beings can only be the result of intelligent awareness of our choices.

In the height of the information age, we are bestowed with more technology than ever. In minutes, we can easily educate ourselves on any subject under the sun. "Just say no" has become a popular slogan for self-empowerment in the modern campaign against usage of these substances. All too often, drugs end up deterring capable bodies from peak performance and even causing potential disaster for many an extraordinary human body.

Ultimately, our free will—our gift of choice—will determine our intent to live with integrity and walk our talk through our values, beliefs, and dreams. We are masters of our actions. We possess the discipline and self-control to give ourselves a command—and follow it through. We can take ourselves seriously and know in our heart that we have integrity. The world will then begin to see us as we are—living examples of our purpose moving in harmony with the Universe and just as importantly, having a blast. As coined by Nike, "just — —."

So how do we get started? How can we change years of bad habits? First, we congratulate ourselves for that decision, that moment of honesty within ourselves. We must be willing to be honest with God—and ourselves. We must also trust ourselves, and believe in the universal birthright of abundance and love for all, letting go of our scarcity consciousness. We can let God guide us in our desire to enjoy this good and plentiful life. Once firmly planted, we nourish our desire and need to grow every day.

We are life; we are energy; therefore, by nature, we grow.

We do not desire just to survive, but also to thrive. We excite in playing to win—not just playing not to lose. My mentor Larry Wilson has helped many people with life-changing strategies on this very concept, discussed in more detail in Chapter Ten. In fact, he has written the book *Play to Win*. Larry represents a new genre of business, leadership, mentoring, and interactive change through fun and adventure. Leaders such as Larry Wilson will carry this world into a spiritual evolution of cooperative-growth based on abundance and prosperity and away from competitive-fear based on lack and limitation. Dare to ask and expect to receive. What a fascinating way of life!

Once we recognize the importance of being honest with God and ourselves, trusting in God's laws of love and abundance, we can begin our change. We can decide consciously on a plan of action in harmony with our truest purpose, moving toward our desires to grow in harmony with the universe. We can employ our mental faculties, our senses, and our subconscious to show us the way. While our conscious chooses what and why, our subconscious (or spirit) will go to work in showing us how, when, and where. We simply trust in our image of the good that we desire and commit to a call for action as the plan unfolds itself. We write down our desired intentions and see the daily steps that we need to put into action. We write them down and commit to action. We call on our imagination, and our senses, to see and feel our bodies in action. We are integrated with our goals, possessing integrity. We take care of ourselves, and, yet, we take bold steps on our journey into the unknown, into the brave new world that we desire to embody and experience.

Like Columbus, we set sail with full intention to chart our personal course of discovery with great enthusiasm and undivided attention. We are committed, and no one is going to stop us now. We hit obstacles, unforeseen challenges, rough waters, and criticism from many along the way—even from family and friends. We stop, challenge, and choose our desired course of actions in serving our purpose. We may choose to ignore; we may choose to modify our course in response to the input. Nonetheless, we are unwavering in our quest to succeed. We seek and receive positive affirmations from an understanding team of like-minded visionaries. When we can include our spouse or children in our support group, our spirits will soar dramatically to heights of unimaginable dimensions. As a family bonded in love, we can move mountains of intent into action—for the entire world to enjoy!

On those first days, it will be difficult to envision ourselves in our new habits. Our bodies might not have yet acquired the keen skills to appear sharp at our new activities. However, we must carry on and congratulate ourselves on where we are in that moment.

Regardless of the accolades that we do or do not receive from other people, we must believe that God is always watching and smiling upon us. When we are weary, God carries us. His heartfelt strength rejuvenates our spirits. We see and believe in ourselves, as we desire to realize this new experience. We have an attitude of gratitude. We read our commitment, and tape our affirmations verbally, so that we can listen to our own voices repeating our affirmations each morning, and before we go to sleep at night. We refuse to be tempted by ease, by chaos, by distraction, by popular trends, by mental worry, doubt, anxiety, fear, or guilt. We take pride in our ability to remain calm and relax with conscious respect for the need for deep regular breaths of fresh air. We hydrate ourselves regularly with pure refreshing water. We enjoy nightly rest and periodic intervals of quiet reflection and repose throughout our day. We balance our daily activities with reverence for our emotional needs and desires, as well as our personal and professional goals—and challenges.

Seem daunting? All you have to accomplish is enough to fill one moment at a time. At the end of the day, you will have accomplished all that is the best of you. Your best each day is an awesome gift—for you and the world!

When is the best time to start? Now. Tomorrow is never here, and yesterday is already gone. If we wait until we are perfectly ready, we will never begin. Yes, the time to begin to be is now. We start right where we are and go forward inch by inch, day by day, with the end in mind—as if it is already in our hands. How do we begin? Well, it is said that old unwanted habits can be replaced in thirty to ninety days with new desired habits after a consistent and committed daily call-for-action program. I share with you a call-for-action program that can be easily remembered through the acronym, **I. B.E.G.I.N. N.O.W.**

"I. B.E.G.I.N. N.O.W."

Intend to begin a call-for-action on a specific physical goal by a target date—like right now.

Become 100% committed with written and verbal accountability.

Enthuse the mind and senses emotionally with daily affirmations and imagery.

Go for it right now!

Increase support with like-minded teammates or a mastermind group.

Nightly and daily recite affirmations and emotionally visualize—the end in mind.

Never give up, but always be willing to adjust.

Optimistically expect your accomplished goal.

Win with conviction in the face of adversity, criticism, or a modified strategy.

Cheri Lutton

Daily stories exist of staggering courage that occurs from the battlefield to the ballfield. I am awestruck by the heroes that have given their lives for the rest of us to embrace a better world. For those who have survived their obstacles in life by the sheer will to live, I can deeply empathize. I close by sharing my story with you on my own will to survive. Bring your imagination, a towel, and a life jacket. . . .

It has been a peaceful ride on the Arkansas River—up to now. The sun is hot and the skies are clear as we take in the views of the red stone canyon and green grass along the banks of the higher-than-average waters. Water levels are at 5500 cubic feet per second (cfs) during this '93 season, compared to a drought season that can be as low as 500 cfs. Up to this point, our trip has been fairly sedate, calm, and pleasant. The waters are smooth and glistening. Steve and I are happy that we decided to join his friend Wayne on this weekend get-away to spend time together in the mountains, while enjoying a day rafting adventure. As a married couple with two children, we like to treat ourselves from time to time. This feels relaxing, I thought as I smile and wink at Steve. He responds in kind, adding a hug. With two rafts full of fun-loving adults, it seems that everyone is enjoying the ride. There is much laughter, splashing, and good-natured play carrying on between the two boats of rafters. After a leisurely break for lunch, however, the mood turns to excitement as we soon experience the infamous whitewater rapids of Brown's Canyon.

Back into our rafts, I bask in the sun's heat along with my other five mates for the last time. Just ahead, I see the white bubbles spraying into the air from the crash of the waters. I hear the roaring sounds, and the air is feeling a bit more chilled and moist. This is my third rafting expedition, and yet, each time it feels like the first because each ride is so different. I am excited—and nervous.

Courage in Body

I focus my eyes on our navigator who begins to change positions with a guide-in-training. I start wondering about the wisdom of this decision as we approach the wildest stretch of the river. In fact, I am stunned at his next move. We are heading straight for a huge rock with fast waters spiraling around each side of it. I am thinking, "What are you doing?!"

Before I could utter a word, we are perched on the rock and the lower side of the raft starts to cave down into the river. White water is everywhere. The waters roar loudly as if they are yelling at us. Two of the rafters, along with the navigator and trainee, scramble to the top of the rock. The other four of us are swept away by the water's momentum deep into the chilling waters. Steve goes under immediately while his ankle gets caught on the rope from the raft. Quickly, he struggles to free his ankle. Fortunately, he untangles his leg while underwater, then swims up swiftly and toward the right bank through the rough currents. The other three rafters, somehow, make it to another rock—standing, shivering, and staring—as they await a rescue.

I am not so lucky. I fall instantly into the icy waters, smack into what is known as "the toilet bowl" rapids. The forces of the spiral suddenly suck me underwater. Then just as quickly, I am spit out into the air a few feet above the river surface, only to immediately splash back below the waves, then back out again—quickly floating on the waves. I remember the guide's advice at the beginning of our journey. I remind myself of his words now, "Keep your feet straight in front to protect yourself from the elements. Stay horizontal on your back with head up and eyes glued to the sights ahead." I brace myself. Okay, I'm thinking, Here we go. . . .

I hear my name to the right . . . It's Steve's voice. I catch a sobering glimpse of my husband staring frantically into my eyes. Would it be my last look at him? Oh no! Is this it?

Dear God, please help me. I am so scared and I am not sure I know how to handle this. What I do know, though, is that there are more rapids ahead with lots of rocky banks to my left side. Suddenly, I go under again and begin to swallow lots of water this time. By now, I am really cold, tired, and delirious. I just want to close my eyes, stop swimming so hard, and go to sleep. Then, amazingly, I catch myself in my surrendering consciousness. I realize that I am very close to death. In a heartbeat, I recognize that the only way I can survive is if I will all of my attention into an enormous fight for my life.

Suddenly, I recall my children back at home being cared for by loved ones. I remember my brother's wedding is next weekend. I think about my husband desperately running along the banks trying helplessly to follow me. I yearn for more of all that I love and enjoy in life. I want to live. I will do whatever it takes.

I call on all of my inner resources now and adapt to—whatever. I quiet the panic within, and maintain a sense of calmness, preparing for the ride ahead. Then, as if he had fallen from the heavens like a guardian angel, I catch the sight of a kayak and a kayaker to my right. He smiles ever so quickly and commands me to jump on top of his kayak. Okay, I go for it. He tips and down under, he goes. Now, I am hanging on to an upside down kayak. Of course, I have to release to save him, so I go under. . . again. This time it becomes harder for me to find my way above the surface. The waters are wilder and stronger in their urge to pull me underneath. I begin to swallow more water and feel like I am drowning. Everything gets so fuzzy and tiring. I resist, though, enough to finally succeed in seeing air. I cough up the excess water and there, again, I see my rescuing angel. He firmly directs me to come onto the left side of the kayak. I plunge all of my energies forward and grab it with all of my might. I latch on to the front and he rows us over to the right bank. He saves my life. Whew, I am ecstatic—and exhausted.

Slowly, I stand up in the shallow waters and begin to recover with very deep breaths. Finally, I can cry, and begin sobbing gratefully. It is quite an emotional release. Then, I feel my shin aching and pull up my wetsuit leg to see a gash. Interestingly enough, the wetsuit is not torn. Apparently, the force of the rock and the water cut me on my initial fall out of the raft. Soon I forget about it, and, instead, I am laughing and thanking God fervently for my life. Steve stares affectionately as he runs to me. We must have looked like that commercial where the two lovers are running in slow motion toward each other. Oh, do we hug. . . for a long, long time. "Hi, honey," I say with a smile as I look into his big brown caring eyes. "I am so glad to see you!" Steve replies emphatically and continues, "Why don't we call it a day?" "That's fine with me," I reply, adding, "Let's go have a drink and celebrate." He smiles and we kiss. "Wait, I need to thank someone," I abruptly said, turning to thank the kayaker who just saved my life . . . but, he is gone. I look down the river and faintly catch a glimpse of my hero strolling down the stream through the canyon. "Thank you!" I scream and then I pray.

Aside from the gash on my shin, I was left unscathed physically by the experience. Emotionally, I am transformed for life. I deeply respect the forces of nature, the power of prayer and . . . my own free will. Amen.

Courage is never having to say I can't . . . always believing that with enough planning and determination . . . anything can be accomplished.

—Steven H. Lutton

Steven Lutton Family

CHAPTER FIFTEEN
Courage In Body

Steven H. Lutton

The Courage to Resolve Life's Adversity

Courage is never having to say I can't . . . always believing that with enough planning and determination . . . anything can be accomplished.
—Steven H. Lutton

"Did my heart love till now? Forswear it, sight! For I ne'er saw true beauty till this night. It is my Lady; O, it is my Love!"
—Romeo

"My bounty is as boundless as the sea, my love as deep; the more I give to thee, the more I have, for both are infinite."
—Juliet

Courage in Body

These passages from William Shakespeare's *Romeo and Juliet* will remain in the treasury of my soul as the chosen words for our wedding theme. Steve has struck me with arrows of love from his heart. I now understand the bravery that is also tucked underneath his heart. For the Lord is mighty in his greatness. My epiphany is so splendid when I see the image of God in my warrior of love, my wonderful husband, for whom the bells toll for me. I thank the Lord for leading me into his life and love.

As a dedicated husband and father, Steve wears his coat of arms with an apparent sense of pride, commitment, and wholesomeness. His shield of unwavering protection guides our family in a manner that embraces the American spirit and enriches my soul with a deep belief in the power of true love, sex, and romance. Yet, conversely, Steve has a way of being one with the earth. His love for nature brings him the gift of wisdom. Lord, you have done well in guiding his light and steadfast manner. His fortitude as a born gardener bears the fruit of his year-round labor of love. I know—for I continually enjoy his delicious garden treats.

Tall, dark, and handsome, Steve is 5'10" with big brown eyes, dark brown hair, and the will of an athlete in-training. Humble and friendly, my quiet hero shares his shy heart tenderly with all. Yet, he is also a person of great character. Steve has the discernment of a lion in knowing what he must do to protect his family and himself. He has the conscience to stand by his innermost convictions . . . and the discipline and stamina to move constantly through obstacles. Most importantly, Steve has the courage to be human and grow. Ladies, he is a winner—one of those hunks who happens to be kind, gorgeous, and in love with me! Gentlemen, take notes.

My dear husband loves to climb mountains and ski in the rugged Colorado Rockies. Steve holds his American heritage

Steven H. Lutton

and its grandeur in high esteem. His dream is to climb all of the 14,000-foot mountains of this spectacular country. He truly loves the land.

One night, when we were still dating, we went skiing together, along with others, for a fun night out after work. Steve was a skilled downhill skier, accustomed to skiing the most difficult "black" runs. I was an intermediate skier, although I could handle bumps on soft not-so-steep slopes. Night skiing, however, could be tricky because once the sun sets, ice could appear over the snow where you least expect it. This happened to be Steve's first experience with night skiing and its unpredictable conditions.

Nevertheless, Steve was a joy to watch. He had that expert look when he turned downhill or traversed the bumps. He smiled and danced around me as we skied down the hills together. The rest of our group was on the beginner slopes, so it was turning into a romantic evening for us. Steve put his arm around me as we sat together riding the chair lift up the slope. He whispered invitingly, "Let's call this run our last one, Cheri, and then we can go back to my home, build a fire, and have some pizza, okay?" I looked up at him and gave him a kiss on the cheek, and then we took off to hit the last run.

I noticed the ice had worsened, so I took it a bit slower. Steve found out in the next few moments. He began skiing down on an icy hill too fast. By now, I had lost him so I had no idea of his fate. He fell, slid down into a ravine, and suddenly hit a tree. He slid sideways toward the tree and broke his right femur upon impact. I was already at the bottom of the hill, waiting and wondering where he could have gone.

By sheer instinct, Steve actually crawled out of the bleak darkness of the trees toward the light and the hill, and screamed for rescue. The pain became agonizing for him as he waited for help. Fortunately, somebody had seen him fall. "I need help!" Steve urgently advised the fellow skier. The unsung hero quickly retrieved the ski patrol to rush to Steve's rescue, while he remained flat on his back in conscious pain—and unsure of his immediate destiny.

I waited at the bottom of the ski slope for what seemed like an eternity. I kept asking myself, Where could he be? This was, after all, a time for cheer and celebration, two days after Christmas and six days after Steve's birthday. I did not want to imagine the worst.

Suddenly, a ski patrolman approached and asked me, "Are you Cheri?" I nodded guardedly. Then, he informed me that Steve has been in an accident; was hurt badly but stable, and was waiting for me. "Oh no!" I exclaimed. The kind ski patrolman assured me that Steve was at least safe. Still, I did not feel calm at all. I followed the man to the patrol's first aid center and, eventually, rounded up the other family members of our ski group. There he was—lying on a stretcher—in excruciating pain. We just looked at each other with both sadness and relief in our eyes—saddened because of the accident, yet, relieved that we were reunited and alive. "Hi, honey," is all we could express to each other. I held his hands as he groaned in severe agony. I stood speechless in heartfelt shock. The first aid staff had stabilized Steve's right leg, but I noticed that he was still complaining about his left leg.

Shortly thereafter, I was comforting him at his side in an ambulance as he was given narcotics for the pain. Everyone else met us in the emergency room where we all just stood stunned and saddened by the turn of events on such an enjoyable evening. Steve's sister Cheryl, and her husband, Scott, soon arrived to comfort Steve. This was only the second time that I had met them since our initial acquaintance at their home on Thanksgiving Day. All we had energy for now was a silent nod of acknowledgment and a focused concern on Steve's screams of pain. Our expressions silently voiced the grief we felt for Steve as we tried to comfort him. Steve continued to scream about his other leg. I was confused and concerned about all of this. X-rays did not show any break in the left leg. Why couldn't someone help him? I thought. Finally, Steve's orthopedic surgeon arrived, and I felt a small sense of relief.

"Hi, Steve," Dr. Rector said with a gentle voice between Steve's screams. Steve grimaced and nodded. The doctor began to discuss the plans for impending traction, surgery, and the predicted course for recovery. Then, Dr. Rector wiggled Steve's left knee and realized immediately that the problem was much more complicated than a broken femur.

"Steve . . . it appears that you tore three of four ligaments in your left knee and will require a totally different course of medical and surgical care. With both legs out of commission, I am afraid you will not be walking for quite a while," Dr. Rector said in a sobering voice. Steve turned his head in silence and became very pale. I held on to his hand, quietly awaiting his cue. Whew. What an evening!

By night's end, my new love would be completely incapacitated in a Boulder hospital wailing for comfort and the strength to endure. As I sat near his bed in a state of shock gazing at the Johnny Carson show for a reprieve, I tried to piece the events together. I was certain that Steve was the man that God had chosen for me. However, I prayed that our time together would last more than these three short months. I remembered the male nurse coming in to take care of Steve, remarking that if I am really his girlfriend, this event would determine how close we were, and if we would make it as a couple. I had no doubt about our bond. I just wanted him to survive.

Courage in Body

I cried for days as I watched Steve agonize 24/7 in pain before surgery, and then after his lengthy operation. One day, his oxygen level dropped so low that he needed to be rushed to a more specialized unit. As a registered nurse, I knew exactly what was happening, but I didn't want to alarm him. Once he was stabilized, I felt more at ease. He was so happy to be alive, and appreciated everyone's help. Each day, Crystal and I enjoyed watching Steve's big brown eyes and smile brighten as we entered his hospital room. "Hi, honey, it's so good to see you!" he expressed. Then, Steve turned to my four-year-old daughter, "Hi, Crystal, what did you do today?" She smiled and gave him a big hug. Steve listened intently to Crystal as she cheered his day with her artwork, stories, and songs. As a single mother who had never been married, I was perfectly at ease raising my daughter alone. Yet, now it appeared that we were both being courted by a good man, and it felt right. We became a family even in such unforeseen circumstances. "Cheri," Steve whispered in my ear and added, "I love you so much!" My heart melted every time he said this, and I knew with certainty that I was blessed, and in my moment of true love.

Two days after surgery and while in rehabilitation, I remembered Steve asking his nurse when he would be able to climb his next "fourteener." If you were there watching him in his immobile predicament, you would appreciate how far-fetched he must have sounded to her. She tried to change the subject. Steve relentlessly returned to the topic at hand. He amazed me. There he was—straddled in traction with obvious discomforts, yet already visualizing and talking about a climb of fourteen thousand feet.

Over the next few months, Steve slowly and steadfastly regained his spirit of enthusiasm. Steve's mom, Lorraine, came out to Colorado from Ohio to help him recover.

Steven H. Lutton

Initially, I was unsure of what to expect as I met his mother for the first time. After I spent time with her, and we were acquainted, however, I felt quite at ease. She was so calm and had such a gentle loving spirit. I can easily understand now why Steve is such an incredible man. Lorraine is such an incredible mom. Over time, I would eventually discover that Steve's dad, Herb, is too.

Day after day, Steve began his relentless effort to rehabilitate his legs. "I have to get my legs back," he expressed to me with a sense of determination as I drove him to his physical therapy session. Steve rarely complained and was always enthusiastic about the progress that he experienced with each day. "Thank you, my two sweethearts, for all your love and support!" he conveyed to Crystal and me as he gave us both a big hug and smooch.

Six months later—on the Fourth of July—Steve and his brother-in-law Scott climbed to an elevation of 14,355 feet to the summit of Longs Peak. On October 31, Steve asked me, "Will you marry me?" The next summer, we became husband and wife. Shortly thereafter, Steve became Crystal's legal dad by adoption and our emotional bond as a family became officially recognized. On April, 8, 1992, we were blessed with a son, Steven Herbert Lutton II.

I often reminisce about those days and the strength that Steve displayed to overcome his physical challenges. I asked him about this while we were driving to the mountains for a camping trip. He smiled and calmly replied, "I just had to harden my resolve because I had to get my legs back in shape. I was going to climb a mountain that summer. It was embedded in my mind and drove me—one day at a time."

Steve continues to show the same zest for life in all of his aspirations. He is steadfast in his commitment and dedication to everything that he sets his mind and body to accomplish. As an executive, he has successfully managed an award-winning commercial printing company, Renegade Press, Inc., for over fifteen years. Steve is the co-owner of Renegade Press, along with his partner, Dennis Durakovich, who founded the firm in 1983.

As a gardener and cook, Steve has started his own line of naturally grown sauces, spices, and other delicacies from seed in our own backyard. Through experimentation, he has provided our family and friends with delicious herbs, garden fresh salads, spicy green chili dishes, and his own delectable spaghetti sauces. I can't wait to write his first garden cookbook! Steve grows a spectacular array of annuals and perennials in our basement greenhouse and transplants them to our gardens for a beautiful show of color in the spring and summer seasons.

As a proud owner of chinchillas and a rabbit, he has used his carpentry skills to build impressive "homes" for his pets to enjoy. As a fitness enthusiast, Steve finds the time to work out, cycle, golf, ski, walk, and/or run on just about a daily basis. "I love being outdoors either in the dirt or just getting exercise and fresh air. I really have a passion to be in touch with the earth." I asked Steve what motivates his stamina and vigor to be so physically active. Steve replied, "Staying fit gives me the freedom to do anything I want in life. My physical health is as important to me as my spiritual and mental health. It's all about balance." On the subject of balance, Steve is a devoted Christian father and husband. He enjoys playing soccer with his son, coaching his daughter in her artistic interests, and writing romantic cards to me. On Sundays, Steve offers his time ushering at our parish,

Steven H. Lutton

and, together, during periodic retreats, we mentor engaged couples on married life. As a couple, Steve and I often speak about our family values and he expressed, "Cheri, family life is everything to me. I grew up with a great family life and just feel blessed by God to be enjoying such an incredible life . . . with you."

Truly, a day does not go by when I don't count my blessings for having met Steve. . . my Romeo. . . and spending our days together raising our Lutton family. I love you, Steve. You really are my dream come true!

◆ ◆ ◆

*Courage is doing the very thing
that you are afraid to do.*

—Steve Siebold

*Steve Siebold
with Partner Bill Gove*

CHAPTER SIXTEEN
Courage In Body

Steve Siebold

The Courage to Go Pro Physically & Mentally

> **Courage is doing the very thing that you are afraid to do.**
> —Steve Siebold

The year is 2001. The continent is Asia. The subject is... the Tiger. The scene is... the panoramic vista of the open azure skies—breathtaking to the human senses—basking in the sun under free-floating clouds. The open range of land seems to extend far beyond infinity. The earth toned wisps of tall green and gold-colored grasses cast a surreal atmosphere as the wind breezes through the endless prairies. Down below, one can see herds of wild antelope, deer, and water buffalo roaming swiftly on course. Then... lurking in the background, a keen eye can observe the camouflage of a lone tigress scouring in the perimeters keeping a watchful eye on her cubs.

Her role in the jungle is no less important than her male counterpart as she instinctively rears her young into their own eventual empowerment. She knows her focus . . . and her purpose. The tigress is clear, concise, and on beat with nature.

Watching her closer, she moves in cunning fashion toward the broad canvas of velvet green trees . . . into the heart of the jungle. There, in the deep of this jungle, lies the mighty one, patiently and voraciously hungry. This mighty leader of power, focus, and victory is none other than the unconquerable tiger.

Notice the senses of the tiger—heightened to full potential. Even in dim light, he sets his gaze on his objective—and cannot be distracted. Observe the hearing skills of the tiger. With cup-shaped ears, these light-footed cats know the importance of remaining silent in absorbing all of the opportunities that are laden in nature's sounds.

Although reputed to be fiercely solitary, the tiger simply needs a lot of space to acquiesce its appetite for victory and to act on its purpose—to hunt, protect, and expand its vital interests. The instinct of a tiger is unequivocally clear: pure energy in raw form. Its focus is akin to a laser beam in motion. The tiger is inherently social, yet at a controlled distance. This leader fastidiously carves out his strategy for action by mapping out his territory. He learns everything he needs to know about every inch of his land . . . and then, when opportunity strikes . . . he pounces with every inch of his body and will. For he is—every inch of him—prepared for victory. For every hundred attempts, the tiger will only succeed at five conquests. In ninety-five of his conquests, he fails. So what does he do? He perseveres. He knows he will win five out of the one hundred times that he takes action. It is a very clear and simple bottom line. Otherwise, he will die. To this day, he prevails as king of the jungle.

Steve Siebold

Accordingly, it has been observed that in history, there were once eight subspecies of the tiger genus Panthera, otherwise known as the big cats. Now only five species of the Panthera remained alive: the Bengal, Siberian, Sumatran, Indochinese, and Caspian. Their closest relatives in the big cat family are the lion, leopard, jaguar, and snow leopard.

Now, in the new millenium, there are confirmed reports worldwide of a hybrid subspecies of the tiger that has emerged onto the planet. This new species is considered hybridized because it is human, and yet, truly akin to the tiger in nature and natural zeal—to move its desires of goodwill into action. It is clear, concise, and on beat with nature. Without hesitation.

In one word, this new form of tiger is—action. This great warrior knows precisely the quintessential importance of focus, preparation, and action to acquire the object of desire. He decides to act—then does it! No thing and no one will get in the way of a true tiger on a mission. With the animal, it is instinctive. With man, however, we have a few more tools of the minds to embellish our image. Nonetheless, man also shares intuitive impulses that can propel his mental victory into an external reality for all to enjoy.

This new "tiger" that I describe has taken the world by storm because of its blend of the best characteristics from the animal that it respects and the inherent gifts it possesses within humanity. As human beings, this new breed of tigers appears to have an invincible quest for victory. The unique characteristic that sets them apart from the pack is their unwavering confidence in the universe as abundant and cooperative.

Originating in Florida near the alligator glades, one king of this friendly jungle has been spotted, and I had the privilege of spending some time with him—in between conquests. He goes by Tiger Steve however, many people—particularly his folks—remember him fondly as Steve Siebold, the "child prodigy, tennis pro gone-tiger-on us-now" guy. Steve begins our conversational prowl on mental toughness with a roar of laughter and enthusiasm. Yet, he is fierce in his beliefs on the power of focused action and follow-through . . . over and over and over.

"Eventually, when you love what you're doing so much that you're willing to stake everything you have on one turn of the wheel, the universe seems to say, 'let him through, he'll never give up, so just let him through.' After all, you can't stop a man who won't be stopped; you can't beat a man who won't be beat." Steve explains. Steve's enthusiasm seems to build as he finishes this thought, "That's when you become a powerhouse, and you get on the road to turning your dreams into reality."—the Siebold way.

What is the *Siebold* way? Well, his energy knows no limits when it comes to going after his passions, dreams, and visions! I remember the first time that I was introduced to Steve. He was conducting a program on telephone communications and rapport development. It consisted of a conference call with Steve leading a series of dynamic interactions that would grab the interest of anyone desiring to sharpen their minds and skills. I was curious, yet, still reticent.

I, like most, had become saturated with the latest and greatest advice from the latest and greatest fast-talking salesperson. It did not resonate with my beliefs, and I was becoming numb, yet, I was still certain that somewhere out there were others who also wanted to really connect with like-minded people. I wanted to attract them to me during our initial phase of business communication, and convey the three V's: vim, vigor, and vision!

I felt cocky that day. I remember even chuckling to myself at his marketing strategy—The Tiger Program. GRRREAT. I thought to myself, next thing, I'll be on a diet of frosted flakes for this upcoming eight-week program staring at Tony the Tiger all day. I envisioned a jungle of

Steve Siebold

crazed business warriors gone primal who were all following the roaring cues of this intrepid new leader. Stop it, Cheri, I thought to myself. I finally stopped musing and dialed the number. I decided to give this fellow a chance. After all, I had heard that he was a former tennis pro, and who knows, maybe all professional athletes are tigers at heart. If nothing else, I deduced that the experience would expand my sense of humor.

That moment marked the end of an era for me. No longer could I ever cry again—over the sheer boredom, difficulty, toughness, seriousness of life, nature, or human circumstances. In fact, I had just lost the opportunity to cling to any, and, all excuses, in putting mental courage to action.

Tiger Steve was all and more of what he was cranked up to be in the game of moving vision into action. Steve was raw energy with trenchant enthusiasm. Wow. If I was a +3 (on a scale of 1-10) when I hooked into his conference call, then I was over the charts way beyond +10 when I hung up the telephone. Short, concise, clear, and robust—that was the message that I picked up in his hilarious, yet, stellar introduction. I realized very quickly that this thirty-five-year-young entrepreneurial athlete was indeed the real deal. He had first-class style. He was cut from the cloth of pure-bred sportsmanship, *and* he was a lot of fun!

Fun. Boy, this word seemed to have been omitted from any adult lexicon or genre of corporate events. Fun, laughter, the lightness of being—where did they all go since capitalism became so popular? Yet, Steve seemed to ingeniously create the entire package alongside a tremendous intensity for accomplishment and victory. Yes, the "Siebold way" definitely appeared to embrace a tremendous decision on the part of each player to mentally focus on the vision, along with the complete cooperation of one's inner resources of courage, creativity, and conviction. The objective was to win and have fun playing the game. What a concept.

Now, a couple of years later and as an honorary graduate of the Mental Toughness Tiger Program, I can honestly say that it was GRR—— oh, you know. Steve Siebold's collaboration with the father of public speaking, Bill Gove, has created an unprecedented training program through their multi-media enterprise, Gove-Siebold, Inc.

So, for anyone in sales, sports, communications, or leadership of the highest caliber, who wants to hit the mark in a big way, I urge you to run—not walk—to the nearest seminar and see these two professionals in action. You might ask, what is so great about them? For starters, they show up. I do not just mean literally. I mean they are fully present and totally engaged in being with—you and me! Bill Gove is one of the most gracious gentlemen of all times, and at nearly ninety years old, he is still going strong. Secondly, they pay attention to their audience and prove it in their responses. Thirdly, they walk the talk of a professional who is at his best, regardless. Steve never asks anyone to do anything that he does not try himself. "Have cell phone, will call" is his motto—even if he has to hide in a closet backstage in between public speaking performances. Steve remains loyal to his commitments to people. That is his passion and purpose.

I was highly curious about this telephone mentor of mine. I met him in person and heard him speak with the great showman Bill Gove. Standing 6'2" with a young attractive bright face, great laugh, and enthusiastic green eyes, I bet that Steve's radiance could replace solar energy. After he spoke, I introduced myself and we chatted about common ideas. I felt a strong sense of sincerity and friendliness with Steve and stayed in touch with him on professional ideas. His confidence and enthusiasm are contagious strengths that I enjoyed in my life. Yet, what has touched me most about Steve is the sheer brilliance that he has attracted into his life through his own courage. Steve courted and sought the attention of Bill Gove as his business partner and won. Not only the deal, but also the admiration and friendship of Bill Gove—only the most gracious spirit and man of great integrity within the speaking industry. That coup alone speaks volumes for both Steve and Bill.

I couldn't take it any longer. I had to get deeper into the heart of Steve's attractive nature. I was intrigued by his prodigious achievements as a seven-year-young tennis pro, so I asked him in a recent conversation to elaborate on courage propelled from the mind into action—before the breakthrough.

"Cheri, I'm so honored to be a part of your project. This is great!" He begins as he immediately lifts my spirit with his attitude of gratitude and delightful charm. I wanted to hear from the tiger himself on how he became a successful tennis pro and, later, a mental toughness trainer.

Of course, it made sense that Steve credited the influence of his parents and siblings for its part in shaping his personal development. He shared reminiscent memories that obviously grew to create a strong sense of love, trust, abundance, laughter, excellence, and conviction for passion. Steve also prides himself in being a very happily married man to his beloved wife, Dawn, for the past fifteen years. "I am also humbled by our only child, our pet dachshund, Robin," he adds with a chuckle.

Steve chimes in over a lively chat about the importance of mentors. "Cheri, besides my family, the most significant individuals who have led the way for me in my athletic success have been my tennis coaches and mentors, like Jimmy Connors. "I believe that if you become a great champion, then you only want to be around great champions. First, you find and decide what you love to do and become just that person. You remain gratefully humble and do whatever it takes to attract their attention and admiration in helping you in your quest. Then you go out and do whatever they direct you to do.

"For instance, with me, when Bill Gove tells me to jump, I just ask, 'how high?' In fact, on the advice of Bill, I spent my first year on the speaking circuit speaking all through Florida—for free! It's that simple for a while when someone is studying under a great mentor or coach. It was the same way with tennis," Steve advises as he proceeds in his great storytelling manner. I wanted to find out the connection between Steve's tiger mentality and his strength in his earlier tennis career. Steve began his story.

"I fell in love with tennis the first time that I picked up the racket," he reminisces. I query, "And, how old were you then, Steve?" He replies, "Six." Okay, I muse to myself on his early advantage. Steve continues, "Whatever success that I had was due to my parents' love and support, my brothers and the greatest coaches. By their living example, I became who I am today. There were ups and downs, wins and losses, laughter and tears. During those years, we developed an unbreakable bond. I think we earned each other's respect, and I feel so blessed just to have had the opportunity to get to know such people as great as them," Steve expresses openly.

"I grew up on the national junior tennis circuit. I spent twelve years traveling the country competing against the best junior tennis players in the world. When I first started, I was winning so often that I never gave the mental aspect of the game much thought. But as the competition became tougher, my coach brought in a team of mental trainers to teach his stable of champions how to think like world-class athletes. Essentially, what these trainers did was to help us reprogram the way we saw ourselves as performers. They taught us how to create images in our minds of our desired accomplishments," he shares.

"My first assignment was in 1979. . . and my job was to see myself as the #1 fourteen-year-old tennis player in Chicago. I was to see myself as the point leader in the Chicago Grand Prix, which was a year long competition with over 500 players competing for a place in the championships in December. The only problems was, I was not the best player! So, I created the image. I saw myself walking into the tournament and seeing myself as number one seed. . . walking around the tennis club with all of my peers congratulating me. I could see the admiration on their faces, feel the pride and accomplishment. I emotionalized the image—of them, the audience, and me. I was told to visualize this scenario every morning and before going to sleep. Secondly, I was to repeat affirmations to myself all day long, such as 'I love playing under pressure; I am the tiger and no one is strong enough to stop me; I am the Grand Prix point leader and City Champion.' At first, it felt awkward, and, then after a few weeks, I could feel the transformation that was taking place. The combination of visualization and self-talk catapulted my confidence, and I was never the same. In fact, on December 13, 1979, I walked into the mid-town tennis club in Chicago as the point leader of the Grand Prix . . . and walked out the City of Chicago Champion," he recalls with clarity.

I was captivated by his certainty; yet, I was also interested in hearing about the difficulties he must have faced as a young boy in the big leagues. Steve laughs as he continues, "Well, yes, it was a challenge to maintain such a rigorous lifestyle of practice. As a ten-year-old boy who has to get up and practice at 4:30 AM everyday, there were times when I would want to be out after school playing with the other kids. I'd watch them riding their bikes while I was always practicing at tennis. Then, my coach told me to go ahead and play with all of the other kids—or take three months and study the tiger. I thought hard about it and finally decided to study the tiger. I recognized his point that I was different than the pack, and I had to pay the price. Sometimes a solitary life would be necessary if I wanted to enjoy my own passions. Like the tiger, I understood the mental game that I had to play to remain focused and confident. Like the tiger, who maps out a part of the jungle, we too, learn every inch of our own territory, business, profession, sport, passion, whatever and go at that one thing clearly until we become—our best. Then, we *are* the unbeatable champions."

I asked the obvious on whether he experienced tough times. "Oh yes," he laughs slowly. "But, it's so much fun that it's worth it! I loved to play tennis and I locked into the discipline and focus that being your best in the universe requires from all of us. I would ask myself daily, 'Are you a true tiger or just a big talker?' I recognized early on that if you stay honest with yourself and your passions, then the universe would reward you with wheelbarrows of prosperity and happiness—almost overnight! In fact, when the tennis circuit became more about the winning and not the playing, I left. For me, I need to be playing to win, not working to win. I have to have the passion in the moment, not as the goal. Now, I just love helping others discover what I've found." I could feel Steve's underlying drive of truth—in those last statements.

"What of the young people who are seeking the courage to go for their dream to become a professional athlete?" I ask. With all of the competition and advertising pressure, how can a bright sports-minded youth remain on the high road of success and fulfillment?

"Cheri, I'd still say to them, find what you love to do and go after it. Listen to your own heart on this one, then keep your mind locked on your vision and passions." Steve advises with sincerity. He pauses, chuckles, and adds, "We need to get more of our youth in front of great leaders. Just whom did he recommend as mentors? His own, of course. Once I heard whom he was about to unveil, I must admit that I was excited since they were being honored in this book as mentors of mine, too!

"Cheri, beyond Bill [Gove], I would say that Larry Wilson and Bob Proctor have been the most significant

Steve Siebold

individuals who have led the way of excellence for me in my personal development," Steve remarks with pride. "Larry is not only an awesome tennis player, but a theatrical genius in personal development and playing [the game of life] to win. Bob is a master of the mind and one of the finest human beings of our day." I had to agree with him. These men are the best in their fields.

Steve and I covered a full spectrum of thoughts and ideas. I felt totally invigorated and we came on the subject of his faith in the Creator. He paused reflectively and then he replied with that Siebold confidence, "I'm not exactly a religious person . . ." he said as he chuckles, "but, I do know that this universe works too orderly. So, there's definitely a Divine Order upstairs that is in charge. It's just too magnificent to be otherwise!" I knew I liked this guy.

Why do I choose a good-looking guy with the greatest upbringing, obvious talents, and charisma as a man of honor? Where is the struggle that qualifies people as great courageous heroes? Maybe, that's just it. Struggle. Maybe that's a choice, too. What I sense from Steve is an essence of untainted and unbridled enthusiasm and a pure zest for life. Sure, perhaps, he was blessed from the get-go. That doesn't mean there weren't any sacrifices and trade-offs. Earnest effort and perseverance—with a genuine respect for everyone and everything—underscored the solid family values of the Siebold homestead. Steve wisely followed the prosperity-consciousness that he gained at an early age. Even as a highly competitive athlete, Steve understood the true nature of a cooperative world in place. . . and never lost sight of the power of gratitude and humility.

As for the influence of these qualities on others, I can share my own experience on the power of the human spirit. I have discovered, especially in the process of writing this book, that when I am feeling low or confused, all I have to do is think about positive individuals like Steve. Almost immediately, I can feel a heartfelt energy that lifts my spirits and . . . can even make me laugh into a healthier perspective. Wow. God is great.

In closing, I ask you . . . what distinguishes a big cat like the tiger, lion, jaguar, and leopard from the little cat like the lynx, bobcat, ocelot, cougar and house cats? Steve knows all too well—big cats roar; little cats do not. Go get 'em, Tiger Steve . . . see you back in the jungle!

◆ ◆ ◆

Word Records Media Communications

Courage is being able to say and do what is on your mind without having any second thoughts, doubts, or worries.

—Rachael Lampa

Tony Baker

*Rachael Lampa
with Word Records*

CHAPTER SEVENTEEN
Courage In Body

Rachael Lampa

The Courage to Sing for God

> **Courage is being able to say and do what is on your mind without having any second thoughts, doubts, or worries.**
> **—Rachael Lampa**

Amidst the holiday crowds of the Christmas season, my daughter, Crystal, and I caught our breath in the local Soundtrack music store at the Boulder Crossroads indoor mall. Suddenly, I felt visually and surrealistically entertained. Talented artists symbolically invited our attention through the displays of CD's, DVD's, and audiocassettes. The playful image of a room filled with a potpourri of vocalists, showering a rainbow of unique melodies, lyrics, styles, desires, and spirit was enchanting to my senses. In fact, it was bedazzling for any music lover to roam such a place. Then, I felt a tug just as I was ready to exit stage right, before surrendering to an over-the-top spending spree. Crystal whispered, "Mom, look straight ahead on the wall at that CD. That's Rachael Lamp's CD. I went to middle school with her. Can we buy it?" she pleaded. I almost did and then I realized that, right now, I simply needed to get home, and away from all of these frantic crowds. I began to think about this whole concept. Although holiday giving may have originated with a kind thought, I truly wondered if, in modern times, the spirit of giving had become a less-than-kind experience. With a genuine feeling of overload, after a day filled with all too much shopping, I replied, "We will, honey, . . . next time."

Next time came in a few weeks while our family was enjoying a quiet holiday week together in the San Juan Mountains of Durango, Colorado. We enjoyed a breathtaking tour on the Silverton train up the rugged terrain. As a wife and mother, it is a dream-come-true to spend relaxing time together in laughter and chatter with my husband, Steve, and two children, Crystal and Steven. We admired the snow-capped peaks and briskly moving river as we peeked out the side of the train. "Wow, look at that!" exclaimed Steven as we passed by so many interesting beauties of nature. We felt blessed to live in God's country of Colorado.

Afterwards, we all decided to take a drive through the charming town of Durango and stopped in at an eye-catching Christian bookstore. This lovely place connected to a friendly coffee shop and attracted us with the sweet aroma of freshly baked goods and brew of coffee flavors. Meandering through the myriad of literary collections, I looked up to stretch my neck and happened to catch the sight of a familiar CD with a close-up photo of a beautiful, yet innocent-looking young lady. An instant later, I noticed the artist's name and quickly remembered my promise to Crystal. I smiled pensively as I quietly purchased the compact disk along with a few gifts for the men in my life before we returned to our majestic getaway on Lake Vallecito.

Rachael Lampa

Once we returned to the rustic, yet cozy, two-bedroom cabin retreat, I was all too anxious to pass out my surprise gifts for everyone. For Dad, I had an action-filled Tom Clancy novel that he had been perusing at another bookstore. He was already nestled in his recliner enjoying the warmth of the wood-burning fireplace, anxious to begin his imaginative adventure. For Steven, I bought an animated Christian storybook, which he couldn't wait to dig into after he curled up in his favorite blanket on the couch. For Crystal, I had the promised CD that brightened her face as soon as she recognized the photo of her former schoolmate. She excitedly retrieved our boom box so we could preview the debut recording of this lovely new artist, Ms. Rachael Lampa.

I walked out to the porch to enjoy the spectacle of stars, twinkling in the night. I gazed into the luminous sky, which absolutely shimmered from the light reflected on the moon and celestial bodies. Just in front of our cabin, we were swept away by the magnificent outline of the empty Lake Vallecito, and the majestic mountain peaks in the shadows. With such breathtaking views, I began soaking in all the exquisite beauties and blessings of my life.

I continued to gaze above admiringly as I began to notice the sounds coming from within the cabin. The lyrical melody was almost dancing with me while inviting me to listen and enjoy the song. The voice of this young artist was captivating, calling on all of my senses to glorify this great universe. Slowly, a feeling began to come over me as I enjoyed the collection of Christian songs on the "Live For You" CD. I begin to understand the sincere intent behind the rich qualities of Rachael's voice, which resonated with ageless passion and purity as she expressed her love for God. I felt compelled to pray.

Even without knowing her, or having ever seen her, I began to cry and comprehend the depths of her own desires to express her love for her Father. I began to hear Rachael's own love for humanity through her God-given gift of song.

Courage in Body

This young aspiring artist inspired me—and I am sure many, many others—to reach deep into my own heart and embrace my own gifts. So that I, too, may express in bold fashion, a passionate desire to express my love for our Heavenly Father, for all of humanity, and for all other living creatures in this marvelous place called life. In that moment, as we all enjoyed Rachael's voice, danced to her music, and felt her artistic passions, I knew that I wanted to know more. I knew that an impulse had stirred within me, and I wanted to invite her to participate in this collection of heroes. I knew that somehow, when I returned home, the way would be shown.

For once in a destined moment, between the twilight of the night and the dawn of the morn, a star is born with the rare sparkle and purity of a glistening diamond. A diamond that beams such clarity and brilliance simply cannot be concealed. Sometimes, it is in the beauty of God's creation that we discover his true message. Shining with boundless love and laughter, the precious star I speak of today is indeed, our debutante, Rachael Lampa.

This rising star at only seventeen years illuminates the qualities of a professional—a young model of faith, hope, and courage. Faith . . . that when we believe and trust in God's plan for our human destiny, the way will become clear. When our ego-driven selves get out of the way, our faith in God will begin to carry us to endless heights that we once simply dreamed and hoped would come true. Hope. . . in the belief that our young can enjoy a fun-filled life naturally—and still behave morally responsible. Courage . . . in taking a stand in defining who we are as God's children and going for it completely.

As I let go and let God, events occurred which made it possible for me to visit with Rachael and her family at her home. On the evening that we met, Rachael and her mom had just returned home from a memorial service for a fellow high school student who had tragically passed away after trying a drug called "ecstasy" at her own birthday party. Even with an unexpected event as this, Rachael was gracious and professional in her welcome to me. Immediately, I could sense in Rachael a rare essence of integrity, which embraces her complete celebration of life through her service to God. I knew she indeed possessed the strength of character—the impenetrable armor of courage—so clearly needed in her stewardship as a Christian vocalist in today's pop culture.

A petite, five feet tall, Rachael immediately warmed my heart with her presence. She attractively captivates one's attention with her long golden brown hair flowing down past her shoulders, her trusting brown eyes, and her enthusiastic smile. Add to this her angelic complexion, and these stunning qualities only accentuate her inner beauty.

My first impression of Rachael only reaffirmed my intuitive feelings that this young woman was happily drawn to her professional singing career—through her natural instincts to please God, and serve others. The most dramatic unfolding of Rachael's success came in one immediate sign—her esteemed family and the warmth and enjoyment they exude in being together. After meeting Rachael's mom, Marianne, I witnessed the strong reflection of amazing grace that is mirrored in such a healthy mother-daughter relationship as theirs. Evidence of Rachael's upbringing and her own Catholic conviction is clear in the central core of her existence. From this core, springs forth her pure desire to dedicate her daily life in Christ's grace . . . as she enjoys every moment! Rachael expresses her passionate and unwavering belief that our Heavenly Father is always there to pick us up whenever we fall as she sings in "God Loves You," written by Brent Bourgeois and Jill Phillips.

The spiritual chemistry in the air among all of us when we visited rang so clear to me. Marianne, blonde and very pretty, sat with us and shared many cherished memories with me on her family life and her own convictions in her Catholic faith.

Rachael spoke so fondly of her family—her dad, Phil; her younger sister, Colleen; her younger brother, Nathan; and her older brother, Ryan, as being instrumental mentors in her daily walk through her life. "Ryan has been a real source of leadership for me," Rachael remarked with sincere pride. "He was president of the student council at our high school, and I have always looked up to him. My brother is so supportive of my career," she added.

I asked Rachael to share with me what she thinks contributes to her successful lifestyle. Her candor and enthusiasm shaped our conversation together as she remarked, "I've been singing since I can remember , , , in church when I was five years old. I've always felt God's hand—and my mom, dad, and older brother, Ryan—have all guided me by their own example in their love for Christ and Christian way of living. Colleen and Nathan have also been great sources of joy and inspiration toward my sense of belonging. To me, that is where it all starts—in home life. Learning to trust others and making a home a real home can make a big difference in whether a young person will rebel, act out, or feel that sense of natural happiness from within themselves," Rachael responded compassionately.

"What of your breakthrough in music at fifteen years of age?" I inquired. She paused, smiled shyly, gazed down and instantly revealed her rare self-confidence and poise as she replied, "Last year, I felt my Father's heart more than ever. I wasn't really attached to any outcome when I sang for him. I knew through my daily prayer that God's love would shine through me because I want to show others the joy that they have in their hearts. Even the week before I signed the contract with Word Records and GET Management, I didn't have a clue about what was to unfold in the next few days. In the summer of 2000, I had an unexpected opportunity to perform in *Praise in the Rockies,* a Christian artists' seminar held in

Estes Park, Colorado. It was at that event that five record companies discovered me, which included Word Records. Cheri, I felt something that day, too. I knew that I was ready and I had trust in God's plan for me. . . . I had a feeling that the time was right," she commented assuredly. Life imitates art, and clearly this is reflected in the lyrics from Rachael's hit song "My Father's Heart" written by Chris Eaton.

Surely, it has taken extraordinary focus and stamina for Rachael to launch a professional career in the music industry, develop her identity, and complete her academic high school curriculum. Rachael has already received an audience with Pope John Paul II when she was invited to sing at the last World Youth Day event in Rome, Italy. She has also performed on the Jay Leno Show, and many other celebrated engagements.

"What of sports, family, and a social life?" I queried lightheartedly as I wondered how she packs it all in. Rachael giggled as she replied, "You're right. My schedule demands sacrifices, and I must practice, practice, practice. Sometimes, it's hard for me to call my family or friends, knowing that I miss them while I am out of town for a concert or event. When I am home, though, I enjoy the same routines that I have always cherished . . . my family, church, choir group, friends, school, basketball, eating, and just being home in Colorado with people that I love and who love me."

Rachael's achievements in pursuing her passions have not come without resistance and, sometimes, even ridicule. After Rachael signed a substantial recording contract, she had to face graffiti written about her on the outside walls of her high school. How does a young leader handle criticism by her peers? How does a Christian youth model her strength of character in a society that sways more toward acceptance with material values, surface beauty, and physical pleasures?

How does a beautiful young vocalist resist all of the temptations and conveniences of fame and fortune? "I walk through my day with daily gratitude and prayer," Rachael happily recanted. "I let His love shine through me and try not to think so much. Anyway, God is really the only one to impress. I stay on my path and know that he is always there with me," she added with confidence and sincerity.

What does Rachael advise to other teens that might want to develop their courage and sense of character? "You can still have integrity, be respected—and be popular. My brother Ryan is a good example of a true leader that everyone likes and follows," she remarked with pride. Rachael smiled, adding boldly, "I think that if teens become more responsible-thinking when they have to make a decision about anything, they will succeed in causing the right actions. They will develop their own strength. Their inner light will begin to shine brighter." In fact, according to my daughter, Crystal, "Rachael was always looked at as a role model in middle school. Someone who was not afraid to be herself."

I asked Rachael what she, too, looks for in a leader? "Someone who is capable of real love and friendship. A leader is someone who takes a chance at his or her dreams and stays positive without holding back at all. A Christian who is willing to 'walk their talk' in secular crowds. That is what I'd like to do with my own vocal ministry—help those who still might not even see their walk with Christ," she chimed earnestly.

On Rachael's perspective of Heaven and . . . Heaven on Earth, she looks for pure and genuine smiles everywhere, peaceful harmony among all humanity, and, with all God's loving creatures. She sees angels singing melodiously, good food, bowling, and basketball for all!

Although, I had enjoyed my acquaintance with Rachael during our visit, I still wanted to hear her sing in person. I took an evening drive into Louisville and attended Sunday

Mass at St. Louis Catholic Church, hoping to hear Rachael singing in the choir. There, I enjoyed her lovely voice in quiet harmony with the other choir members. Again, Rachael displayed a genuine sensitivity to others, as she remained a team player, never taking the spotlight in this time of worship.

Just as Rachael sings, she is living her desire to see the world through the eyes of God, and in his honor. She truly does seem to be headed for the stars on a moonbeam. Rachael has asked God to lift her up and take her farther than she had ever been. I say to you, Rachael, you are well on your way. Your kaleidoscope of beautiful visions has enriched our world. May your lyrical expressions continue to lift the hearts of many, many more!

◆ ◆ ◆

Courage is allowing the real me to become exposed. To be true to myself, regardless of what I think others might think of me. Sometimes that is scary, but since I will probably be fearful anyway, I might as well go ahead and do it.

—Robert Troch

Robert Troch and Daughter

CHAPTER EIGHTEEN
Courage In Body

Robert Troch

The Courage to Inspire Fitness and Fun

> **Courage is allowing the real me to become exposed. To be true to myself, regardless of what I think others might think of me. Sometimes that is scary, but since I will probably be fearful anyway, I might as well go ahead and do it.**
> —Robert Troch

A man on a mission to create fun for himself and those he helps is a man for whom I recommend you stop in your tracks, and enjoy. I have and he is Robert Troch. A marathon runner and owner of the Injury Free Athletics Institute in Brooklyn, New York, Robert has run right into my family's life, and I can't wait to see where he steers his course.

Courage in Body

I met Robert a few years ago through a mutual friend at a Starbucks near Times Square. I had only a tiny sense of Robert's true grit and determination. I knew he was a bit of a sports enthusiast, but these days, who isn't? As an entrepreneur, he talked like he would act on his words, but then again, so did everyone else. What set him apart?

I had yet to experience his striking boldness, and his unwavering desire to actualize physical and spiritual truths. I had not yet known about Robert's unstoppable thirst to coach his fellow man along his or her journey for self-expression. I had not fully appreciated the dimension of loyalty and commitment that Robert shows for his friends. Now I realize that Robert is not only the epitome of a life coach, but he is also an expert in sports and fitness. More significantly, he is a truly caring professional-at-heart.

An eclectic individual, Robert stands 5'7" with brown hair, a handsome, yet youthful look and the sincerest blue eyes you will ever find in New York. A son of a successful entrepreneur in the oil and coal business, Robert left Chicago in the eighties in search of personal freedom, fun, fitness, and balance. Financial prosperity, although just about guaranteed if he had remained in the family business, was an element that Robert was willing to chance on his own terms.

Robert can make me laugh so hard it aches. In the process, he delights me in the wonders of my own behaviors. As a colleague of mine on a weekly mastermind call, he has a gutsy knack of walking directly into everyone's hearts and minds, and questioning the generally unquestionable. He projects his desire to inspire, help, and uplift everyone with brotherly love. Robert is an effective leader for one important reason—he walks his talk.

I have heard this man laugh, cry, cajole, befriend, honor, listen, empathize, inspire, challenge, and, most of all, calm the hearts of many into a place where life feels friendly, and dreams are possible. The launching gear he sets in motion becomes sassy and inviting like the saying, "Pour Quoi Pois?" or, Why Not?

Oh, but make no mistake about it, Robert's acts of courage lead him into rough clouds of resistance and, sometimes, thunderbolts of crackling rejection. He himself admits lightheartedly, "It can get scary. Sometimes I just don't go there if I feel that someone isn't ready or in the right space. Yet, I am always prompted to help a friend in need or one who desires to grow. When I help them, I grow and help myself get out of my own box. I simply like to call a spade a spade."

Robert has learned the importance of balance in his pursuit of truth. He holds his family life with his wife, Kelly, and his young daughter, Georgia, in high reverence. "I want to create a destiny for us that offers a spontaneous lifestyle, the freedom to travel to faraway lands, and visit friends everywhere. I want to provide my wife with an impressive art studio for her to live up to her potential. I want to create opportunity for my daughter, and help her to be better than me. Most importantly, I'd like to help her to develop an attitude of being on purpose every day. I want to be in the moment with my family and myself, growing as my wife's best friend," Robert affirms as he professes his passions for the future. Robert chuckles, "I want time to play with my toys. I have a collection of vinyl prehistoric models like Godzilla, and I really enjoy building them." Build these vinyl figures he does, as their market value approaches a hefty investment. Serious about his fun, Robert has won several awards for his creative displays in the Godzilla genre, even attending a worldwide event in Japan to heighten his involvement. "I set a goal to attend and made it happen. It was a big dream of mine to experience that event and it was definitely worth it!" exclaims Robert.

Courage in Body

Robert's proficiency at blending mind, body, and spirit into a seamless whole has earned him a reputation as an expert in his field. Robert offers his clients a variety of choices through his yoga classes, sports training and therapy, mental coaching, and technologically advanced wellness products. "I'd also like to incorporate track and field coaching into my goals," Robert adds with definite purpose. "I have always been fascinated by the powers of the mind trained in synchrony with the powers of the body, combined with the Source of all powers—flowing through the heart or spirit," he remarks. When I set my mind to accomplish something—physical or otherwise, I get focused, learn to master it, then practice, practice, practice," he comments.

O the world is so much more fun with you in the race, Robert. Thank you, Lord, for such a winner!

◆ ◆ ◆

Courage is overcoming extreme obstacles in an honorable and productive way . . . even when you're going against the grain.

—Steve Immer

*Steve Immer in
concert on Vibraphone*

CHAPTER NINETEEN
Courage In Body

Steve Immer
The Courage to Be Real

> **Courage is overcoming extreme obstacles in an honorable and productive way. . . even when you're going against the grain.**
> **—Steve Immer**

In my dear pal Steve Immer one can enjoy the spirit of genuine enthusiasm even when the chips are down and tumbling fast. "Thud, thud, thud" he likes to chime as the man, probably most known around Breckenridge, Colorado, shares his tale of transformation and penniless perseverance to succeed.

"I came to Breckenridge, Colorado in 1982 because I wanted to redefine myself," he begins a story, pacing in front of his fireplace. "After some tumultuous times in a variety of careers, including college teaching, government, and investment banking, I found myself with a very cynical feeling about people, trust, and my own position as a human being. People had deceived me, and it hurt. I had lost virtually everything, and was drained both financially and emotionally. I was forty years old, broke, unemployed, and in the midst of a classic textbook mid-life crisis. However, I remained optimistic and hopeful. I wanted to be more and give more—especially to folks who proved to be real and trustworthy. I wanted to enjoy myself, life, and others," he giggles and adds, "even though all I had left were my beat-up car and a 250-square-foot studio condo. I had previously purchased the condominium in my more affluent days as a weekend skiing crash pad. It's funny how a tiny studio grows more attractive when it is all I had left to call my own," he reminisces.

"I started working at a local bank for sheer survival, and, before long, I knew almost everyone in town. I quickly discovered that virtually everyone in Breckenridge was basically broke, except realtors and property managers. I thought, Why don't I try real estate? Eventually, I began my own property management company, then found a more experienced partner. Together, we built a successful rental property and real estate firm from scratch. We sold it for a considerable profit in only eleven years, and then retired."

I asked him, "So what of this thud, thud, thud you keep laughing about? He smiles as he replies, "Cheri, have you ever gone to a laundromat, in the cold of a winter's night, without enough funding to finish the job?" I couldn't say that I had, but I knew where we were heading now.

"When I began my business," he continues, "I did all the work on less than a shoestring budget. If it meant laundering the linens from my condo rentals myself, then guess what I was doing at night! When it's cold, and the sheets are wet after I just spent my last quarter—before getting kicked out of the laundromat—well, the wet linens get rolled into my car until morning. Back at it, now fresh in the morning with a new pocketful of quarters, I barely managed to carry

Steve Immer

the now frozen logs of linens out of my car, and back into the laundromat for drying. 'Thud, thud, thud' was the unexpectedly loud sound that the frozen sheets made in the drier when I first started the machines," Steve roars merrily, recalling his eighteen-hour days as he was getting started as a rental and property manager. He now continues to enjoy the equity payout of that business after selling it in 1996. His big smile and gentle blue eyes reflect nothing but sincerity and spontaneity, during these well earned days of freedom and financial independence.

Steve has proven that one can forge ahead in the face of a knockdown battle with delusion and disappointment. He reexamined his history and beliefs, to redefine what was beautiful to him through his mind's eye. Thereafter, Steve was freed to nurture his inner self, ultimately experiencing his true purpose in life. Enter Breckenridge.

This is where I met Steve. We were both at a networking function through the Summit County Chamber of Commerce. I immediately found him an affable and fun-loving spirit. We eventually became friends and business associates. In Steve, I am inspired as one who holds the commitment, "To Thine Own Self Be True," yet not without compassion for his fellow man.

Steve was willing to risk many career changes in search of his true self. I knew it was often not that easy for Steve, as I have heard the pain in his voice, and seen the tears well up in his eyes, during candid discussions with him. Although Steve's sincere nature attracts many friends now, he confessed that as a young man he had struggled painfully to be loved and accepted. "I felt like a nerd. I was terribly shy and skinny, and it was a long and lonely journey for many years," Steve shares. I asked him how he managed to transform himself from a less-than-confident introvert to an at-ease-with-himself extrovert. "I believe it is an acquired skill. I know my limits, and I have taken the time to self-reflect, and care enough about who I am. One must become self-aware and then go for it! I used to make lots of compromises and bargains with my own integrity. Well, no more bargains," he advises lightheartedly. Never too short on words, it is hard to imagine Steve as the shy youth he likes to describe himself as in his past. However, it has developed him into a person who has sincere concern for others, especially for the underdog.

"Slowly I learned to discover new skills . . . new potentials to be realized. I learned to focus on what I could do well, and Voila! I discovered that I could ski—expert slopes at that. I could play music and record with professionals. I now run, bike, sing, and entertain, so I joined an acting troupe, the Summit County Choral Society, and my church choir," Steve proudly expresses.

Above all, Steve discovered that he was even braver than he ever gave himself credit. He dared to dream a lifestyle that he could own and embrace. With vision and a sense of purpose, this community-spirited pied piper has moved toward the realization of his own worthy ideals—the celebrated Earl Nightingale's definition of success.

Living in God's country, just a walk away from the ski slopes, Steve savors the majestic beauty found in his natural surroundings. "More importantly, I get to enjoy this beauty everyday with peace of mind and a relaxed attitude," he admits with pride in discussing his decision to chuck the corporate existence in which many ambitious Americans currently find themselves trapped.

Steve says of his lifestyle, "I may not be high on the hog, but I am definitely on the hog's anatomy somewhere." Having earned enough from investing the proceeds of his company, he now enjoys diversifying his resources, time, and talents into a range of activities. He is proud that he is sixty years young and still weighs the same 150 pounds he did in high school. Steve's interests include skiing, bicycling,

Steve Immer

investing, and entertaining jazz audiences in a band playing the vibraphone. "I love music, having fun, being fit and healthy, and helping other people do the same. Combine that with my love for the outdoors, and I guess my life is right on track," he reflects with candor, pride, and a great big smile.

Steve has a clear commitment to enjoy life to its fullest, growing as a better human being in the process. This philosophy explains his attraction to CCQH, Inc., the company that I founded with a mission to help humans be more rather than do more—by celebrating their centered qualities—like courage. Steve also spends much of his time volunteering for causes such as Shaping Our Summit, Make A Difference Day, Chamber of Commerce Volunteer Days, and Adopt-a-Bike-Path. Although Steve would like it to appear as if he is just out having fun all day, much of that fun time he truly spends giving back to his community.

What about Steve's experiences with love? He has learned to love and forgive himself—and others. As for Steve's soul mate? Steve is the everlasting bachelor and quite happy being single. He explains complimentary, "Well, Cheri, I really respect you, your marriage, and your beautiful family. Yet, the way I see it—there's the gold ball of love—like you have. Then, there's the silver ball of freedom—like I have, which includes lots of great friendships. Sure, the gold ball is the age-old desire, but silver is just fine . . . for a happy bachelor like me! Since Immer means "always" in German, I guess, once again, I'm just being true to my name!"

Here's one for my buddy, Steve! We love you, tiger. You will *always* brighten the world with your shimmering spirit of silver and your generous heart of gold!

◆ ◆ ◆

PART FOUR
Courage In Family

Pray and Laugh Together, and Stay Together

Mom, here's a card to remind you daily

how much we love and support you.

Love,

Your Two Greatest Accomplishments,

Your Daughter, Crystal

and Your Son, Steven

CHAPTER TWENTY
Courage In Family

Pray and Laugh Together, and Stay Together

Mom, here's a card to remind you daily how much we love, support, and are there for you. Love, Your Two Greatest Accomplishments, Your Daughter and Son, Crystal and Steven

Ode to the nest, where nature seeks to soften life's beginnings and nurture, protect, and share the common bond of family. Serving as the safe haven for our weary wings to rest; this is the launching pad from which we learn to fly and, then, soar through our human journey at becoming our best.

Has our nest of family life served its duty? Can we look into the face of life with wings of courage? Do we soar as we enjoy the reflections of our nest, mirrored in the unconditional love and support we have shared as a family? Will we fly to great heights, each with our own wings of destiny, yet come together voluntarily because we are still attracted back to the nest? Isn't it our birthright to seek such a nest? Do we not deserve a foundation of unconditional love, worthy values, and mutual respect? Do we not crave a home that nurtures the expansion of our unique wings of self-purpose?

Yes, for this is where it all begins . . . where fun and spontaneity blend with growth and self-development. It has been said that Mrs. Kennedy Onassis has poignantly expressed that if we bungle raising our children, nothing else much matters in life. Certainly, she deserves true recognition for her walking her own talk, and having achieved it all alone. Truly, a family that loves, and a husband and wife in love, can change the world . . . .

Come with me now and reminisce on the wondrous experience of new love. Recall or take a new glimpse at the feeling of love in the air when you discover or rediscover your soul mate. When do you realize that, together, the two of you can build your lives as one?
Through the vows of matrimony, God guides a man and woman in consummation of their love to heights so powerfully reverent that it can only be described as miraculous. The transformation of a husband and wife in love who surrender themselves unconditionally carries them into a sea of intimacy that has a spiritual energy all its own. As the honeymoon fades and the realities of life set in, each then draws on the inner strength necessary to continue unveiling their truest nature—their most human side—weaknesses, vulnerabilities, and all. Each, reflecting love and growth to the other, which, in turn, nourishes and expands their bond, starting the cycle all over again. The creative power that can be derived from the delicately balanced chemistry of the marriage triad—love, sex, and romance—is a fascination that has been with humanity since the beginning of time.

This chemistry ignites our desires and passions beyond comparison to exhilarating dimensions of life.

A man and woman devoted to each other through genuine love are in communion with their godliness as one. Feelings of joy, serenity, and enthusiasm will refresh their daily lives. They will expand through each other, as they reflect their desires to give freely of themselves. The harshness of the outside world, the monotony of practical routines, and the confusion of the unknown future will all appear sweetened with the softening touch of spiritual love.

Add to this element of love the delicacies of romance, and, suddenly, the pie is even sweeter! Juliet says to her Romeo, "My bounty is as boundless as the sea, my love as deep; the more I give to thee, the more I have, for both are infinite." And, Romeo returns to his Juliet, "Did my heart love till now? Forswear it, sight! For I ne'er saw true beauty till this night. It is my Lady; O, it is my Love!" The desire to please becomes a delicious obsession of the heart, which tames the beast and unveils the beauty.

The "a la mode" of relationships is the tantalizing passion of sex, which completes this phenomenal triad unique to happily married couples. A sensual experience of fulfilling pleasure through the sexual life of a married couple is God's desire for humanity. When the chemistry that combines love, romance, and sex is triggered, the human spirit is most closely united with the state of mind known as rapture. This experience can spark the creative genius within each human being to create a flame so intense that is melts the barriers between the finite mind and Infinite Intelligence.

This kindling of the fire in our soul can drive our capacity for courage to extraordinary levels of achievement, all for the betterment of humanity. For the human spirit can either shrink or expand, depending on its association with the positive emotions of life, especially the emotions that have the power to induce our creativity. These emotions include faith, desire, enthusiasm, hope, and the triad of love, sex, and romance. A marriage blessed with the sprinkling of this important triad will stir the spiritual nature of bliss, and only serve to delight our Creator. For the union of husband and wife is the most precious gift and important act of life that God has bestowed upon humanity.

There is an almost visible quality in married couples who possess an unwavering faith, particularly if God is included in their daily lives. My husband and I received a beautiful poem as a wedding gift, which hangs in an inscribed frame in our home's foyer.

Marriage Takes Three

*I once thought marriage took just two to make a go,
But now I am convinced it takes the Lord also.
And not one marriage fails where
Christ is asked to enter
As lovers come together with Jesus at the center.
In homes where Christ is first, it's obvious to see
those unions really work, for marriage still takes three.*
—Perry Tanksley, 1986.

If you are of a faith other than Christian, certainly the inclusion of God or the Highest Creator at the helm in your marital vows will guide your hearts and fill your lives with much peace, joy, and splendor.

Often times, I take my cue in finding my own strength by observing my husband, particularly during his quiet moments. I watch his selfless acts of thoughtfulness. I observe his genuine respect for others. I see how he handles his own struggles with grace under fire. I watch him in his kind actions toward me. I experience a great sense of joy when I surrender to gratitude and humility. I feel calm and cherished with a happy sense of fulfillment that spurs my day, knowing how deeply he loves me. I think of him throughout the day and smile, knowing that I cherish him with all of my heart and soul. I feel a joyful sense of confidence because I know that he walks through his day knowing how deeply he is loved by me.

When the days become dark, weary, or turbulent we draw on our reservoir of steadfast fortitude. When the decision of commitment in "let no man put asunder what God hath put together" is held sacred, all the creative options for problem solving become available—and quitting is never one of those options.

Yes, the bond of marriage begins in romance . . . propels into high gear through the passion of sexual pleasure . . . and endures in eternal commitment through the growing understanding of a true selfless love for each other, in pursuit of your individual purpose. Mix these emotions with the visions that a married couple has for their family's journey, and one can experience the magic of boldness and creativity in action.

Here comes the fun. No longer are the mornings of Saturdays now quietly filled with the aroma of a freshly ground café au lait sipped while tasting sweet blueberry muffins, artfully carved pineapple slices, omelets with finely crushed garden tarragon, warmed bagels, real cream cheese, and a delicious array of homemade preserves.

Now, newborn feedings, early soccer games, and/or volleyball practice take time away from the gourmet moments of romance. The advent of child rearing in family life can be one of the biggest curve balls known to humankind. The days of wine and roses transform suddenly into milk and cookies. Albeit, pleasant and filled with wonder, take care to recognize an important message that is missing from the newborn arrival:

"No Instructions for Care or Assembly Included.

Learning how to raise a family becomes the great surprise of the mystical Universe. God's masterpiece in family design has to be the most awesome miracle in all of creation. He must be grinning at this very moment. You did good, my Lord; You've got us all bewildered, bewitched, and begging for more of those little pitter-patters we call our children.

Yet, in truth they are yours and not ours. We, as their earthly parental guardians—ready or not—are bestowed with the privileges and responsibilities of their tender loving care and rearing. What do we do? There is certainly a wealth of resources out there ranging from a to z in opinions of what should go on in your household. I emphasize *your* household, as this is the operative ingredient. For it takes a strong dose of courage to know thyself and thy will for the mission of your family. It takes patience, understanding, and genuine effort to confer as a couple, and, then again, as a family, on the values and vision that are in harmony with your family's mission.

Indeed, the mission of your family has far more significance on your life than the mission of any other institution. It can be a collective synopsis of each member's individual purpose, or it can be a combination of the flavor of the family's ideals. For some families, it can be summed up in one sentence, and, for others, it might be expanded into a paragraph. Whether the family's mission is written or spoken, the spirit of the vision is spearheaded by its very creation. This process serves to unite a family to stand for a common cause.

In our family, we have a blend of earth, air, wind, and fire as our four spiritual natures. We strive to embody all of these natures and we have combined phrases that each of us has contributed to our family mission. I give credit to the works of the Covey family in their books and audio programs on the *Seven Habits for Highly Effective Families*.

We have incorporated many of their suggestions into our own family routines. Having family sharing time has helped our family to try out new ways of giving and receiving on a level playing field where we can break new grounds of communication and forgiveness—as adults and children on equal turf. Believe me, it felt awkward, at first, and still, it is not always top priority for everyone to come together in building upon our family mission. Yet with fun, creativity, and a desire to create goodwill a loving mom can usually entice her fans into a cooperative meeting.

Time invested together on a regular routine without authoritarian roles, where each member can share without trepidation, can gradually inspire many a heartfelt and/or humorous revelation. When sons and daughters feel that they have the undivided attention of their moms and dads in a quality setting, they soar with self-esteem, belonging, and enthusiasm. Once their values and input are recognized as highly regarded, (not necessarily agreed with, but respected) then the fostering of the family spirit of togetherness solidifies to an immutable bond. This family bond quenches and nourishes the human spirit like no other.

"You know, Mom, parents are role models—whether they know it or not—from the moment they have kids," expresses my daughter. I see it as the "hot potato of life" and suddenly, tag—we're it. Only the pass stops here. It's a 24/7 mirror to check and see if we are really growing in harmony with our truest purpose. Regardless of their age, our children are always watching us to see if we can rise to the occasion and lead the way in this human journey. Sometimes, I think that God made children to help show their parents how to grow more humanly just as much as we show them. So, isn't that the crux of it all anyway? We must demonstrate our adulthood in our willingness to show our humanness. Do we have the courage to reveal our propensity to err and fall? Can we expose the fact that sometimes we make lousy choices, forget, regret—or not get—our desire to get back up, and try again?

The wisdom and courage that our children seek from our leadership is in our willingness to show forgiveness and humility. They are not looking for our perfection; they are looking for our humanity. They are also looking for our ability to stand for our convictions and carry a vision from the moment onto fruition. This courage in family life is the essential element that strengthens and nourishes our families to grow and fly with wings of confidence. When our children know, see, touch, hear, smell, taste, and feel the values of the family through the modeling of ourselves, integrity has arrived. When our children are able to experience our own serenity and candid response to the harder sides of adulthood, they are comforted in knowing that we share in their journey of both dark and light. They are given a path of leadership that they can now follow as they begin to try their own wings of independence.

In John F. Kennedy's *Profiles in Courage* inner character is the measurement that determines true courage in leadership. If the leader knows how to lead, he or she takes stock in genuine values. Leaders exert the true wisdom they possess to make decisions based on the best interest of the entire whole or, in this context, the family. Just as great leaders do, great parents make decisions with the family's mission in mind over there own best interests. These are the mighty waters that great courage carries us over, especially when the weight of our egos burdens our capacities to give so selflessly to the whole. Sometimes, we will be tempted by self-doubt, popular vote, immediate gratification, economies of scale, or even outside influences to question our own abilities to lead our families. These are precisely the moments of growth where God can make the difference.

If we trust in our spiritual faith, our true purpose will guide the way. We can let go and let God, for he will never abandon his children.

When our children are clear about their esteem, along with their family's mission and values, the integrity of the bond will shore up the boundaries. If a family freely chooses, their own moral guidelines based on respect for humanity, voila! Character has been born. Families who bring character to society bring their best to the dance of life. The light of God shines upon them. The love of God is within them. The power of God flows through them, wherever they are, God is, and all is well. Prayer is a direct line to our higher connection with God. When we pray daily with gratitude and humility with our true purpose as our vision for life, then, we can smile and go about our daily activities in a calm and purposeful manner. God will surely show us the way to our heart's delight.

In remembering that thoughts are things and energy just is, we can command our focus in family life toward positive energies that nourish happiness and fulfillment. We can acknowledge the negative emotions that arise and then let them go! Be wary of any uninvited hints of the seven negative emotions of: fear, jealousy, hatred, revenge, greed, superstition, and anger. Chances are great that when we are personally willing to face these emotions and even talk about them as a family, we can more easily let go of them. We can understand more clearly their origin and find the strength to move on toward states of being that will bring us more fulfillment. We, as a family, can become invincible in our spirit of happiness.

I hope that our family has helped yours. You have certainly helped me in simply allowing me this opportunity to

⚛ Courage in Family

explore my own ideas and share our experiences with you. I feel confident that the more we uplift the spirits of our children and ourselves; the stronger our wings will be to soar toward new heights of peace, love, and joy as we become all that we were born to be!

Go now and take delight in reading the profiles of individuals who have shown unwavering Courage in Family.

⚛

.John F. Kennedy Library/Funeral March

. . . Jackie was a pillar of strength and resilience. It helped all the rest of us to sort of carry on.
—*Senator Ted Kennedy*

First Lady Jacqueline Kennedy

John F. Kennedy Library

First Lady Jacqueline Kennedy in a Riding Session

CHAPTER TWENTY-ONE
Courage In Family

First Lady Jacqueline Kennedy

The Courage to Walk Through Darkness

> ... She was a pillar of strength and resilience.
> It helped all the rest of us to sort of carry on.
> —Senator Edward Kennedy.
> First Lady Jacqueline Kennedy

When I reminisce about America's Queen of Camelot, I see many faces, many moods, and many emotions. I see true grit remarkably blended with the essence of elegance. I see a classic thoroughbred with poise, showmanship, and the tenacity to persevere through any race to the finish line. I see a timeless beauty from a bygone era where exquisite taste was appreciated like

Courage in Family

a fine wine. I also see a shy and very private woman who just wanted to love and be loved.

Yet, one memory stands out, embedded in every American living in 1963 on that very somber twenty-fifth day of November—days after her husband, President John F. Kennedy had been assassinated. This is the image of America's First Lady standing tall with her two young children at her side as she prepares to lead her country and the world through our late President's final parade. In Jacqueline Kennedy's face, we experience the darkest of dark strikes upon humanity. Nonetheless, she affirms, "I am going to walk behind the casket."

Moving closer through her black veil, we see the puffiness of her beautifully tender dark brown eyes from an endless ocean of grief-stricken tears. We feel the fatigue from every cell in her slender body from the most perilous week.

We hear the silent voice of pride and daunting certainty that her "Jack" would be remembered in the time-honored tradition personified by one of the great forefathers of this country, President Abraham Lincoln. We will always remember her quiet dignified courage, as we also remember her brave husband cut down in death like President Lincoln was almost a hundred years earlier.

We smell the sweet nectar of a fragrant blossom, almost frozen by the stark chill of a sudden, calamitous frost that struck across the country. We taste the bittersweet gestures of protocol and parenthood as we bow in respect alongside our widowed First Lady and her ever-so-respectful son, John and her loving daughter, Caroline. Together they gave their final salute to their father, her husband, and our revered leader of the free world, the late President John Fitzgerald Kennedy.

Her brother-in-law, Senator Ted Kennedy recalls Jacqueline Kennedy's valor. "I think we [he and Robert

First Lady Jacqueline Kennedy

Kennedy] had extraordinary respect for her inner strength and fortitude at the time of that walk beside her, and for her presence in the church. She was an extraordinarily powerful example for all the world, for all Americans, and for the family. While others were sort of trying to find themselves, to put this whole tragedy into some kind of context, she was a pillar of strength and resilience. It helped all the rest of us to sort of carry on."

Who can ever understand where such courage springs forth? Making sense of it all is so difficult with such an inexplicable tragedy as the one endured by Jacqueline Kennedy, where destiny and duty collided so violently right in her lap.

On the infamous day of November 22, 1963, the day that started so bright and ended so dark, Mrs. Kennedy made her first official domestic trip as First Lady to Dallas, Texas. She had personally delivered a speech in Spanish to a Latin-American audience in Houston the evening before they arrived in Dallas. On the day that would end up to be her last as our First Lady, she spent five hours in a plane, four hours in a motorcade, shook hands with thousands of enthusiastic citizens, and received three bouquets of yellow and one of red roses.

She was beginning to enjoy the sense of being needed and loved in her role. "Jackie," the crowds roared for her as she bedazzled the world in her now—legendary pink suit and pillbox hat. Even the president was truly in awe of his wife. She did more than complement his presence . . . she completed him.

Then with shots fired in mass pandemonium, it was all over. At Parkland Memorial Hospital in Dallas, she stood numb to the world, yet in sobering recognition that her husband was now gone forever. She quietly insisted that she be allowed to be alone with him before they left. She remained at his side with her hand on his casket as it was taken to the hearse and then to Air Force One. Steadfast in her intent to ride in the back seat near his side, she remained close to the slain president on that sad flight. Wearily, the former First Lady embraced her brother-in-law, Bobby, at Andrews Air Force Base. Now with her family, the all-too-young widow allowed Bobby to escort her and the late president's casket to Bethesda, Maryland, for an autopsy. Finally, the exhausted lady of Camelot arrived back with her beloved to the White House before dawn of the next day. Jackie made one request. She asked her parents to spend the night at the White House with her. This would be a week full of many tender tears for an all too brave woman.

I believe it is in these quiet acts of courage that the world began to understand her brilliant light. The First Lady touched us privately and publicly. Her poised essence of strength illuminated us through the darkness, even with the unimaginable pain she must have endured during that week. Jacqueline Kennedy remained centered and everyone else around the world simply took her cue.

Her personal secretary, Ms. Mary Van Rensselaer Thayer wrote a poignant memoir:

"At ten o'clock the next morning after that terrible night, the family, half a dozen friends, and as many presidential aides and some members of the White House staff gathered in the White House for a private mass. A temporary altar and chairs were set up in the Family Dining Room. Those who had been invited stood stiff as statues, separately, eyes averted from each other, in the adjoining State Dining Room. The President's flag-draped coffin could be seen in the East Room at the end of the long corridor. . . . The design was similar to that used at the funeral of Abraham Lincoln. . . . Suddenly, those in the State Dining Room were aware of Mrs. Kennedy's presence. A slim figure in stark black, she stood facing the coffin, holding her children by the hand. She turned and the three walked slowly along the red-carpeted hall toward those who were waiting. . . . Those gathered for the service could not bring themselves to look and stared down desperately at the complex design of the new Bessarabian rug.

"Mrs. Kennedy glanced briefly into the Family Dining Room and walked away. Robert Kennedy returned and softly announced, 'Mrs. Kennedy wishes the mass celebrated in the East Room.' The altar and the rows of chairs were moved, and those waiting walked in misery through the three glowing State Rooms. There, near the coffin, they knelt on the hard oak floor. As the friends left Mrs. Kennedy stood in the hall and thanked each one for coming. She wore no makeup. Her pale features seemed luminous with a sustaining inner strength."

Mrs. Kennedy's inner courage was observed throughout the tough week. After she lit the eternal flame at Arlington National Cemetery to complete the burial ceremony, Jackie continued to hold up as an almost surrogate president, personally thanking each of the sixty-two heads of state who had attended President Kennedy's funeral.

In her last days at the White House, Jacqueline Kennedy successfully lobbied President Johnson to change the name of the space center from Cape Canaveral to Cape Kennedy. She also persuaded the new president to support several of her important causes, including the Historic Preservation Act, the Pennsylvania Avenue Redevelopment, and the National Cultural Center, eventually renamed the John F. Kennedy Center for the Performing Arts.

On the final night before Mrs. Kennedy was to leave the White House, she sat up until 4:30 A.M. hand-writing notes on prayer cards bearing the likeness of JFK, personally thanking every member of the White House Staff. The next morning before saying good-bye, Mrs. Kennedy did not forget to comfort her children. The United States Marine Band honored both Caroline and John in celebration of their birthdays while masking their own sorrows as they respected Jackie's desire to offer her children some sweeter memories in a bitter week.

Mrs. Kennedy spoke to the nation on television from the Justice Department awhile later, thanking everyone in the world for all the kindness and support that she and her family had received since her husband's death. Her soft voice only enhanced the strength of her character. The First Lady encouraged the world to visit President Kennedy's upcoming Presidential Library, eventually dedicating her time generously to the successful opening of the John F. Kennedy Library and Foundation located in Boston.

In her own words of timeless wisdom, Ms. Jacqueline Bouvier conveyed her essence in an inspirational piece "Be Kind and Do Your Share," written many years earlier when she was an eighteen-year-old student at Farmington Boarding School. In reading the short essay, I was touched at how clearly and succinctly she expressed important values such as kindness, generosity, accountability, honesty, and others. As young as the First Lady was at that time, she conveyed a mature understanding of the essence of character, selfless love, and true happiness. The essay can be read and enjoyed in *We Remember Her.*

Indeed, dear heavenly angels, we are grateful for the touch this fine woman bestowed on our hearts, and our heritage. We ask, "Where would this country be today if our brave and beloved Jackie had not the inner wells of strength and vision to turn the pages of history from despair to hope. . . for the land of the free and the home of the brave." We ask, and instantly, we realize that we are blessed. May the wings of her indelible spirit carry us forever.

◆ ◆ ◆

Yvonne Kalench and Sons

Courage is being able to draw on your own inner strength and count on yourself at any crossroad in life.

—Yvonne Kalench

Yvonne Kalench and Sons

CHAPTER TWENTY-TWO
Courage In Family

Yvonne Kalench

The Courage to Love Unwaveringly

> Courage is being able to draw on your own
> inner strength and count on yourself
> at any crossroad in life.
> —Yvonne Kalench

When a heart opens up and cries out for help for the tender attention of selfless love. . . are we ready for the calling? Who among us could indeed step up to the plate? Who could pour forth the unconditional acts of commitment promised in those often declared vows, yet not so often put to the ultimate test, "From this day forward, for better or worse, 'til death do us part."

One person stands clear in my mind as a model heroine, Mrs. Yvonne Kalench, affectionately known as Yvonne, widow of the late business and civic leader John Kalench.

Courage in Family

O heavenly Father, how your work comes to us in such mysterious ways. How majestic you appear to us through the light of the courageous, in their acts of love. Your essence of infinite kindness unfolds before our eyes through Yvonne.

Unfolding through Yvonne is her boundless desire to fulfill the last days of her beloved husband's life, which has made many of us stand in her honor and take note for this unassuming, yet, so courageous, lady.

I am confident that John is smiling down on us from heaven right this very moment. I am sure he affirms my belief that his beloved wife is one of those rare and precious pearls. One that God chose to glorify and reflect the grandeur of life, love, and the unwavering strength seated inside the universal soul of humanity.

I speak so admirably about Yvonne, a striking woman of slender stature, standing 5'8" with tender green eyes. I speak of a vibrant lady who, while relaxing at her pool, met and fell in love with a man who, unbeknownst to her at the time, would become one of, if not *the* leader in relationship building or partnership marketing. A brilliant master at networking, John Kalench, well-esteemed author, speaker, and founder of an international company Millionaires in Motion, spoke in one of his books (dedicated to his wife), *Being the Best You Can Be in MLM*, about looking for the pearls in a world full of oysters. He spoke of seeking mentors and he chose his father . . . and his wife. His words are touching and especially poignant in this hour, and I share them with you.

"I personally have a number of mentors, one of whom is my father. Not because of his entrepreneurial example, but rather because of the unconditional love he continually displays for my mother—his wife. I've never met a man who is so open and proud in showering his affection for the number one person in his life. I can't tell you how this makes me feel every time I see them. I can tell you, I want to create that same kind of love in my life. So, my father, is my life's reminder, my hero, the shining example I try to follow!"

Life mirrors its desires as I speak of the true pearl that John attracted and cherished so much—his wife. Together, they dedicated their lives to each other, and between them, they shared the joy of life with the birth of their two sons, Jackson and Cole. Their love was a real fable of giving and receiving in the most complete sense, and their life together was the successful reflection of their individual will and desires. As Yvonne describes, "Our sixteen years together simply felt like a continuous date. Our live-in nanny of the last five years even noticed that special quality about us."

Yet, earthly tragedy was to strike havoc in the Kalench home, and Yvonne would be faced with the dissonant music of reality in the shattering news that her husband would soon die. His unremitting battle with pancreatic cancer would escalate, and as grim odds began to overshadow their optimism, the couple would have to accept a new fate for their family's journey.

Throughout the brief eight months that transpired before John's passing, Yvonne would be tested in the toughest battle of inner resources that she had ever experienced in her lifetime. I asked Yvonne, in an intimate conversation, where she felt that she was able to draw the strength she carried in these tough times. As she sincerely searched her heart and wept, she told me, she speaks to God and to John. Through our conversations, I realized that Yvonne knows no other way. Her genuine respect for the word and essence of commitment is paramount in her fiber. I see now that as John was so highly respected as a man of his word, he also recognized this rare jewel in his loving wife. Yvonne would not have had life any other way, but to take care of John's needs herself as his condition worsened and took his life.

Courage in Family

"Of course, it was pretty tough," Yvonne reminisces. "Three years ago when John was first diagnosed with a tumor, we were relieved after he underwent a successful surgery. We had a great life. We have always been goal-oriented and we would achieve what we set out to accomplish. John was a great father, and yet, we still made time to do what we enjoyed as a couple and as a family.

"Then, in January 2000, we discovered that the cancer was spreading again and had begun taking over John's health. I knew that I would have to prepare the children and myself for the time that John would pass away, although I had always hoped for a miracle. It was difficult, and it is still hard, but I really feel that we had a full life together . . . only our years together were cut short. We always made time for ourselves and we knew that the 'let's wait for the right timing to talk about the unpleasant' approach just wouldn't work. We made a decision to always talk and that is what got us through . . . I feel that we—John and I, as well as Cole—were able to talk about all that we needed to share before John left us."

Yvonne adds warmly, "I was especially sensitive of my sons' needs, and I talked Cole through much of his grieving process, so that he actually did okay once John did pass on. In fact, she muses fondly about her son, "As Cole touched John's back, he actually said he felt John's wings to Heaven."

My first personal experience with Yvonne was during a conference in which John spoke and introduced his family. As the seasons passed, I noticed a shift in her role, as John's illness became public. Yvonne began to emerge as the leader of the family and of their business affairs. I began to see a subtle, yet dramatic, change in her force. I saw a woman who was certainly nervous about suddenly speaking in front of 10,000 people; however, she had a raw level of determination and strength that seemed to grow unconsciously within her.

Yvonne's unwavering expression of optimism always carried through in her public speaking as she tried to console, and, yet, update the large audiences that also loved and cared for John.

In Yvonne's words, "I guess I've just realized in such a sad way that you can feel free to love another human being totally and still be at peace with your own self-reliance. At the end of the day, it is only you. You have to be able to trust in your own wisdom and instincts to do what is next . . . and that is important to accept, I'm still working on it."

On the subject of purpose, I share words from her husband:
"What kind of a person builds a pattern of setting and getting their goals? A successful person—a person who is building a growing resource of passion to be used in pursuit of their purpose. A powerful person. A person who empowers other people. And I'll give you a little hint about a person's purpose that comes from working with all those extraordinary people—it always has to do with helping and empowering others!

"Your purpose is a honing beacon that keeps you on track and prevents you from being distracted. Your goals are valuable stepping stones that lead you to 'being' your purpose. That's why I say your purpose is unending. Purpose isn't something you do. Purpose is something you be. This is a big and very important difference. Living your purpose is the way you are. That's being. Remember, they call us, "human beings," not "human doings."

"With a clear, articulated purpose, no matter what comes up in your life, you won't stray. You know which choices serve your purpose and which ones do not. When times get tough, your purpose can pull you through. Without one, you're unclear as to why you're going through the difficulties.

"When your life's purpose is held high and you're down in a valley of despair, you'll always be able to see a glimmer,

Courage in Family

just over the next hill. So, you take your struggles in stride and turn your stumbling blocks into steppingstones. Eventually, you climb up and out into the bright light of success."

—John Kalench, 1944-2000.

Because of you, Yvonne, and your model of courage, John, Cole, Jackson, and the rest of us . . . are in a better place. Thank you for being all that you are!

◆ ◆ ◆

*Courage is the willingness
to stand up for your beliefs.*

—Doc Moody

*Doc Moody
with Lutton Family*

CHAPTER TWENTY-THREE
Courage In Family

Doc Moody

The Courage to Model Unconditional Love

**Courage is the willingness
to stand up for your beliefs.**
—Doc Moody

Sometimes in life, we get lucky and a sincerely generous soul, akin to Santa Claus, comes passing through our hearts more than once a year. Better keep your eyes open though, because these folks are incredibly humble and calm in their godly works.

If you're too busy, too noisy, too materialistic, too pretty or too scared, you might just miss their prolific gifts... gifts of immeasurable wealth and timeless value. Oooh, the kind of gifts one would find at Tiffany's, Fifth

Courage in Family

Avenue, you might ask? Or perhaps, FAO Schwarz toys, for the young-at-heart?

No, my friends, these are intangible pearls for life, only available to the brave and warmhearted warriors of life. Wait . . . do I dare to share this special person with you? Promise to treasure him and you may join me for a peek at this great, yet humble man.

What caught my eye about . . . Doc . . . was his dance step. Prancing delightfully in his own peace and harmony, he and I crossed arms in a playful jig during a personal development seminar for parents at a youth academy where he was the clinical director and full-time psychologist. I caught the bright contagious twinkle in his eye. From that moment forward, I knew that I had accepted the invitation to an extended dance with Doc Moody, as he is affectionately and professional known, trusting him to guide our family through the waltz of our lives.

It was in June of 2000, when my husband, Steve, and I called on God to take the steering wheel of our family's journey and simply show us the way. At the time, our children, Crystal and Steven, were fourteen and eight years of age, respectively. Crystal was struggling though her early teen life, and, along with our son, Steven, we were all becoming frightened and confused as a family. Eventually, the heaviness in all of our hearts became too heavy and the pathway became too foggy. We prayed fervently and our prayers were soon answered by leading us to a school for troubled youth known as Sun Hawk Academy.

We traveled with great hopes to St. George, Utah, led by our intuition; yet, not without . . . the anguish . . . caused by our trembling thoughts and fears of the unknown. As a family, we were in search of refuge in the most paradoxical act a parent may ever need to do for their child—to let go and let God.

We did, and it worked. The heaviness and cloudiness slowly lifted, and our hearts soared with praise in the glory

Doc Moody

of God. Hope and vitality soon renewed our spirits. As soon as we arrived at Sun Hawk, we knew instantly that we had followed the right path and made the right choice for Crystal and our family. We finally felt a sense of calmness.

Clarity began to emerge, and, now, the four of us were embracing our new sense of vision. We realized that we could rely on professional support to redirect our family dynamics, and empowered ourselves with a plan of action. We all worked together over the next year and a half, and, on many days, the growth was painful and confusing. Yet, it was worth every moment of trial and error. We had our daughter and her loving attitude back again, and she was emerging as a blossoming new rose with healthy roots, and buds of new fragrances and colors. As a family, we continued to grow and build our bond and vision for our future together.

I certainly would credit Kevin Baron, one of the founders of Sun Hawk Academy, and his staff for their professional yet loving expertise in nestling the young-hearted in from the cold for the experience of their early lifetime. Like a cup of hot cocoa or chicken soup (as so well edified by my mentor, Mark Victor Hansen and his partner Jack Canfield) to soothe the weary from the wicked. Empowering their students with healthy values and the discernment to self-actualize in a society filled with elusive choices. Yet, my deepest admiration rings clear for the clinical director of the therapeutic program, Dr. Richard Moody, our daughter's one-on-one therapist, coach, and true friend. Dr. Richard Moody, Ph.D. is a well-respected leader, expert, and skilled practitioner in many fields of psychology, especially, personal development, youth crisis intervention, and family counseling.

"Doc Moody has been such a mentor to me. Next to my father, this is the man I respect and listen to the most. I have learned so much about myself through Doc's leadership. He is humble, yet confident," expresses colleague Dean Nixon.

Doc has a quiet calmness about him that offers solace to those he encounters in his day. His rugged country persona quickly emanates an invitingly relaxed atmosphere of confident, yet, caring mentorship. Doc and his staff competently and tenderly wipe off the tarnish and confusion that has jaded their students' attitudes. They inspire these teens to discover their inner beauty and strength, and polish their characters and personalities to a sparkling brilliance that the world—and they—can now behold and enjoy. Then, they lovingly and proudly send them off to their families with tools of love, compassion, discernment, self-esteem, and empowerment. Most often, these graduates return to society with an expanded awareness of their potential and purpose, deciding to begin their lives anew, and become effective leaders. Many even desire to courageously claim their stake of success and mark their place in the pages of their own destiny.

Since Doc's trademark is his quiet leadership, I chose to ask others about his qualities rather than pressing him to reveal himself through a candid interview. Even my own experiences with Doc attest to his surefootedness in establishing values and boundaries as the foundation to a healthy self-esteem. "My dad has always been a great role model for me," expresses Doc's adult son. The two of them spend many weekends camping in the high country of Utah together. I asked my daughter, Crystal, what defined Doc's leadership and courage. "Mom, even when Doc is quiet, everyone listens to him and watches how he handles issues. I think what I remember most about Doc is how he encouraged all of us to love ourselves first, and never give away our power. He seemed to be real clear on his own values and the natural consequences of life's choices," Crystal

Doc Moody

explains. She pauses and adds with a heartwarming smile, "Even though Doc would be calling me on myself, I always felt like he really cared about me. I miss Doc."

Our eyes are the portals to our soul and, make no mistake about it, with Doc, as I have never experienced more descriptive eyes than his. Doc will look into your eyes and help you see yourself, as you invisibly desire to become. I am certain that many a hardened teen has rebuked his reflection of them to such a cutting degree that it makes me wonder what drives Doc to even continue his work. I can think of nothing nobler than the contribution that Doc has made on the future of our dynamic society. He is truly building new hopes and dreams in our young adults day by day, talk by talk, walk by walk, heart by heart, tear by tear, hug by hug, and smile by smile. Through Doc's sensitive eyes, his warm and open heart, his patience and attentiveness, his gentle, yet, wise words, his commitment to love these young folks unconditionally, he firmly, yet, successfully sets the ground rules for respectful behavior. Then, almost suddenly, just like Santa, Doc seems to orchestrate along with his staff, a medley of miracles, which are exalted from parents and youth alike.

To a mother, there is no more precious and priceless of a gift than what Doc has given me in the rekindled light of love and joy that shines so brightly now in our daughter, Crystal, and in our home.

Thank you Doc, we love you and the world is a better place because of you!

◆ ◆ ◆

*Courage is walking to the edge
of all we know . . . and
taking . . . one more step.*

—Renee Sisney

Renee Sisney at Work

CHAPTER TWENTY-FOUR
Courage In Family

Renee Sisney
The Courage to Model Respect and Value

> **Courage is walking to the edge of all we know . . . and taking . . . one more step.**
> —Renee Sisney

Walking to the edge and sizing up the challenge ahead is a choice that Renee Sisney welcomes without any hint of hesitation or regret.

Watching Renee in motion is a joy in itself, as she certainly must have been sent to minister by orders of the highest Commander-in-Chief. I honestly believe that our Heavenly Father broadens his smile as he watches Renee unveil herself through her calling, to serve the hearts of his families.

When I first met Renee, I knew there was something special about her (as there is within every human being). Anyone who can be that calm, and, still, hold her position as director for youth ministry certainly has my undivided attention. Renee has a huge thirst for assisting young and old in their own walk to the edge. She sees the beauty within people, earning their trustworthiness and rapport almost immediately. Rita Levine, a former adult group leader under Renee's direction, described Renee's stamina and strength. "She has been one of my strongest mentors. Always nonjudgmental and tactful while acknowledging the hand of God, Renee is a true leader who embraces everyone's talents as part of the bigger picture," Rita says.

My husband, Steve, and I began to notice Renee's true strengths as we became involved in our children's religious education programs at Sacred Heart of Jesus Catholic Church. Crystal began attending the Tuesday evening teen meetings and started to share some positive feelings with us about the program. Before long, I, too, became more interested and befriended Renee as I watched how steadfast she was in her desire to produce a rewarding experience for the middle and high school-aged parishioners. Renee's leadership attracted me like a pied piper into volunteering to assist the youth program. On many occasions, Renee would even become a great source of wisdom and guidance for me during times of strife and confusion as I struggled through my own life's journey. As a mentor for Crystal, our teenage daughter, Renee gently, yet, boldly walked to the edge with her on many issues—the easy and the tough. Crystal has become a stronger, more secure leader through her relationship with Renee.

Just as a conductor carefully orchestrates a symphony, Renee magically coordinated ministry activities into a melody of good times for all to enjoy. Renee succeeded in balancing the program with a social, physical, spiritual, and emotional focus. For instance, one week would be devoted to time in the gym shooting hoops on the basketball court, while inviting enough free time for all the teens to visit, and just have fun together. Other weeks included theme topics of interest with biblical references. Still at other times, the teens enjoyed going out for field trips to local restaurants. Always sensitive to any new or shy participants, Renee placed importance on reaching out to everyone.

During that year, Crystal attended a weekend retreat in Estes Park, Colorado that encompassed a year of planning by many of the Catholic parishes within the regional archdiocese. Renee, along with other adult leaders, was instrumental in creating and implementing this youth event entitled, "Voices that Echo."

As Steve and I had hoped, this retreat offered our daughter a spiritually uplifting, yet, fun-filled environment. Crystal staffed as a mentor to the sixth, seventh, and eighth grade participants, while bonding with like-minded peers whom all shared common hopes and concerns. Crystal even had the opportunity to express her passion as a solo vocalist and lead the keynote address with a heartfelt story of her own mental battle between good and evil voices. As typical of Renee, she downplayed her role in the success of the event. Yet, when I picked up Crystal and saw all of the teens parading off the bus, there was a sense of great fulfillment and value reflected in their weary yet enthusiastic faces.

These examples of Renee's daily acts reflect the small footsteps in life that create solid foundations for our young. Renee has touched many in her tireless desire to reach out and recognize human value. However, her unwavering acts of courage are not necessarily the type of heroism one typically reads about in extraordinary portrayal. In fact, her valor stems from her ordinary deeds of listening, counseling, and handing families what they need when they want it. Then, suddenly, all these quiet moments add up and lead to pivotal transformations for all those who are ready to get closer to the Inner Light of God.

With her tender green eyes and genuine ear for empathy, Renee can soften the hardest of hardened hearts with a simple glimpse of warm recognition and her understanding smile. Her 5'4" stature and raring-to-go demeanor invite teens and adults alike, to join her in the fun. In joining her, you subtly notice that your presence makes a keen difference to her. Your feelings are valued and your spirit is uplifted. Then, and often suddenly, truth begins to emerge and reveal itself while you enjoy her companionship.

As I met with Renee on various occasions and we began sharing with each other, a stir in my soul started to capture my attention. I did not know what was happening, yet, I began feeling a stronger closeness to God. Then, I mused quietly to myself with the question, How did she do that? Well, of course, she didn't, and Renee is all too humble to embrace herself as anything more than an instrument for God's works. Yet, her gift of holding a person's hands as they unfold their innermost self and reveal their heart becomes the forbearance to an extraordinary event. In particular, when one comes face to face with their own likeness and the image of their Creator.

Sitting in Renee's office, I noticed the inviting ambiance created with the cozy sofas and beautiful portraits of Mother Teresa and, especially, one of Christ. I asked Renee many questions about herself, her work, and our work together in serving society. Her answers resonated strongly with my own views, instantly placing me in a positive vibration with a feeling of certainty about our acquaintance.

"We simply don't connect anymore," Renee begins. "The sense of family is greatly skewed, and that [family] is an important anchor for all of us. Little things aren't wrong anymore, and so, there is no clear definition of the path of goodness. A strong sense of God, morality, and humanness is truly needed more than ever. In earlier days, such as the sixties, we had causes to defend, and, now, there is hesitancy before the majority of people are willing to put themselves on the line. We are in dire need of clear values and boundaries as guidelines. We need heroes to emulate," she adds with sincere concern. I am not sure that Renee realized what a hero she had become to many people.

"Renee, please tell me how you came to discover your calling to minister to families," I ask. She replies thoughtfully, "After a respectable career in sales, I wanted to go beyond encouraging people to buy something. I wanted to give back some of what I have received in my life. I had always been connected to God and found myself drawn to Catholicism coming into the church as an adult. I believe that my growing relationship with Christ led me to connect my way in faith to younger individuals. Before I knew it, opportunities were in my focal point, and I went to work full-time in youth ministry once this position became available to me eight years ago."

Realizing for herself, the importance of a strong relationship with God—later, rather than, earlier—Renee feels that one way she can contribute to today's society is by helping more youth to discover the truth and love of God—as early as possible. "Once someone can connect and really hold on to their relationship with God, with Christ, with the Holy Spirit—the Holy Trinity of their Catholic faith—I know with great confidence and happiness that this special person has, indeed accessed the great gift of life. I know with deep fervor that once one enters a relationship with God, they will find that they are . . . less alone and more content in their search during their life's journey. Defeats are not as great and abandonment is impossible because God is their constant and loving companion in the journey," she affirms with certainty.

Renee warmed my heart with joy and serenity beyond words. I say this—emphatically—because deeper convictions, which impart these expressions of joy and serenity, are not derived merely from an emotional experience, as much as, from a spiritual awakening. I have noticed that emotions can change constantly throughout the day; yet, the inner qualities of joy, serenity, purposefulness, and happiness remain steadfast, regardless of human feelings.

"What of Christ?" I ask. "Oh," she smiles, briefly closing her eyes as she confides, "Although I draw comfort daily from God, I surrender to Christ in his Grace. I take comfort in his desire to share our humanity, as he did for us in his living example while on Earth. Christ gives me the strength to persist during times of struggle."

"What advice would you offer today's parents?" I ask as Renee calmly listens and then replies, "Cheri, I would ask them to stay closer with the Lord themselves and recognize that their children are children of God. Therefore, they can take comfort as this helps set the standard and ease the control. When we parent through God's eyes, we are free. Above all, we need to strengthen the family bond and provide more intimate and physically present time together. This is so critical for us . . . not only to survive, but to thrive!"

For anyone looking for the courage to stay the course and walk to the edge, Renee advises, "Stop and stand in your walk of darkness and please don't be afraid. Take the time to look for your Inner Light—the Light of Christ within the light—and then go forward with God to the next step. Walk with like-minded people who represent God."

Renee's vision of Heaven on Earth reflects an ultimate state of love where no one is without the total experience of God's love. Her eyes well as she tributes her dad who passed away a few years ago, and she sees a reunion with those she loves as her desire for eternity. Renee's mom has

Renee Sisney

since passed on, as well, and her memorial funeral was on September 11, 2001. In spite of all that became history that day, Renee maintained her spirit of love and devotion for her mother, in her honor; all the while, encouraging all those in attendance, to pray, together, for the country. We did, and the memory of that place of gathering, in such a spirit of love and comfort, will be a source of warmth in my heart forever.

In closing, I share a memory of one particular Christmas Eve. Renee had directed the Nativity scene reenactment at our Children's Mass with volunteers of boys, girls, and young adults. I offered both of my children's talents, along with my own assistance in dressing the children and announcing the play. I smile now as I remember the backstage scenes of light-hearted calamity with little boy shepherds losing their sheep, shoes, and rods. Renee simply kept smiling with a cool and calm style of leadership, while she directed the play to its glorious finale.

Once again, Silent Night reigned as a Holy Night through the gentle tenacity of heroines such as Renee! May God bless you, Renee, and bring you all the love you bring to us!

◆ ◆ ◆

Courage is having the heart and faith to do what you believe is the right thing to do.

—Melissa Montoya

Montoya Family

CHAPTER TWENTY-FIVE
Courage In Family

Melissa Montoya

The Courage to Embrace a Christian Family Life

Courage is having the heart and faith to do what you believe is the right thing to do.
—**Melissa Montoya**

Look into the night and up into the deep blue sky and gaze for hours at the spectacle of light. See the shower of illumination throughout the Universe . . . the Milky Way and all its glory. . . the constellations, meteors, and heavenly bodies all parading by—just for our amazement.

O do look again! My sweet Mary, Mother of our dear Lord, you have enjoyed casting your say in the who's who of the stars. You have chosen the bright star in the northern direction to guide the indomitable spirit of the lovely Melissa Montoya, affectionately known as Missy. I do thank you, Mary, for your hand in creating such a brilliant beacon of light . . . shining today . . . in this lovely lady.

With her blonde hair neatly sweeping along her shoulders and her hazel eyes and ivory complexion highlighting her inner beauty, Missy forges ahead in her day with the might of Joan of Arc. A rising star of hope and integrity, she will radiate your world with her passion for humanity.

Always delighted to spend much of her day with her daughter Sydney and her loving husband, Marty, Missy renews her vision daily through earnest prayer and the silent example of piety and fortitude. To know this heroine is to feel her strength and convictions in the goodness of God and his universe. In the face of darkness, Missy looks to Christ for the light of purpose. With steadfast fervor, she gracefully journeys one step at a time toward self-actualization.

To emulate Our Blessed Mother's sweet woman, one would first have to become very tidy and ambidextrous. With her own cleaning business, Missy has skillfully mastered the challenge of scouring clean four or five houses in a working day's time. When I visit Missy, I always enjoy the bright and cheery warmth of her, yes, beautiful home! I delight in the huge smiles and warm greeting that I receive from Missy, Marty, Chelsea, and little Sydney. There is a certain sense of pride and wholesomeness that one feels instantly in the Montoya home. No doubt, this organized wife and mother gives an enormous amount of her heart and time to her family. Her most recent endeavor has been to assist her husband in launching a family landscaping business.

Missy expresses during a poignant chat, "My desire is to spend as much quality time with my family as possible. I am most happy when I am helping my church and loved ones. In my youth—after my father passed away—my faith and purpose were reawakened. Before that, I was just following the crowd, only concerned about having fun. I had lost my way

Melissa Montoya

with God, and I didn't feel right about myself. Dad's loving attitude inspired me to take a serious look at my faith and my life. He had a strong faith in God and Christ. Once I received Christ in my life, I knew I was on the right path, although I received harsh ridicule from some of my friends for awhile. It hurt, but it only made my faith stronger. Ever since then, I have been led by God to serve others through a strong family life."

Missy has expanded her mission to include possibility thinking that offers her multiple sources of income through a variety of home-based businesses. By sharing and caring, Missy will take part in a growing phenomenon that is helping people take ownership for their health, wealth, and balanced lifestyle.

Missy epitomizes valor and it is evident in every fiber of her being. Her conviction to protect extends not only to her daughter, husband, and loved ones, but, also, to all people and principles that she believes are good and just in the world. Her deep faith and integrity are apparent as she humbly, yet fervently, walks through her life's journey.

To really depict the true nature of Missy's courage, one might ask, What would it be like to be Missy's child or inside of her heart? I believe, the answer is—exquisite. For my intuition tells me that within Missy, there lies purity, safety, and a warm light brilliantly glowing toward eternal life with our Creator.

With quiet strength and a calm understanding of all that she has become, Missy moves forward in her daily life, with triumph in her heart. She radiates the glory of God and his love for humankind. She is truly an awe-inspiring instrument of inner strength displayed through all her radiance.

Thank you, Blessed Mary, for your hand in shaping our beloved Melissa!

◆ ◆ ◆

PART FIVE
Courage In Work

Live Today Like There is No Tomorrow

*Every act rewards itself in like manner.
Cause and effect, means and end,
seed & fruit, cannot be severed; for the effect
already blooms in the cause, the end
pre-exists in the means, the fruit in the seed.*
—Ralph W. Emerson

CHAPTER TWENTY-SIX
Courage In Work

Live Today Like There is No Tomorrow

> **Every act rewards itself in like manner. Cause and effect, means and end, seed and fruit, cannot be severed; for the effect already blooms in the cause, the end pre-exists in the means, as the fruit in the seed.**
> **—Ralph W. Emerson**

These acts we call our work, shall they be fun? Shall they be the sincere rendering of our truest purpose in life unfolding as we breathe into the newest day? Shall they be our acts of gratitude played out in physical form for the world to enjoy? Yes indeed.

For as we, as a civilized nation of loving human beings discover our gifts, we, in turn; will follow our nature to perform in the best manner possible. This production of our innermost being sows sweetly the harvest for future generations to come. We now reap the harvests of all life before us.

Shall we not put our greatest seeds of passion and purpose into the great soil of life? For it is in our daily work that we learn to love God more, love ourselves, and truly become humane in lending our hands in a common cause to serve, grow, and belong during this precious experience . . . our lives.

Certainly, it is our birthright to be born with an abundance of all things necessary to live out our lives in the manner that best besets our nature. When we understand our own nature; we can truly recognize the joy of our purpose. We can begin to witness our day in a state of balance when our work becomes our play, shared with the world in a genuine state of gratitude. In turn, the world will thank us through this law of cause and effect or as so eloquently described by Emerson earlier in this chapter, the Law of Compensation. This is the evolving cycle of success—expanding higher and larger, elevating an individual to a level of self-actualization or . . . greatness.

Today, the primary compensation that we receive is in the physical form that we have coined money. It is merely the instrument—no more and no less—serving as a thank you from the universe in the exchange of goods and services. These exchanges of goods and services were originally seeds of ideas sown from every one of us. Day to day, we can witness the shape of our human character as a whole, by the extent of the thank you we render for the various exchanges we choose for our daily lives. For what are we willing to trade our time, money, and focused energy? How will we, as a society, determine the value of ideas—transformed into goods and services—that we incorporate into our daily lives? Once decided upon, we will reward that exchange, that act, that work, accordingly. In economic terms, it is the law of supply and demand determined by what the market will bear as maximum compensation.

Yet, we as an evolving group have the decisive power to carve this cycle of economy toward the good that we desire in our lives and for our children. If we want to know ourselves, all we have to do is look out at what we have become through the looking glass of our results. The Laws of Supply and Demand, Cause and Effect, Compensation — call them what you wish—will go on just as certain as the sun has set and risen since creation. All we have to do is observe the consequences that take shape in modern society and we see these immutable laws in action. If we allow circumstances and others to seduce us, then we can be tricked into an ego-oriented doom. However, as God's children, as masters' of our thoughts, and captains of our souls, we have only to confer with ourselves in our quest for peace and prosperity. We are endowed with all that we need, and we are reminded in all books of God to "seek and behold the gifts of plenty." Once we ask, we shall find within the universe. The Bible states, "The Lord already knoweth what you ask before you speak." We must, therefore, know and ask, for what we desire to receive.

This is part of our work. This is the courage that we tap into from all of our resources to put our best efforts forward in our daily missions. Courage leads us to:
1. become clearer in our hearts about our true passions
2. trust the Universal Laws enough to go out and do it.

What if by trusting our own self-competence, we would be contributing precisely our proper share toward the greater whole? Isn't that what happens in nature? Does an orange do the work of an apple, or does it simply follow its true nature? Can we imagine a world in which we all followed our natural passions, putting forth a day's work toward our truest purpose? How would our productivity levels measure if everyone were enjoying their work? As humans, we are divinely blessed with a multitude of gifts and talents, which all serve to support our core purpose.

In the act of drawing from our own strengths to trust ourselves, we can begin to feel strong, connected, joyful, valued, and, useful in our service to God, our fellowmen, and the entire universe. Once we are centered on our truer purpose, passion rises spontaneously from within us.

We begin to notice love in action through our work. This wisdom sings loud and joyfully within individuals who capture their calling. Can you recall being in the presence of people who are passionate about their work? They seem to release that energy of elation to all with whom they are in contact. Watch someone who is in the act of their work when it becomes their play. It is almost an effortless experience. They seem to be having so much fun that it becomes indistinguishable to notice when the play is finished and the work begins. For some onlookers, there is a sense of envy or frustration as to why they themselves do not possess such a natural state of success. Yet, they can, and it is their duty to their self-esteem to discover that precise place within themselves to draw their own courage in work. Just as success breeds success, abundance breeds abundance. The universe truly rewards those who have given purely of themselves. "Joie de vivre" or the joy of life is passed on from their essence—to be shared with you!

The antithesis to this giving attitude is the paradigm that one works *for* money. Perish the thought of a precious human being placed on this magnificent place in their physical existence—to work for money? Toil for most of our lives for a paper instrument designed by man? No, my dear friend, money works for *you*! You are the master of your fate and the captain of your soul, fully in charge of determining the manner in which you propose to share your true self with the world. To the degree that you are honest with your true self—in your desire to become all that you have been designed to be—is the exact degree to which your reward will result in the form of a thank you from the universe. The great riches of life appear in at least a dozen human desires, and will be elaborated upon later in this chapter. For now, it is worth noting that money is the least desired of all that we desire.

It takes mustering up our own innate resources of strength in our spirit, mind, and body, especially, as we continue to break through the time, space, and fear barriers of our human journey. No accidents occurring, we must simply awaken, at that precise moment in our destiny, to the happy fact that we, too, can move the mountains of our worlds. We can do it with great ease and success . . . once we make the decision and commit to keep on keeping on! Earl Nightingale, considered the father of the American movement in leadership development, defined success so brilliantly and succinctly as the "progressive realization of a worthy ideal." An ideal is an idea with which we fall in love.

However, those individuals that still wander and begrudge their work generally do not enjoy their lives. They only get by in a sometimes hypnotic, frantic, or even worse, a wicked state. Yet, ironically, how can one put forth meaningless service day after day, and actually expect anything greater to arise in their feelings of satisfaction and reward? Observing an adult out of harmony with his or her chosen path of work is like watching a child required to eat a particular vegetable that they do not like. It is also akin to a couple dating without any mutual attraction, or a sun-loving blossom being planted in full shade. We can cajole a resistant nature forever; however, we will never see its true nature in bloom until it is planted in the conditions that trigger its natural passion.

Alas, it is in that very notion that one can understand the origin of misgiving. This dichotomy in nature is often experienced not once, twice, or quarterly, but as often as five days per week for the average working person. This dichotomy in nature is not just in our waking hours, but the sensation also reckons with us in our sleep. Our souls stir in our subconscious thoughts through our dreams. Then, our restless battles of avoidance or resistance become labeled as insomnia. The battle between the conscious and the subconscious—or what is and what desires to be—carries on relentlessly without any control. For some individuals, this battle of the wits can linger on and haunt them right into their graves. As said in the Bible according to Matthew 12:25:

"A house divided against itself cannot stand."

I cannot presume to understand this model of strife. I only pray that these souls may someday find peace in their chosen eternities. I do take consolation in the understanding that all humans are under the same precise laws; and therefore, with the luxury of our free will, as our birthright, we are able to choose our own Heaven on Earth. We are all granted the grace of courage to being anew each day. Each day we are free to face our fabricated demons and conquer them in the trust of our inner gifts and talents—with our positive drive to break free and go for it! We can unleash our fears and say, "So what if I am afraid? So what if I fall? I would rather live for something than die for nothing. I am tired of watching everyone else have fun. I want to play!"

O yes, our innate desire to be ourselves, and the best at that, is a true gift of love that the world can embrace tremendously. Our world needs each one of us so tenderly that it shows its aches through universal stress and turmoil. Please reread that last sentence. It is that important. Through our disservice, we produce the inequities, which can only be reflected in its makers. As we said earlier, that success can only breed success, then, we can also reason that a worthy ideal sought after by its master is sure to reward a worthy result, that can multiply and feed a nation in need. What a splendid idea indeed! For each of us to mind our own business rather than that of our neighbors, in that moment, would begin the miracle of world peace. Once we know our own business—for that can be a life long end in itself—we can render the proper service of our business to others.

How will we recognize the true merits of our deeds? Shall it be measured through the "thank you" we receive from the universe in monetary wealth? After all, the circulation of money is an excellent vehicle for the free-flowing distribution of wealth. Moreover, our inherent birthright endows the abundance of wealth to each of us in our labored harvest.

Alas, we must be weary of only the reliance on paper money as sole indicator of our wealth and abundance in life as the reflection of our true merits. In fact, according to Mr. Napoleon Hill, the great thinker and literary architect of the internationally acclaimed book *Think and Grow Rich*, there are actually twelve great riches of life, which are sought after by humanity.

The Twelve Great Riches of Life

1. A positive mental attitude
2. Sound physical health
3. Harmony in human relationships
4. Freedom from all forms of fear
5. The hope of future achievement
6. The capacity for faith
7. A willingness to share one's blessings
8. A labor of love as an occupation
9. An open mind on all subjects
10. Self-discipline in all circumstances
11. The capacity to understand others
12. Sufficient money

ॐ Courage in Work

Although, money serves as an ideal instrument to use in creating extraordinary economic wealth, opportunities, or buying power for other goods and services, it cannot overpower the other eleven riches of life. Money cannot buy any of these centered qualities within humanity. It cannot buy success, or the elusive states of mind called peace and happiness. However, it can indeed serve to make our lives enjoyable, so that we can experience all that we desire, and deserve in life.

Paradoxically, money—under our generous and guiding care as an instrument in the circulation and increase of wealth—can serve to induce noble acts of servitude, enhancing favorable conditions for the other great riches of life to follow. These riches also include lasting friendships, joyful family relationships, harmonious cooperation between business associates, peaceful discourse among nations, creative progress throughout industry, eternal love for God and the universe, and a sense of awe for each day's wondrous gifts.

As if that bundle of optimism is not enough to savor, I shall intrigue you with more good news for your days ahead. Napoleon Hill continues to say in his book, which has been read by well over twenty-five million men and women, that "when riches begin to come, they come so quickly, and, in such great abundance, that one wonders where they have been hiding during all those lean years." This encouragement alone should provide sufficient impetus to excite one toward a proper means to their own well-deserved treasures of wealth.

Napoleon Hill, under a commission by Andrew Carnegie, set out to research a new economic philosophy, interviewing many of America's wealthiest statesmen and businessmen. All of these individuals possessed a passionate definiteness of purpose that is inherent in self-actualized people. Mr. Hill interviewed the likes of Thomas Edison, William Taft, Dr. Alexander Graham Bell, Woodrow Wilson, John D. Rockefeller, Theodore Roosevelt, Henry Ford, Charles M. Schwab, and many others. I only regret that I am not aware of any great women mentioned in his interviews. However, when one studies Mr. Hill's work, it becomes apparent that he has a keen sense of appreciation for some of the finer qualities inherent in a woman's nature. He also recognizes these inner qualities of women as fundamentally significant in a man's success, and to the whole of life's grandeur.

How can we begin in our desire to tap into our resources of courage and creativity within our work? One pearl that I have enjoyed hearing by Bob Proctor, one of the most fascinating thinkers of modern times is:

"We must go as far as we can go with each day and when we get there; the way will be shown for the next."

For each day that we pick up our heads from our pillows of rest, we begin anew to thank God for another chance at becoming all that we have been designed to become during this human experience. Another anecdote warns, humorously, however, "If we are not at the edge, then we are taking up too much space."

This reminds me of a very similar perspective stated by Bill Gates of Microsoft in Peter Lowe's *Success Magazine*. "I don't hire bozos," says Gates. "In terms of IQ, you've got to be very elitist in picking the people who deserve to write software." Gates does not tolerate mediocrity. "If you have somebody who's mediocre, who just sort of gets by on the job, then we're in big trouble. The biggest problem with a mediocre employee," as Gates sees it, "is not the bad mistakes that they make, nor is it the good things that they fail to do. The biggest problem with mediocre employees is that they take up space that could be occupied by brilliant people."

In looking at some that have tested their strengths and weaknesses, we can take comfort in the assurance that we, too, can become great—not in shunning, but in embracing our challenges, weaknesses, and fears as seeds of equal or greater opportunities. It only takes a decision to ask and be ready to receive while we do our share, regardless of the sacrifices. Then, luck will come knocking at our door, usually when we least expect it, and, in the most unlikely circumstances. As it is said, that luck appears—almost magically—at the intersection where preparation and opportunity cross paths.

If you are one of those individuals who have been called to your purpose early in your life, then I applaud you and invite you to contact me with any further insights that might be available to share for future books or interviews. As well, if you are one of those individuals who are in conflict and confusion about your purpose in life, take heart in the fact that you are at least willing to be honest with yourself, and continue to listen to your inner guidance. I can suggest a few books and audio programs that I have found to be beneficial in leading my journey here and list others in the back of this book. The first, *The Winner's Image*, is by Bob Proctor through Life Success Ventures. The second, *Thinking Bigger Than You Ever Thought You Could Think*, is by Mark Victor Hansen through Mark Victor Hansen & Associates. The third, *Lead the Field*, is by Earl Nightingale through Nightingale-Conant. The fourth, most importantly, is the Bible, or the corresponding book of your particular faith.

Whatever our work may be, it is important. Walt Disney produced an endless myriad of playfulness for families through Mickey Mouse, and countless other animated characters. Ray Kroc connected the globe through McDonald's, and its cheeseburgers. Another area of important work is in the home. The work of parents is tremendously significant to society. Mothers and fathers who consider the role of raising children as their primary mission will shape the lives of generations to come. Think of all the countless people who have influenced us simply by living their mission in life. For example, Steve and I feel that our marriage has been touched forever by our former pastor Father Madden, through the blessings he ministered to us during our recent anniversary. Each of us has the capacity to influence the world if only we can reach out with the courage to work through our true mission in life.

In an address here in Colorado, Mikhail Gorbachev, the former head of the Soviet Republic, advised, above all, "Take care to know and go along with your own nature. Then, act accordingly to go about your purpose, your mission, your work." He said that although you will be tempted and tested along the way, if you are clear with your own understanding of yourself, and you vow to do and be your best, then, you will—and must—carry on. Gorbachev viewed these acts of leadership as the acts of "leading others through the unknown and through change."

As we wrestle with the lofty words that follow, written by a wise poet from yesteryear, we might find debate in the absurdities of the world's reward of great economic fortune toward the strange, the ugly, the useless, or sadly, the harmful. How can this paradox fit into such absolute laws toward the evolution of growth? They do, and they will, as long as humanity determines it fitting to reward it so. Observe again, the vast fortunes of economic wealth, bestowed on producers of goods and services, which do *not* contribute to the collective betterment of life. These tides of demand will serve out their own truths and purposes, until they fall to demise in their own contradictions. Observe the recent catastrophes in the stock market and major accounting firms to understand this principle. Eventually, the good that we all desire will attract the good that we all deserve!

Courage in Work

In closing, I'd like to express that I have thoroughly enjoyed this journey of self-discovery with you, and I leave you with one request. When you feel broken and lose your way, re-read this book, forgive yourself, and know that you are important. You are important to God, to the universe, to humanity, to me, and to . . . you. Join me now as I share with you this delightful prose before continuing our journey in honoring the fine individuals, profiled in the upcoming chapters for their . . . Courage in Work.

"If You Think You Are"

"If you think you are beaten, you are.
If you think you dare not, you don't.
If you like to win, but you think you can't,
it is almost certain you won't.
If you think you'll lose, you're lost,
for out in the world we find,
Success begins with a fellow's will
—it's all in the state of mind.
If you think you are outclassed, you are;
you've got to think high to rise,
You've got to be sure of yourself
before you can ever win a prize.
Life's battles don't always go
to the stronger or faster man,
But sooner or later the man who wins
is the man who thinks he can!"

—Unknown Poet

John F. Kennedy Library/Civil Rights

Moral courage is a rarer commodity than bravery in battle or great intelligence. Yet it is the one essential vital quality of those who seek to change a world, which yields most painfully to change.

—Senator Robert F. Kennedy

John F. Kennedy Library

Robert F. Kennedy and Son

CHAPTER TWENTY-SEVEN
Courage In Work

Senator Robert F. Kennedy
The Courage to Care Regardless of Consequence

> Moral courage is a rarer commodity than bravery in battle or great intelligence. Yet it is the one essential vital quality of those who seek to change a world, which yields most painfully to change.
> —Senator Robert F. Kennedy

'Twas never a more caring knight born of Camelot who dared to tamper with the crooked, the crafty, and the cursed than that of America's own Sir Lancelot; Robert Francis Kennedy. Moving ever so bravely to defend the brokenhearted and the downtrodden, this modern day knight in shining armor crossed the land of the free on his white horse with visions for a new frontier.

In so many ways, Robert F. Kennedy epitomizes the character of the American spirit: in one word, multi-dimensional. Robert Kennedy is not easily summed up in any one direction. Was he a bit too ambitious? I suppose so. Was he a bit cavalier? Probably. Was he filled with idealism and moxie? Of course! Was he altruistic? You bet. Was he perfect? Far from it. But, who is? Was he impervious to his own infallible nature? Sometimes. Did he push the envelope? Obviously. He was, after all, the brave, young investigator for the United States government who brought organized crime into the federal courts for hearings, exposures, trials, and eventual convictions. He would later become U.S. Attorney General and finally, Senator of New York. He was a modern-day David who took his chances with the goliaths of crime, civil rights, and politics.

One of Robert Kennedy's favorite passages from classical Greek literature reflected his tireless quest for human progress, "Let us dedicate ourselves to tame the savageness of man and make gentle the life of this world." Bobby, affectionately known by friends and family, loved ancient as well as modern wisdom. In fact, one of his sons, Maxwell Kennedy, published *Make Gentle This World*—a collection of many of his dad's favorite thoughts and prose—in honor of his father. Maxwell's mother Ethel inspired this project, demonstrating her larger concern for the world to continue to hear her late husband's wisdom and heart.

Robert Kennedy was a person of great complexity and contradictions. He was a man born into a Bostonian family of great wealth, position, education, and power. Yet, he championed the hopes and dreams of America's poor and disenfranchised. He served as the nation's Attorney General, a position of awesome power that can easily be

Senator Robert F. Kennedy

abused if the position is filled with one who has self-serving interests. Kennedy, however, chose to use his authority on behalf of justice, freedom, and human dignity.

Looking closer at this man, I see a leader of deep inspiration. Imagine his grand vision, his quest for goodness and equality, and, ultimately, his respect for the Almighty General from above. The two greatest laws taught in the Bible guided Robert Kennedy's life:

1. To love God with all our heart, mind, and soul like no other.

2. To love and respect our neighbor as we earnestly love and respect ourselves.

Robert F. Kennedy (RFK) became a defender of his neighbor's rights early in his career of public service. He was always willing to work in the trenches alongside less educated comrades. In the military, young Kennedy served as a Seaman Second Class in the United States Navy during World War II. In the government, RFK served as chief counsel for the congressional committee created to investigate organized crime. The young attorney took on tough and formidable adversaries, such as Mafia hit man, Joe Valachi and the Teamsters' President, Jimmy Hoffa, exposing organized crime and union corruption. In his book *The Enemy Within*, Bobby writes:

"It seems to me imperative that we reinstill in ourselves the toughness and idealism that guided the nation in the past. The paramount interest in self, in material wealth, in security must be replaced by an actual, not just a vocal, interest in our country, by a spirit of adventure, a will to fight what is evil, and a desire to serve. It is up to us as citizens to take the initiative as it has been taken before in our history, to reach out boldly but with honesty to do the things that need to be done.

". . . The tyrant, the bully, the corrupter and corrupted are figures of shame. The labor leaders who became thieves, who cheated those whose trust they had accepted, brought dishonor on a vital and largely honest labor movement. The businessmen who succumbed to the temptation to make a deal in order to gain an advantage over their competitors perverted the moral concepts of a free American economic system."

From 1951 to 1964, Robert Kennedy would build an impressive career serving in the United States Justice Department. Beginning as a trial attorney in the criminal division, RFK eventually, earned the highest-ranking position in the department as the 64th U.S. Attorney General. In between these periods, Robert would serve as the campaign manager in the election of his brother, John Kennedy, as the 35th President for the United States of America. On January 21, 1961, RFK was officially appointed Attorney General under President John F. Kennedy. RFK had been reluctant to take on the position in the face of the obvious claims of nepotism, but it apparently became a fortuitous coup—for his older brother, the country, and the world. As the closest advisor and confidante to President Kennedy during the 1962 Cuban Missile Crises, Robert Kennedy's thoughtful and humane insight gave way to the successful outcome prayed for by all of us during those sobering thirteen days.

"RFK," according to Ronald Goldfarb, a lawyer who worked closely with Kennedy in the Justice Department and author of *Perfect Villains, Imperfect Heroes: RFK's War*, "accomplished much of what he set out to achieve. The statistics with respect to the organized crime and racketeering section of the Justice Department were impressive. Kennedy's crusade had ample immediate successes, and it changed the law enforcement landscape permanently. Robert Kennedy tapped into a wellspring of energy and high-minded public service that seems unique in retrospect.

Senator Robert F. Kennedy

. . . Most of us in our relatively small group at Justice were there to accomplish a task, to follow the goal of a leader in whom we came to believe, and to do something we thought was good for our country. . . . Kennedy and his crusade against organized crime did that."

By the end of RFK's four-year tenure at the Justice Department, there would be 201 indictments against Teamster officials and associates with 126 convictions won in court. However, despite all of his hardball determination, Bobby was considered by many of his key advisors as personable and genuine. According to Goldfarb, "Kennedy always paused his conversations to greet arriving aides individually with a handshake, direct eye contact, and offer some personal comments. Even with the enormous agenda that Kennedy held both at the Justice and all over the New Frontier, he knew us [his staff] and what we were doing." Goldfarb applauds and adds, "He clearly cared and we as clearly appreciated it."

As an eloquent speaker, visionary, and political leader, RFK revealed his own values, as well as America's, on a worldwide goodwill tour in 1962, during the following speech given in Japan.

"This is our vision of the world—a diversity of states, each developing according to its own traditions and its own genius, each solving its economic and political problems in its own manner, all bound together by a respect for the rights of others, by a loyalty to the world community, and by a faith in the dignity and responsibility of man.

". . . We deeply believe that humanity is on the verge of an age of greatness—and we do not propose to let the possibilities of that greatness be overwhelmed by those who would lock us all into the narrow cavern of a dark and rigid system. We will defend our faith by affirmation, by argument, if necessary—and Heaven forbid that it should become necessary—by arms. It is our willingness to die for our ideals that makes it possible for those ideals to live. . . .

"Freedom means not only the opportunity to know but the will to know. That will can make for understanding and tolerance, and ultimately friendship and peace.

"The future stretches ahead beyond the horizon. No mortal man can know the answers to the questions which assail us today. But I am not ashamed to say that we in America approach the future, not with fear, but with faith— that we call to the young men and women of all nations to join us in a concerted attack on the evils which have so long beset mankind—poverty, illness, illiteracy, intolerance, oppression, war. These are the central enemies of our age—and I say to you that these enemies can be overcome.

"Let us therefore pledge our minds and our hearts to this task—confident that though the struggle will take many generations, we shall be able to look back to this era as one in which our generations—joined as brothers—met our responsibilities and furthered the cause of peace at home and around the globe."

Bobby had a natural magnetism, which attracted the best in all those employed in the Justice Department. His momentum for passionate productivity was almost unstoppable, almost . . . but, unfortunately, not quite.

On November 22, 1963, it would come to a crashing halt. President John Fitzgerald Kennedy was assassinated and Attorney General Robert Kennedy's heart was ripped open and left vulnerable for much time to come. Bobby had lost his big brother, while the nation lost its president. He became devastated with shock. The country lost its innocence. The New Frontier seemed to disappear.

Senator Robert F. Kennedy

Yet, somehow Bobby found the inner strength to get back on his white horse immediately and look after his beloved brother's widow, a damsel in such an unthinkable distress. Despite Bobby's own overwhelming grief, he still had the fortitude to console the First Lady, Mrs. Jacqueline Kennedy, through a very dark time in history. Bobby's quiet acts of chivalry greatly comforted his sister-in-law during her hours of foreboding despair after the fateful trip in Texas. In that most critical time, when the arrows of evil tore through the hearts of all Americans, particularly through the hearts of a mother and her two now fatherless children, Bobby Kennedy was as solid as a rock. A man of courage, Bobby was doing what he did best—supporting and comforting his family, and his nation.

John F. Kennedy was gone, but Robert F. Kennedy was very much alive and in high demand. As U.S. Attorney General, RFK was still in a commanding position, a leader of America in its darkest hours. As Dad and Uncle Bobby, he was now the leader of the extended Kennedy family. Despite his heavy heart, Robert Kennedy persevered with the same standards of excellence. The Attorney General worked with his brother's successor, President Lyndon B. Johnson, to help pass two pieces of legislation that best defined the idealism of the 1960's: the Civil Rights Act of 1964 and the Voting Rights of 1965. While this vigilant leader kept the heat on organized crime, he also continued his big brother's spirit of "vigah" by climbing Mt. Kennedy, a 13,880-foot Canadian mountain named in honor of the late president. Bobby and his team successfully climbed to the summit with very little skill and preparation—and in frigid conditions. No doubt, John Kennedy would have been proud of this tribute.

Yet, a chord strikes in my heart during a particularly poignant period—Bobby's transformation between the period of the late President Kennedy's assassination and

Bobby's decision to run for the senate and eventually, the presidency. These critical moments underscore this young patriot's legendary leadership. The emotional and political stakes for RFK as a public figure in a troubling world were tremendously high. Probably more than anyone in the world at this time, Bobby Kennedy realized the risks he would take in order to remain true to his own nature as a defender of justice, equality, and freedom. His own brother just gave up his life for his country. Would he be willing to continue in the same path, knowing the odds against him as a potential target of an assassin's hand?

Where does a loyal brother, husband, father, son, and U.S. Attorney General of the most powerful country turn for guidance and strength while he is in such a beleaguered state? How does he turn to his beloved wife and children, and offer any words of hopeful encouragement for their future, his future, and the future of America?

In September of 1964, Robert Kennedy resigned from his position as Attorney General. Bobby paused from public life. In this deeply introspective period, he found great solace and guidance in his spiritual faith. As a devout Roman Catholic, I can empathize and surmise that Bobby indeed found his way through his inner dialog and prayers with God and Christ. Bobby remained poised and calm through the chaos and somehow even managed to stay in the main arena of his life. Although he took refuge in his own personal grieving process, Bobby never appeared bitter or reckless in his public conduct. However, Bobby's future public service now became a very sobering personal risk. Would it be wise of him to subject his large family to the outcome of his own potential assassination? Would he and Ethel have the courage to face the consequences of raising a family of eleven children without their father?

Senator Robert F. Kennedy

In Bobby's words, "Our liberty can grow only when the liberties of all our fellow men are secure; and he who would enslave others ends only by chaining himself, for chains have two ends, and he who holds the chain is as securely bound as he whom it holds."

In a serene manner, he boldly moved toward his vision. Robert Kennedy resumed his political career winning election as a United States Senator for the state of New York. In spite of the fears that surely haunted his thoughts, in spite of the enormous odds, in spite of the adversity and potentially disastrous outcomes, RFK remained true to his own vision, and his own earthly purpose. Bobby held his head up, rose above the fears he faced, and modeled to his family—and country—a portrayal of intense desire to become all that God designed him to become in life.

Serendipitously, the time was ripe for fresh leadership. The Vietnam War was going nowhere for America. Casualties were mounting, and there was no end in sight. Additionally, the southern states were engaged in massive resistance to civil rights for African-Americans, again, with many deaths and intimidation to civil rights workers in the south. The two great movements of the time, anti-war, and civil rights, were dividing America and raising passions for and against the war to unprecedented levels. President Lyndon Johnson was in the eye of the storm. Yet, even with all his executive power, he was unable to resolve the foreign war or stop the domestic violence. Americans, particularly younger generations, turned out by the thousands in demonstrations, protesting the war and the bigotry against African-Americans. Race riots broke out in many cities with tremendous destruction and serious loss of life. America cried out for new leadership.

In 1968, President Johnson realized that the tide of public opinion had turned against him, and he wisely decided not to run for re-election. In turn, this powerful vacancy created a dire need for strong leadership at the nation's helm.

Senator Robert Kennedy, along with Senator Gene McCarthy from Minnesota had now emerged as leaders in the U.S. Senate opposing the war. Senator McCarthy decided to challenge the Democratic candidate, Vice President Hubert Humphrey, winning the Wisconsin presidential primary in the spring of 1968. It was another pivotal decision for Robert Kennedy. Should he stay out of the race, back McCarthy, or risk everything by running for the presidency himself?

In Bobby's prophetic words, "No one—no matter where he lives or what he does—can be certain who will suffer from some senseless act of bloodshed. Yet it goes on and on and on in this country of ours. Why? What has violence ever accomplished? What has it ever created? No martyr's cause has ever been stilled by his assassin's bullet. . . . A sniper is only a coward, not a hero; and an uncontrolled, uncontrollable mob is only the voice of madness, not the voice of reason.

"...And let no one say that violence is the courageous way, that violence is the short route, that violence is the easy route. Because violence will bring no answer to us here in the United States, as a people.

"...We all struggle to transcend the cruelties and follies of mankind. That struggle will not be won by standing aloof and pointing a finger; it will be won by action, by men who commit their every resource of mind and body to the education and improvement and help of their fellow man."

In 1968, Senator Robert Kennedy decided to run in the race for the 37th President of the United States of America. On June 5, shortly after midnight, Senator Kennedy was celebrating the California victory in the Democratic Primary for the upcoming presidential election. While leav-

Senator Robert F. Kennedy

ing the Ambassador Hotel in Los Angeles through the kitchen, the senator and others were shot at from an assassin's hand. A Jordanian immigrant, known as Sirhan Bishara Sirhan was arrested and charged for the senseless crime. The senator died the next day, sacrificing his life for his country, just like his brother, President John F. Kennedy (and his even older brother, Joseph, who died in action while in service for his country).

Robert Francis Kennedy may have died a hero on that sad day in history, but his spirit vigorously lives on in the courage he displayed in his work—the work of fighting for the ideals of democracy and a love for humanity.

On November 20, 2001, marking the 76th anniversary of Kennedy's birth, President George W. Bush and Attorney General John Ashcroft announced that the Department of Justice main building would be named after former U.S. Attorney General Robert F. Kennedy to commemorate his accomplishments during his term as Attorney General. In a ceremony laced with poignancy, the Presidential Memorandum came in the aftermath of the tragic crises from September 11, 2001. At the ceremony, President George W. Bush remarked, "To millions who never knew him, he's still an example of kindness and courage." Attorney General John Ashcroft added, "The Justice Department building is being named after an Attorney General who led an extraordinary campaign against organized crime and who made great efforts to protect the civil rights of every American. We are not merely relabeling this building in the memory of Robert Kennedy, we are rededicating the Department of Justice to the causes he served."

We, honor you, Bobby, and we feel a sense of kinship to you for your free spirit, your why not examination of life, your bold, and daring genius. We send our love and admiration to you in the heavens . . . and to your beloved family. We miss your leadership, and your love for all of us, humble and rich alike. Most of all, we miss you. Like your big brother, you also were cut down before your time. However, your dreams for a better world live on. As optimists, we will prevail to carry the torch of light rather than succumb to darkness. Watch over us, though, Bobby, we need your pull from above!

◆ ◆ ◆

Courage rushes in after you do something difficult. It is a by-product of risk.

—Dean Nixon

*Dean Nixon
with Lutton Family*

CHAPTER TWENTY-EIGHT
Courage In Work

Dean Nixon

The Courage to Push the Envelope

Courage rushes in after you do something difficult. It is a by-product of risk.
—Dean Nixon

Did you ever have a feeling deep inside your soul that shocked your entire being . . . in the presence of someone . . . for the first time?

Someone who rocked your spirit with such a thunderous jolt . . . a force of life rushing through your veins like the rapid whitewaters of the mighty rivers rushing over the calm streams. . . with startling speed and a fresh vibrancy?

Have you ever experienced the energy of a lightening bolt in spirit? If not, then close your eyes and take a deep breath... and another. Go ahead, one more deep breath... in... and out....

Now, shake your arms and legs and get psyched. You know what I mean. Get excited! Mark this moment. For you are preparing to change forever. Oh, you may not feel agreeable or you may not feel comfortable, but I guarantee that if you show up and engage your attention on this particular person... you will feel. You will notice and expand because the laws of nature will move in divine, yet humble expression through Dean Nixon, a wonderful facilitator for adult and youth behavioral growth seminars.

What is so special about this guy? I mean, after all, Dean himself admits he can be arrogant, vain, proud, and even a bit cocky. One might even imagine a humorous reprieve after sitting in one of Dean's emotional growth seminars where you are eyeball to eyeball and ready to say to him, "Get out of my face!"

O yes, God picked the best of the best in choosing Dean Nixon to assist teens and adults alike to face their true selves. I will certainly never forget him. After all, I think I was 5'1" tall when I walked into the Sun Hawk Academy Seminar in St. George, Utah on a Thursday. I am certain that I left the following Sunday an inch taller with all the stretching exercises—physically, mentally, and emotionally —that I had experienced under his leadership. All his rules and sergeant-at-arms approaches surely did not give me the impression that life would be cozy and comfortable during this party, I mean seminar. After all, the first two parental participants called upon by Dean stormed out after fifty seconds worth of emotional growth. Furthermore, during similar youth seminars, Dean informed me that he had been spit on, hit, kicked, punched, pulled, bitten, and attacked, but also gratefully hugged by many a teenage participant. Since my husband and I considered the seminar fee significant—

Dean Nixon

and we did not have the moxie to admit to our teenage daughter that we could be dropouts—quitting was not an option for us. We could hardly wait to begin.

So commenced our journey with the man of the moment, the facilitator of our so-called adult awakening seminar (as if sleeping could even be considered).

How did I feel after this seminar? I have to agree with some great thinkers that in the school of hard knocks called life, many people are sleeping through a hypnotic routine of their everyday existences. They cautiously tiptoe from birth to death trying in between to avoid any pain. What I realized after this seminar, and the next, was that an awakening—and an awareness—were critical requirements for every one of us. Yet, as I looked around, I remembered that most of us were at these seminars because our teenage sons or daughters had inspired the cause. In that heart beat. . . time almost stopped for me. . . and I felt so incredibly privileged. I realized that through our troubled children we were all moving into new heights of awareness and growth. I wondered how we could share this gold mine—this enlightening and exhilarating opportunity—with the rest of the world.

What I also realized was that all of the reasons I felt compelled and inspired to write this book were wrapped into the essence of Dean's passions, as well, both of us, being driven by our God-given desire to tap the spiritual genius in people and celebrate all humanity. With due respect and honor, I realized that this genuinely kind leader has a heart that burns boldly and brilliantly with the fire of eternal love for his Maker and his fellowmen. Indeed, Dean Nixon is a brave warrior of the twenty-first century, blazing the trail for excellence as he unveils the true spirit of humanity.

Strutting 6'1" tall, Dean is rugged, handsome, in excellent shape, and holds a smile and a charming wink of his big brown eyes that can brighten even the haughtiest of attitudes.

Courage in Work

Watching Dean in action during the seminars, he looked like a master at the craft of his desire. He skillfully rides the wave of human confrontation until he can effectively penetrate the defensive crest of human masks. Dean has an uncanny gift for calling people on themselves, meeting their resistance, and then assisting the ready to openly recognize their own misguided behaviors.

During a sincere conversation, I asked Dean candidly how he had grown to become such a courageous facilitator and individual. "I have just learned how to get out of the way," he chuckles with humility and continues. "Make no mistake about it, Cheri, out there in the seminars . . . the work I do . . . that is God speaking through me. God is huge . . . the key to who I am today. For my part, I am simply honored to be an instrument in his hands."

As he offers me insight on the sources of his strength and gifts, Dean adds, "I just love helping people see their own light. Once I see someone make the shift and realize how their current behavior may be self-sabotaging to their own growth, I know that all of the resistance I encountered from them was worth it. Once a person gets it and expands their self-awareness, the rewards are truly so valuable. I know they can never go back on themselves, at least consciously. In fact, the natural high one can experience in elevating awareness and becoming closer to our Maker could completely obsolete any desire for artificially-altered states of consciousness. . . if only we would invest the time in ourselves."

Dean's paradoxical approach blends a tough love attitude with his genuine respect for all people. In his words, "So what? Get rid of the crutch and let's see what you are going to do about it." Dean works to capture his participants' attention until there is a sentiment of "enough is enough" and "I am getting sick and tired of being sick and tired." In so doing, he expresses, "I want these wonderful individuals

Dean Nixon

to capture a full knowledge of being okay with who they are . . . right now . . . in the moment."

As I laugh lightheartedly, I just have to ask Dean how he handles all the tantrums of both teens and adults alike that he faces in his work. Laughingly, he replies, "Cheri, as long as my own ego is out of the way, I really don't take it personally. I've learned to accept where people are for the moment." He pauses now with a hint of sadness. "Many of those that I see simply don't understand how bad they are hurting. They really don't express their painful behavior to be ugly . . . they express it to heal!"

In my own love/hate experiences during the seminars, I remember my eyes welling up as I let go of my own issues, looked outside of myself, and saw another deeper side of Dean. As he exposed his own vulnerability, his eyes also tearing at this time, he began to share a glimpse of his history. Recently, during our conversations, I discovered more. . . .

For Dean, life did not parade through in easy fashion. In fact, the challenges that Dean encountered as a young boy were enough to suppress Goliath. In kindergarten, teachers informed Dean's parents that he was not catching on. Then in second grade, Dean's educators described him to his family as "dyslexic and severely learning disabled expecting to be financially dependent thereon." Onward through high school, teachers would blindly allow standard test scores to continue to rule their human judgments about Dean's abilities. "I wanted to go to college. I worked hard, and still I was shut down. I knew that I was capable. I didn't believe the rejection. I had tremendous parents and siblings who supported me, and I made a conscious decision that enough was enough," Dean reminisces with a quiver in his voice.

With such a discouraging start in life, I ask Dean, "What on earth drove your exuberance toward your purposeful work?" He replies fiercely, "I decided I would do everything

Courage in Work

in my power to help other human beings move beyond labels and paradigms to become self-empowered in their own brilliance."

Dean knew that he wanted to focus on helping other young people with similar challenges facing them. Thereafter, Dean sought out a career in counseling and turned his life around. Rather than believing that he was defeated, Dean believed that he was destined for success. Dean attracted the desired circumstances and soon opportunity enveloped itself around his ideals for human development accordingly. How marvelous the universe rains circumstances perfectly in place, allowing our humanity to nourish and unfold its glorious image. Providence is a masterpiece to observe and behold!

Beginning his counseling career in 1990 in Utah, Dean eventually found his way to St. George and became one of the pioneers of Sun Hawk Academy, a residential high school designed to assist thirteen-to-eighteen-year-old teenagers and their families discover healthier models for successful living. Dean is also a happily married family man with a devoted wife, Andrea, and five lovable children: Megan, Zach, Alex, Garrett, and Faith. Dean has steadily pursued his academic interests in college and plans to continue his studies toward a doctoral degree.

Where do we go from here? How can this beautiful place that we call Earth move forward to bring forth this essence of goodness for all mankind? I ask Dean. "We start at home. With God at the helm of daily life in prayer and scripture reflection, one can become centered. That spiritual core can begin to guide if parents can offer their children a strong sense of self, genuineness, values, and firm boundaries. Lastly, we need to take the time to focus on being together rather than just doing together," he expresses emphatically.

Dean believes in the value of family life. The bond of a family adds the most precious gift of all to the human spir-

Dean Nixon

it because the greatest human need is the desire to be valued. As society continues to search for its own moral fiber, the current rite of passage for teens remains confusing and leaves our youth in a quandary about many defining issues at the brink of their independence. How even more significant the work of vindication becomes for today's leaders.

So once again, we close in honor of a true hero and his acts of goodness toward society. For it is through Dean's core adversity and his willingness to battle his own fears, that this extraordinary example of a soldier for human dignity discovers his genuine tour de force. It is through divine order that all things occur, and for this, we are so lucky to have the love, laughter, and order of the one that we know as Dean Nixon!

◆ ◆ ◆

*Courage is the belief that one has the
ability to handle any situation with
amazing strength and bravery
even in the face of adversity.*

—Anita Sanders

Anita Sanders and Husband, Son at Lutton Wedding

CHAPTER TWENTY-NINE
Courage In Work

Anita Sanders

The Courage to Honor Conviction

Courage is the belief that one has the ability to handle any situation with amazing strength and bravery even in the face of adversity.
—**Anita Sanders**

O dear Jesus, you must be so proud of your beloved Anita Sanders, my courageous sister-in-law. She stands tall as a benevolent soul and, yet, so brave to risk her life for her country.

How ambivalent she must have felt when she received the letter notifying her that she would be sent to the Persian Gulf for active duty in Operation Desert Storm. Anita knew this outcome was a possibility to expect as an enlisted official in the service. Yet, as a mother and wife, the news as an immediate reality gripped her entire body and soul. For Anita, knowing that she may never see her husband, Shannon, her daughter, Krystal, or son Kameron, once she left home, had to have caused her tumultuous grief. Anita's impending overseas duty would be a heart-wrenching disruption for her entire family, and, of course, it would put her in harm's way. Yet, she never wavered in her conviction to defend freedom on behalf of her country. In fact, as Anita explains in her own words, "The trials of life can be accepted with your faith that God will be your constant companion." I ask Anita, during a welcome family get-together, "Were you afraid when you found out that you had to go to war?" She looks down, pauses, smiles, then remarks, "Oh yes, Cheri, very much so, but I just tried to think positive, and I never questioned my commitment to the army. That and my faith in God is what kept me going."

Anita's courage was clearly revealed to me when her brother Steve and I were engaged to be married. It was January of 1991 and President Bush had announced an air attack on Iraq. The world became somber. We watched a live air attack televised worldwide before our eyes for the first time in history. Steve had just given me my engagement ring, and we caught the news while at the shopping mall.

Later, we went for dinner at Steak and Ale where the mood was clear as we all gazed at the television, viewing a dark sky and shower of bombs and anti-aircraft missiles. I could only wonder what those innocent Iraqi folks were feeling because of the evil acts of leader Saddam Hussein.

The next week, we heard that Anita would be leaving rather quickly for the Gulf, assigned to the 101st Airborne Division of the U.S. Army. She would work in the supply department, managing the inventory of equipment in and out of battle. I tried to imagine myself in her shoes, but I

Anita Sanders

could not even dare. We had chosen Anita to light the opening candles during our wedding ceremony. Now, we wondered what kind of a world we would be living in by next June on our scheduled wedding date. Would Anita even be able to attend with us? Sadly, we wondered if we would all even be alive to enjoy, much less, plan a wedding.

The months passed by, and the world watched the Persian Gulf War live on television and radio everyday— reading endless details and commentaries in print. American and Iraqi soldiers and their allies were being killed and were killing each other. Death tolls and casualties were developing while tensions were escalating, with many concerned about our reasons for involvement. Fellow Americans would incur many sacrifices in casualties and resources.

Steve and I were saddened after hearing of his parents' anguish over his sister—their daughter's—plight. It made us think about how we would feel if our children were in this situation, and what other parents were experiencing during this war. Anita sent us a letter and never complained, except about the sand in everything, including her dreams. Anita expressed her desire to free the Iraqi people. On a more personal note, she shared her happiness for our future and her desire to attend our June wedding in Boulder, Colorado. Above all, Anita expressed her longing to be with her husband and children, closing her letter optimistically.

Thankfully, Anita returned home unscathed from Operation Desert Storm much to the credit of her own courage along with that of her comrades and leaders. As planned, I enjoyed the good fortune of meeting Anita Sanders and her family for the first time during our happy occasion. Just as I expected, this brave heroine was beautiful with love and loyalty peering from her hazel eyes and big smile. We proudly watched as she, alongside my Aunt

Courage in Work

Irene, lit the opening candles at Sacred Heart of Jesus Church for our ceremony, forever symbolizing our faith in our country, our soldiers, our God, and ourselves.

I admire Anita for the passion she conveys in her convictions. She is poignant when speaking on her careers in the military and now as a counselor for youth in a juvenile probation program. With a master's degree in this field, Anita feels, "Young people need to be strongly encouraged to go for their dreams and pursue a solid education. I am glad that I did. If you are willing to do whatever it takes to achieve your goals, you will succeed. If you believe in yourself, God will help you, and guide you along the way."

How lucky I am to have Anita as my sister-in-law. The world is a more beautiful place because of her! Thank you, Lord, for such a lovely example of courage and humanity. The world loves you, Anita, and so do I!

◆ ◆ ◆

AP/ Gardner/Liberty Medal

We have to keep trying, and risk failing, in order to solve this country's problems. We will continue to flourish because our diverse American society has the strength, hardiness, and resilience of the hybrid plant we are. We will make it because we know we are blessed, and we will not throw away God's gift to us.

—Secretary of State Colin Powell

AP/Mallory

Colin Powell with Janet Jackson reading for America's Promise

CHAPTER THIRTY
Courage In Work

Secretary of State
Colin Powell

*The Courage to Protect
Human Dignity and Freedom*

> We have to keep trying, and risk failing, in order to solve this country's problems. We will continue to flourish because our diverse American society has the strength, hardiness, and resilience of the hybrid plant we are. We will make it because we know we are blessed, and we will not throw away God's gift to us.
> —Secretary Colin Powell

**U.S. DEPARTMENT OF STATE
OFFICE OF THE SPOKESMAN, WASHINGTON, DC
DAILY APPOINTMENTS SCHEDULE FOR SECRETARY OF STATE POWELL:**

July 9, 2001:
10:00 AM   Attend America's Promise Events at the White House.
11:00 AM   Meeting with Warren Christopher, former Secretary of State.
11:45 AM   Meeting with Members of United Nations Association – USA.

Courage in Work

July 13, 2001:
- 11:40 AM — Attend the President's bilateral with the President of Costa Rica Miquel Angel Rodriquez, at the White House.
- 4:00 PM — Officiate Swearing In Ceremony, The Honorable Ruth Davis as Director General, Foreign Service & Director, Human Resources

July 20, 2001:
- 9:30 AM — Press Briefing on upcoming travel to Asia in the Department of State Press Briefing Room. Secretary of State Colin L. Powell will brief the press on his upcoming travel to Japan, Vietnam, the Republic of Korea, People's Republic of China, Australia.
- 1:30 PM — Meeting with Bishop Macram Max Gassis of Sudan.

I hung up the online connection that described Secretary Powell's intense schedule and peeked at my own. I decided to change plans and go for a walk since the sky was inviting me with its spectacular parade of colors.

It was dusk and another glorious sunset was beginning to emerge in the Colorado heavens. I became amused at my thoughts as I wandered north on the dirt road alongside the nearby pasture of horses. I thought to myself, What if I had Secretary Powell's agenda for a day, and he had mine? Wild idea, Cheri, I mused to myself with a grin as I continued my curious daydream. Would he finish this book for me? Could I handle the press? Would he send my teenage daughter off to her summer job forgetting her lunch? Would I get lunch? Would he help my young son get the lemonade stirred for his entrepreneurial business? Would I end up in the wrong country? O wouldn't I love to see the Rose Garden! Would he weed and water my garden of hearts? Would I know which telephone to use? Would he? Would he enjoy helping my husband rebuild his jeep? Would I be fruitful in helping the Secretary's wife, Alma, in building America's Promise – The Alliance for Youth?

I would say that we would both do just fine handling each other's duties with a resounding yes for victory and enjoyment! Given the four-star general's impeccable work ethic, his love for America, family life, and his hobby of tinkering with old cars, I would bet that his unwavering desire to serve would, again, prevail. As for me, aside from the enormous shoes in which I would be striding, and the funny faces that I would receive from the president and other senior government officials, I would delight in the honor—for a day.

I take heart in knowing that such a quietly courageous hero, rising from meager beginnings to the top appointed position in our national government, is filling those great big shoes. He is America's most famous soldier, the former Chairman of the Joint Chiefs of Staff and retired general, our respected Secretary of State and protector of the free world. I am comforted at knowing that America has such a leader in Colin Powell.

Many times, we as Americans take for granted our freedom and prosperity, conveniently forgetting that a majority of the world's people live in less fortunate circumstances. My personal experience with the other way of living dates back to the 1990's in my corporate years as an international marketing executive of a dental manufacturing firm. I had been invited by a client to spend a week at their dental firm with their distributors in St. Petersburg, Russia, to build stronger relations and increase our business opportunities together. I was also asked to speak to an audience of dental professionals, along with the Russian Minister of Dental Health on the applications and composition of modern dental materials. The Russian/American firm was in partnership with the American government under a grant to develop a free market economy in Russia. I did my best to help the Russians through a sometimes, painful transition from a communist to a capitalist society. They in turn were of great help to me in expanding my understanding of the world's complexities. I experienced a warm and gracious hospitality from them that left an indelible impression on me.

Culturally, I was transformed by the visit to the Hermitage museum and the Russian ballet. The memory still lingers with me. I realized the pride and value that these folks held about the arts. Their respect and support for the classical arts was clearly an area of interest that was unmatched in America. It was a novel experience for me to watch Russian teenagers choosing to go to the ballet on a Friday night. I also enjoyed the cute kindergartners attentively wandering through the art galleries of their world-renowned museum. It was such a splendid respite from my own culture. These were different scenes than I had grown up with in contemporary America.

Professionally, the Russian people that I met were kind-hearted, friendly, and warm. They were eager to learn about everything in my experience and expertise, especially on how to create a prosperous business. They were well educated; yet, they had so much to learn. The paradigm shift from communism to capitalism would be huge for many to embrace, and on occasions, I knew that some would not make it. In spite of the best desires and intentions, I could sense the hints of corrupt methods of business looming in their government. I could see the gray signs of indifference, lackluster effort, despair, and defeat on the streets and felt a twinge of unease that I had never, ever felt in my own country. That feeling propelled me to take heart in the freedoms that I so easily take for granted as a native-born American. I understand now what drives Secretary Powell to hold so dear his inherent desire to protect and expand the free world.

In such times of modern life, when dramatic changes are affecting our society, we, Americans, have a craving for leaders of great moral character and integrity. We have a longing—consciously admitted or not—to be assured that the American dream and its system of free enterprise is attainable for all people. We have a hope to be embodied by the passion that we feel deep within the recesses of our

Secretary of State Colin Powell

beings. We realize the great sacrifices that go along with this noble ideal. Yet, we want to be comforted in the assurance that there are role models out there who are realizing these visions for us. . . for our children . . . and for those to come beyond our time. We want to see courage in work and victories in action. Moreover, we want it now.

We have all that and more with a leader such as Secretary of State Colin L. Powell. He is a veteran soldier and officer, a war hero, and a devoted family man. Now in his mid-sixties, Secretary Powell has been happily married to his beloved Alma for forty years. He is a proud father to his son, Michael, and daughters, Linda and Annemarie. He is also a doting grandfather to Jeffrey and Bryan, children of Michael and Jane. Colin Powell epitomizes the defining qualities for which our founding fathers deliberated upon in shaping this fine country of equality and free enterprise.

Born in New York City and raised in the Bronx by his parents, Luther and Arie Powell, who immigrated to America from Jamaica, the young Colin knew all too well the challenges to the human spirit that leap out upon the journey toward equality and freedom. All black Americans face moments of racial discrimination throughout their lives, yet, Colin Powell has kept his dignity intact. This American leader stands tall with grace, pride, and respect toward his African-American heritage. As a white American, I can benefit tremendously from the insight on compassion and courage derived from anyone who is labeled with the term, minority.

In his own words, "I have lived in and risen in a white-dominated society and a white-dominated profession, but not by denying my race, not by seeing it as a chain holding me back or an obstacle to be overcome. Others may use my race against me, but I will never use it against myself. My blackness has been a source of pride, strength, and inspiration, and

Courage in Work

so has my being an American. I started out believing in an America where anyone, given equal opportunity, can succeed through hard work and faith. I still believe in that America."

Colin Powell describes the painfully senseless times of U.S. racial discrimination that he experienced in the south while in the earlier years of his 35-year Army career. He depicts, again, in his best-selling autobiography, *My American Journey*, his humanity on occasions where anyone might be caught off-center with the ridicule of racism. Even so, this young soldier continued to cultivate his growing love for the Army. Here, he indeed finds the American dream in action, through a system that fosters advancement based on true desire, merit, and performance.

This man has an amazing ability to steer his professional course on the high road. Even in the face of racial discrimination, life-threatening dangers in the battlefield, pressures from his career of high-profile positions, constant media scrutiny, and diplomatic tensions with the war on terrorism, he maintains a relaxed quality of excellence. Secretary Powell's foundation of solid moral courage is the asset that he has so aptly harnessed and shared in his ever-growing love for public service. On a personal level, one can easily see within this revered soul a deep sense of love for his family and their private lives. His public and private qualities merge into a seamless whole as he shows the same respect for every nation's families and their quality of life together.

In Secretary Powell's public life, he has demonstrated a clear desire to wield support for our nation's families, especially our young people. Before his confirmation on January 20, 2001, as the Secretary of State, retired General Powell had been the founding chair for a non-profit organization called America's Promise – The Alliance for Youth. Founded after the '97 President's Summit for America's Future, this Alliance was a result of a call-to-action summoned by

Secretary of State Colin Powell

Presidents Clinton, Bush, Carter, Ford, and First Lady Nancy Reagan. Co-sponsored by the Points of Light Foundation and the Corporation for National Service, this organization, under General Powell's leadership, has led a mission to mobilize people from every sector of American life. Their aim is to build the character and competence of our nation's youth by fulfilling Five Promises for young people:
1. caring adults
2. safe places
3. healthy starts
4. marketable skills
5. opportunities for their own service.

According to the founding chairperson, "America's Promise is pulling together the might of this nation to strengthen the character and competence of youth. And, it's working." Currently, more than 550 community and state partners, spanning all sectors of society, including corporations, not-for-profit foundations, higher education establishments, faith-based groups, associations, federal agencies, and arts and cultural organizations are in cooperation. They have all formed grassroots coalitions in unity to fulfill the five promises. Voluntarily, individuals and organizations work in harmony and in agreement to expand existing youth programs, create new services, or, as General Powell describes, "serve as a force multiplier" in collaboration with other fine youth agencies by enlisting additional contributions of time, talent, and treasure.

The former chairman continues his message for support of America's Promise even in his current role as Secretary of State. He wears his little red wagon pin faithfully on his lapels. Recently, the Secretary demonstrated his good character on national television when he was escorting a couple of exchange students that he was mentoring on Capitol Hill through the America's Promise program. The secretary, as always, displayed as much courtesy and respect for these students as he would for any adult individual in his presence. These moments of genuine dedication toward mentoring were no less important to him than the diplomatic proceedings for which he was bearing testimony. His candor, charm, and dignified wit set the tone for the other public officials in the room. Suddenly he captured everyone's interest. An atmosphere of camaraderie began to spread amongst all of the U.S. legislative leaders in the House of Representatives.

As a private citizen and a family woman, I value these moments most in discerning whether our chosen public servants are doing their job for all of us. The rhetoric that goes along with the political position will never outweigh the quiet acts of respect displayed for human dignities.

To look upon this great leader's entire career and to reflect upon his acts of bravery is, of course, the arc that connects you and I with him here in these words. His mission has embodied a passion for life, liberty, and the pursuit of happiness. As a public servant, Colin Powell has sought to protect our inalienable human rights for his fellow man. He has witnessed the darker side of life without these freedoms in combat zones throughout the world. Most of us have not seen first-hand these terrors of war. Yet, from his earliest beginnings in the ROTC, Colin Powell knew his calling would be to serve his country as a proud American soldier. He devoted thirty-five years in military service in defense of democracy and lived the army motto, "Be all that you can be." Powell succeeded up the ranks all the way to the incredible position as the chairman of the Joint Chiefs of Staff. Through this soldier's eyes, we can share a renewed sense of collective pride for our nation's military accomplishments.

Secretary of State Colin Powell

In 1991, as we watched the Persian Gulf War live on television, we as private citizens had to support and entrust our Joint Chiefs of Staff. We had to hope that the causes and objectives for our American actions were clear. We had to sacrifice our soldiers and support their risks with the belief that it was the right decision, regardless of the outcome. For many Americans, including myself, it was a very personal commitment. My future sister-in-law, Anita Sanders, was in Desert Storm as an Army soldier. I prayed for Anita nightly during the war, although we had not yet met. I can still recall the anguish that I felt during that time. We were counting on this fight for democracy to be a worthy cause. We all—each one of us in the free world—were counting on the leaders. Of all of the individuals on the planet at that time—the world was counting on the leadership of one—the 12th Chairman of the Joint Chiefs of Staff, the highest military position in the world, Four-Star General Colin L. Powell.

His preparation had been there all his life, and, now, he would be called upon to draw upon his courage and creativity to win a triumphant victory for the verities of human liberty and set a new tone for the strategic meaning of war.

On January 22, 1991, Secretary of Defense Dick Cheney and Chairman Colin Powell briefed the press and the American public from the Pentagon on their strategy for Desert Storm. I remember watching the chairman elucidate the battle plan with confidence. He explained that first we would use our air power to destroy the Iraqis' air defense system and breakdown enemy communications. Thereafter, we would destroy the logistics in Kuwait that supported their military forces. Then, he came to the pinnacle statement. He closed with a bang. "Our strategy in going after this army is very simple. First we are going to cut it off, and, then we are going to kill it." Although the general felt that war should be the politics of last resort, he felt that when we

325

do go to war—we go with a purpose that its people understand and support. He believed that you go in and mobilize the country's resources to fill that mission, and then you fight for one clear and swift purpose—to win!

Americans from all lifestyles rejoiced over this swift and decisive victory. The strategy directed by the chairman was praised by many, including contemporary military historians. His execution was viewed as almost flawless and serving order at the highest level of purpose.

After the general retired from the army and before he was appointed Secretary of State, Colin Powell addressed many audiences around the country. Surprisingly, the questions that he attracted did not pertain to his years as a war hero. "They seem to be searching for a guiding star that we have lost sight of. They see good order breaking down. They see violence so commonplace that it has lost the power to shock. They see a judicial system that threatens to become a form of public entertainment, losing its majesty and authority," he conveys.

General Powell answers the people of America by addressing the questions, "How do we find our way again? How do we re-establish moral standards? How do we end the ethnic fragmentation that is making us an increasingly hyphenated people? How do we restore a sense of family to our national life?" His ideals suggest that we have to stop constantly criticizing, which is the way of the malcontent, and instead get back to the can-do attitude that made America. He suggests that we need to restore the social model of married parents bringing into the world a desired child, a child to be loved and nurtured, to be taught a sense of right and wrong, to be provided opportunities for work and a fulfilling life. This empathetic public servant acknowledges that this may be simple to say and more difficult to achieve. However, he believes that we must never stop striving for this vision. Colin's transparency is so often revealed through his honest-to-goodness persona that we can almost feel the fabric of his heartfelt sincerity as he speaks herein.

"My travels since leaving the Army two years ago have deepened my love for our country and our people. It is a love full of pride for our virtues and with patience for our failings. We are a fractious nation, always searching, always dissatisfied, yet always hopeful. We have an infinite capacity to rejuvenate ourselves. We are self-correcting. And, we are capable of caring about each other."

"As one who has received so much from his country, I feel the debt of service heavily, and I can never be entirely free of it. My responsibility, our responsibility as lucky Americans, is to try to give back to this country as much as it has given to us, as we continue our American journey together. . . . This is a magnificent country, and I am proud to be one of its sons."

If that is not enough inspiration, the general has also come up with a list of practical steps for successful living or as he coins them, General Powell's Rules. They are his rules because he demands adherence to these rules for his own daily living. A true sign of a solid leader is always one who has mastered the art of self-control—to give oneself a command and to follow it!

Colin Powell's Rules

1. It ain't as bad as you think. It will look better in the morning.
2. Get mad, then get over it.
3. Avoid having your ego so close to your position that when your position falls, your ego goes with it.

4. It can be done!
5. Be careful when you choose. You may get it.
6. Don't let adverse facts stand in the way of a good decision.
7. You cannot make someone else's choices. You shouldn't let someone else make yours.
8. Check small things.
9. Share credit.
10. Remain calm. Be kind.
11. Have a vision. Be demanding.
12. Don't take counsel of your fears or naysayers.
13. Perpetual optimism is a force muliplier.

Secretary Powell, I suppose you thought that you could quietly exit stage right in thinking that we would view your secrets for success as nothing more than hard work and a willingness to serve. Don't think for one moment that you could fool us! We are perceptive enough to recognize extraordinary greatness when we see it. I am sorry, but you fall into that category. We caught you being completely honest and human in your candid autobiography. You could have just hidden from your weaknesses and mistakes, and we would have only known your successes. You chose to share your vulnerabilities, your misgivings, and your heart with all of us.

Your greatness is peeking through again, Mr. Secretary, in your ability to come clean with your own humanity and enjoy it! O there it is again, in your deep affection and devotion to your family. There are no mysteries to your history and family values. There are no glamorous tales of exciting intrigues, dualities, and hypocrisies. Instead, all we have are just good old-fashioned love, integrity, and commitment. How unsensational! How real! How commendable! Are you really going to think we do not see past all of the tough sacrifices that you must have experienced when you were in the army away from your dear wife, Alma, and your growing family? We saw it, Sir.

We read between the gracious remarks on your reluctance to leave your family as duty kept tugging at you. This was not just a perfunctory example of your willingness to obey respected authority. This was not just personal sacrifice for the sake of your future investment to your career. This was heartbreaking torture. I am certain of it, as a fellow human being that loves all too much the company and emotional reward that I reap daily in being so close to my husband and children. Can we not imagine that you desired the same for your own heart? Your country asked you to move all so often. Many times, you were asked to move toward the White House, rather than remaining with your professional love as an army commander. You always remained polite and obliged your country before yourself. During the Middle East Crisis against terrorism in 2002, your personal and professional stakes were high; yet, you remained focused and committed to your purpose and passion for peace.

I know about that love of yours, for my sister-in-law told me about your true form during Desert Storm. She was a soldier from the 101st Airborne Division stationed in the trenches of Kuwait. She knew of your sincerity. "As a supplies officer, I personally didn't get to know that much about him. However, I can tell you that there was a lot of talk about him coming over to see the soldiers. He seemed to be most concerned about the soldiers . . . and their morale during the war." These are candid words from Staff Lieutenant Anita Sanders. Thanks to you, my sister-in-law Anita is back home with her family and building her own career of service.

Courage in Work

Perhaps, you can blame it on your ideals or your modest "I was just being myself and I didn't know any other way" persona. That would be fine. We would accept this plea of purity. That is indeed your biggest flaw—that you have remained true to the values that Luther and Arie have instilled in you from childhood and have only grown into one of America's great men as a result of your just cause. However, I must be honest, Sir Powell, in expressing publicly that you are not merely, an ordinary man who has had extraordinary opportunities. You are an extraordinary man who attracted like-minded people, opportunities, and circumstances that could only perpetuate your cycle of growth and success into the greatness from whence you came and deserve to own.

The question, however, lies in whether your extraordinary being distinguishes you from ordinary beings. The answer is no, and I believe that is the point that you are so humbly expressing in your own speeches, writings, and briefings. The answer is no because anyone of us is capable of catapulting ourselves into extraordinary events and capturing our own greatness—just like you.

So, now what? You are the leader that four presidents of the United States have called upon for advice. That is quite a calling card. Are even greater times ahead for you? Might America ever invite you into that special chair in the oval office reserved for a commander-in-chief? Regardless, we should never forget how much you, Alma, and your family have already given us. We shall not discount the spirit that prevails between a husband and wife who have chosen to consider their marriage a sacred vow of unity. We recognize that Alma must be an incredible woman to reflect such greatness in you and similarly, you in her. We shall never take for granted the sacrifices we asked of your entire family during your years of service.

We shall also not be so politically sterile as to ignore your devotion to your own spiritual faith. You have provided a model of stewardship to your own congregation. Your level-headed views on church and state have silently opened more doors than we probably even realize at this time.

We shall never forget how lucky we are that you are you, and not merely by chance. We are all indeed lucky by the true definition of luck: when preparation meets opportunity. You had the opportunity to succeed by choosing a career in a well-integrated and non-discriminatory institution, the U.S. Army. More importantly, you put in years of preparation through self-discipline, focused effort, and passion. Just after the intersection where your extensive preparation and enormous opportunities crossed paths, you paid enough attention to take heed, only then, did luck emerge—on course—as success.

I once heard Doug Wead, former White House Special Assistant, say to a group of us that the bond of three—as in a braid—is the strongest bond known to man. This braid of commitment you hold to: 1.) God and your purpose; 2.) your family and your devotion; and 3.) your country and your mission is indeed a great example of Doug's wisdom.

We thank the Lord for your wisdom. We thank you, Secretary of State Colin Powell, for loving us all so much. God Bless you and God Bless America!

◆ ◆ ◆

Courage is trusting that inside of myself I have all that I need—whatever that may be—love, time, or vulnerability—to engage completely with heart and soul in whatever life presents to me.

—Patricia Krown

Patricia Krown

CHAPTER THIRTY-ONE
Courage In Work

Patricia Krown

The Courage to Reach Out and Touch Others

> Courage is trusting that inside of myself I have all that I need—whatever that may be— love, time, or vulnerability—to engage completely with heart and soul in whatever life presents to me.
> —Patricia Krown

When King Arthur found himself troubled and confused, he would go to the enchanted forest of Camelot and sit under the lush trees where he sought the counsel of the wisest of all, Merlin the Magician. Wherefore art thou wise souls of modern days?

Take comfort for there is a place in Boulder, Colorado where one can rest his weary head and heart in the solace

Courage in Work

and counsel of the wise and caring soul of Patricia Krown. I, for one, have thoroughly enjoyed sharing my life's journey and vision with such a beautiful yet bold visionary as Patricia.

On what grounds do I honor this charismatic lady of such courage to portray her in this prose? Join me in this walk into the wondrous forest to discover a tiny spectacle of the many facets of Patricia Krown. Behold and witness her glorious heaven on earth. For it is in the everyday moments of Patricia's joie de vivre, her joy of life, that her power of love awaits us—patiently and purposefully.

It is January 27, 2001, the celebration of Patricia's birthday. My husband Steve and I along with her friends are gathering in her home, awaiting Patricia's presence. Outside, a luminous wintry evening causes falling snowflakes to glisten, casting sparkling hues of color on her snow-covered lawn.

Patricia's home is full of friendly guests and appetizing aromas of delicious foods, giving pleasant testimony to the affection and charisma she attracts and conveys—regardless of weathering conditions or circumstances. At last, she enters. With her blonde curls cascading down her shoulders and her tender hazel eyes, Patricia is adorned in blue. She holds an almost mystical, gracious presence in her sleek satin outfit with soft shades of electric blues, purples, and silvers. Her shimmering blue heels finish off her look as the belle of the ball along with her own magical spell of warmth and happiness.

As Steve and I mingle among the different circles of guests, I ask, "What brings you to know Patricia?" More or less, everyone replies, "It's her powerful yet loving presence." One guest Art, smiles and remarks, "It's Patricia's love for discovery that makes her so attractive. She is a remarkably gifted woman whose quest for the truth has

Patricia Krown

drawn her to her own power. I love the way she flutters onto the unknown and catches the pollen from every flower of life." It is through her daring pursuit for truth that Patricia has transformed herself, just as a butterfly does, into a beauty of great character.

Travelling from Pennsylvania to Los Angeles, Patricia's inner search for purpose eventually led her to Boulder in 1990, where she began a career in metaphysics and self-actualization. Patricia's spiritual strength has empowered her to serve as a successful life coach using modalities from hypnosis, bodywork, and alchemy to empathy, through good old-fashioned conversation.

My first experience with Patricia was at a professional women's networking function. We then met for coffee a few weeks later. I don't remember much about the taste of the latte; however, the dialogue immediately began to transcend the ordinary. Wow. It was akin to a really good book, movie, or concert, where one leaves the mundane and no longer feels captured by time or mindless chatter. Sitting in Patricia's presence, I felt that all of my senses would be called upon to experience the infinite world of wonder. I felt her sense of comfort and courage almost saying, "Anything is possible."

Fearlessly venturing toward the truths of life, Patricia clearly recognizes the forces of goodness and evil, which beckon for the attention of our free will. Yet, as a spirit in desire for light rather than darkness, she yields happily to her calling for goodness. With a splendid display of spontaneity, Patricia will bedazzle you with wit, wisdom, and charm as she engenders the human spirit upward and outward. A master of rapport, she has one purpose in mind—radiating her spirit of vitality in each moment while attracting fun-loving playmates along the way.

One sunny afternoon, we enjoyed lunch together at a quaint restaurant nestled against the majestic Flatiron foothills of Boulder. During our conversation, I caught a glimpse of the world through Patricia's eyes and heart, experiencing emotions from incredible joy to pure sadness.

As a mother of two grown sons, Patricia possesses the sensitivity a loving parent keenly acquires through the act of child rearing. She poignantly reminisces with me about the hardships she experienced from the searing pain of divorce. Yet, in spite of the breakup, Patricia's focus remains positive on the happiness she has enjoyed as a wife and mother. Midway through our meal, she pauses and smiles proudly as she speaks of her recent visit to California to meet her first and only granddaughter, little Piper Skya.

What of the stellar role she plays in the lives of many clients within the community? Patricia retorts with one of her favorite rhetorical queries when digging deeper into the hearts of others, "Are we having fun now?" I nod amusingly, prodding further for insight on her gracious tenacity. "I attribute my success to my willingness to cooperate with God or Spirit, if you will," she replies with candor. "I feel that one of today's greatest human struggles is a person's unwillingness to trust their own inner knowingness. I see Spirit as a clear, quiet, all-knowing voice within each human being. Once realized, a person can begin to develop a strong sense of truth, guide oneself through inner spiritual light, and eventually lead with unshakable purpose."

I ask Patricia, "How do you create such chemistry in your connection with others?" How does she succeed at encouraging people to push their envelope even when there may be arduous resistance? I thought to myself. "Through trust, sensitivity, commitment, and rapport. I walk hand in hand, slowly and invitingly, as I listen and empathize. Again, having fun is the key ingredient in this dance," she hints amusingly.

"What of the desire to overcome adversity while self-actualizing?" I ask. Patricia comments, "I fully succumb to the moment and commit to complete self-expression. If I suddenly notice an emotional clamoring for attention, whether it is positive or negative, I consciously raise the thought to self-awareness and allow it to become expressed physically. Once expressed, it is released and I can then let go and move on and grow in the process of this enlightenment. Sometimes this movement is simple and sometimes profound; yet, I always feel a thrust forward in growth and expansion of my oneness with God and Universe."

Cognizant of the universal laws of life, Patricia respects the laws that energy is and that our consequences are directly related to our actions or—the causes we choose to act upon. "Whoever creates the most joy, wins," she muses lightheartedly as she quotes her mentor Ana Lazar. "I recommend that anyone interested in acquiring spiritual power must dedicate at least ten minutes daily listening to one's inner voice," Patricia advises, "Follow your bliss" as the sign reads in her therapeutic environment and remember that F.E.A.R. simply means . . . forgetting everything's all right. Just decide to take a stand on every daily act and let possibility express itself. Once accomplished, expansion of self will prevail because, of course . . . all things occur in Divine Order," she concludes with a tone of absolute certainty.

In so doing, Patricia expects some failure to follow risk-taking; yet, defeat is simply not an option. I ask her to describe her own daily challenges in her quest for self-expansion. "Oh, you are referring to my desire to become more patient and accept disappointments more gracefully?" she teasingly admits. "I grow daily as I allow Spirit to guide me," she continued.

I invite Patricia to share with me more about her vision of Heaven on Earth. "Living a life that is fully expressive in every modality. . . in both receiving and witnessing myself

Courage in Work

and all others . . . living a completely full life . . . that is my Heaven on Earth," she serenely explains.

Just to know that Patricia is there in the forest of life to guide and counsel all those whom she touches is so reassuring . . . just as Merlin was for King Arthur in the forest of Camelot.

This woman of insight has touched my life and many others in her focused and generous desire to reach out and unfold the spiritual power of humanity. For those of us who have witnessed her acts of goodness, we are blessed by our common connection to Patricia. For those of you who have yet to experience this woman of intuitive valor, rest assured—her universal love will find its way to your heart.

Thank you, Almighty Spirit, for the sparkle that Patricia adds to life. We thank you, Patricia, for all that you are and all that we enjoy with you. You are truly valued by God and our universe!

◆ ◆ ◆

PART SIX
Courage In Society

Love Thy Neighbor as Thy Self

Imagine . . . if just for one day . . . that every human being had the courage to show the world all of their inner goodness and beauty, regardless of the perceived effects. What would society look like? If not while on Earth, what are we waiting for?

CHAPTER THIRTY-TWO
Courage In Society

Love Thy Neighbor as Thy Self

Imagine . . . if just for one day . . . that every human being had the courage to show the world all of their inner goodness and beauty, regardless of the perceived effects. What would society look like? If not while on Earth, what are we waiting for?

It is this courage that transforms a physical journey on earth into an eternal spirit that carries its legacy into the future to shape our society forever. I once read by a lovely writer, Pam Brown, that "the courage of very ordinary people is all that stands between us and the dark." We are all ordinary people conducting ordinary acts every day that almost, suddenly, create extraordinary events . . . sometimes called . . . miracles.

Will we invest our energy, exploring our finest wealth of resources within our spirit, body, and mind? Will we reach out to the universe for the excitement and experience that we desire? Will we swim with all our might and experience the entire journey? Will we fall back and let others help us along? Will we ponder on the difference we will bring to the whole? Will our difference move humanity toward a new art form, music, appetite, technology, or natural beauty? Will we leave a quieter imprint in the sands, reflecting the love and kindness that we so courageously shared even when we were afraid?

Do you ask, "How can I really make a difference?" Not one of us is exempt from our global influence, try as we might, some days to remain aloof. Even in our choice to stand back, to not choose, to squander our time and resources, to hide and to retreat—we are making a choice. Even in our decisions to fall prey to the neglect of our spiritual purpose and cause harm to ourselves and/or others through temptations of our ego, we are sadly contributing our vital share to the grandeur of the seas. Our tiniest ripples, through the absoluteness of the universal laws, will move the seas one way or the other. Yes, we have arrived to the moment in our lives where we must jump off the diving board and take our place in the sea of humanity. Are you nervous? Great! So am I. Then, we are alive and on target as humans. Now let's jump.

This reminds me of a story of a little girl by the sea who was throwing starfish that had swept onto the shore back into the waters. One by one, she would gently toss each starfish back into the seas as she gazed at the unique patterns and colors of each one. Strolling along the sands, an old grumpy fellow yelled at her in a deep voice, "Young lady, what do you think you are doing?" The girl stood tall and looked the man straight in his eyes as she replied, "I am saving these starfish." He laughed cynically and retorted, "Do you really think that you are making a difference? Why, there are hundreds of starfish here that have been swept up from the storm." The saddened young girl stopped for a moment as if to halt her plans. Slowly, her smile returned as she picked up another starfish, turned to the old man and proudly said, "Maybe so, but I know I am making a difference to this one, and that is all that matters."

On a more interactive note, I'd like you to join me on an imaginary visit to one of my favorite places. All you will need is your willingness and your vivid imagination. Now sit calmly, enjoy yourself, and sit with me near the pond.

For as we sit serenely in the quiet of the day and take in reflective moments, we can surely move our minds to a beautiful pond. We can sit together side by side as friends and rest as we sit on the finest and greenest grass of the lands. There in the sun-laden mist, we can enjoy the sweet fragrance of the newly blossoming lilacs and the earthy scents of the hay across the fields. The tall oak trees nearby remind all of us of the awesome cycles of majesty in nature. We can feel the mild breeze of the moist spring air across our faces and smile for all that we have become so far in our tiny lives. We can breathe deeply and cleanse our lungs with a renewed spirit of vitality and opportunity. We can catch the antics of the butterflies fluttering through space always seeking a better attraction. O look at the little critters! The squirrels are scampering throughout the grass and trees looking for nibbles of food. We can allow the melodious songs of the robins to mesmerize us in their sweetest rapture.

Now, we get ready to experiment together . . . to participate in an adventure. We each pick up a red pebble to throw into the pond. Clunk, clunk. Yours lands first. I look in the silence that follows and hear the repercussions of your actions. I see the circles that take shape in the water waving precisely in an ever-expanding pattern. I see a floating tree branch bobbing quicker now as the water circle moves its direction. I see a red robin jump off the bobbing branch and fly over to the edge of the pond. There, I see another robin, and the two begin to play. They jump back together in flight into the tree branch, which is now closer to this edge of the pond. They begin to nuzzle, and a song of indescribable beauty begins to reach my ears. I am filled with a sense of joy, which I had not ever experienced before this moment. The two birds fly into the oak tree and continue playing as they sing now in unison.

The wind sends a gentle breeze through the air and a few leaves and an acorn fall from the tree, landing somewhere close to your side. You pick up the acorn in your hands and amusingly put it in your pocket to plant in your yard at home. We gaze at each other and smile with a sense of companionship for we know within our hearts and souls that our time together has made a difference.

We can even create an impact on each other through our creative minds and our generous spirits. Our impacts can come in all sizes, shapes, and qualities. We can move mountains with one thought, or we can dry a teary eye of a friend or foe and uplift a spirit. We can just be there to listen and care. Small acts of kindness can save a life.

Listening can be one of the noblest acts that we can give to our society. Not judging, talking, pitying, or enabling; just listening, with all of our self-control under discipline, listening with all of our senses and intellectual resources keenly directed toward the attention of one special human being . . . you! I listen with my heart as if I were in your shoes. . . and, for a few fleeting moments, allowing myself to get out of the way and truly experience you. What would that feel like to you? When is the last time that you felt so valued and understood? It is just this experience that has been noted by many great thinkers and, in particular, William James, a great American psychologist. He said that the greatest need of the human spirit is the need for appreciation, this need to feel valued, acknowledged, and understood. I believe that he was right.

Cheri Lutton ☙

Indeed, the, the greatest contribution that we could offer to our fellow man is this gift of reflection. For the beauty within each of us begs to be discovered and springs forth like a fountain, showering expression with effortless grace. Our inner resources are a curiously funny element of truth and can be compared to the precious resources of gold and silver that we mine from the earth. Once we tap into our own natural qualities of goodness and genius, they flow bountifully, leaving one to wonder, Where have you been all of my life? As we open each cavern of our inner riches and share them with the world, another new dimension to ourselves springs forth, requiring time and care for refinement. Therein, lie the ultimate truths of our greatness —our precious and true selves. This is where we find the courage we bring to the grander mosaic of humanity.

Lest what stirs in us, but the urge to give, drawing from our strengths and errs to come together toward a common cause to serve, grow, and expand this spirit of energy. . . we know as life. This elusive urge to connect and help one another keeps pressing us forward in a collective mission to enjoy our days to the fullest and leave our legacies of accomplishment for future generations to behold.

Yet, what kind of attention do we pay to our legacy? We may wonder on occasion or we may not. Either way, our legacy is in the making. Just as we have benefited from Thomas Edison's discovery of electricity and other inventions illuminating this planet, we will have the same potential to benefit from your greatness. What will it be?

Have you ever reminisced about your days and longings as a child living out your dreams? Think back and imagine the whimsical nature you embraced in those days. Were you inventive, thoughtful, creative, curious, daring, artistic, mechanical, analytical? Were you visionary, diplomatic, humorous, or perhaps, the quiet humanitarian who kept everyone feeling part of the whole? Are your days still filled with the zest for life and purpose that you felt back then . . . as a boy or girl? Are you actualizing your true nature?

If your answer is yes, then the advice, "to thine own self be true" has served you well, and I congratulate you! For you are well connected to the fabric of society, weaving color in our lives with the strength and durability of truth and happiness. You are like the acorn that you planted after our visit to the pond. Your acorn, properly nourished in adequate soil, will attract all that is necessary from the force of nature to fulfill its desire to become an oak tree. Surely, the oak tree is not in the acorn just waiting to sprout, and, of course, it is not below the soil of the precise spot where the acorn has been planted. It is only through the unique urge of life in the acorn and by its expression of purpose into the soil that the universe reflects on in responsive harmony. Focused desire + action = results.

If you answered no to my earlier question, then by your very interest in being present in these readings, you are expressing your longings to self-actualize your true nature. You are to be commended for that courage. For if we are alive, that is God's message to us that another day awaits our reunion with our true nature, our calling, our truest purpose to unfold and behold as witness to our eternal beauty and wealth. You will know that you are fulfilling your unique legacy by the fruits of your labor. As stated in the Bible, "By their fruits, we will know them"; by our contributions, our legacies will live on.

If you wander through your days aimlessly, then immerse yourself in the actualizing of your dreams and desires, and, you will have transitioned into a life that is serving all of society. When you are generous in your own nature just because it brings you so much joy, you will be well on your path of self-fulfillment. When you are giving, for the sake of giving, without any concern for the personal gain of these acts, then, you will be making a tremendous contribution to society, influencing future leaders for generations to come.

We, as a people, can no longer excuse ourselves—from ourselves—out of ignorance or scarcity. We live in a world of abundance. Think of the freedom, wealth, resources, and opportunity that has evolved into a global network—spawned by the superhighway of information. In this high-tech era, a growing phenomenon is encouraging us to direct our time and attention to electronic media through television, radio, telephone, or computers. A trend is emerging in today's society toward a high-tech connection to one another, particularly on the Internet. Does this hint at our desire to be a part of a whole? Is high-tech and low-touch, as coined in *Megatrends*, ultimately very healthy? Can we embody this desire more humanly by being physically engaged with our loved ones and community in a truly heartfelt manner? Isn't the point of technology—just as in anything else that we create—to further our missions of becoming fully realized human beings and not mere technical wizards?

Can we orchestrate technology so that it is an instrument of our service? In so doing, can we become more honest with ourselves and employ our innate gifts and talents toward our truest purpose? Can we manage technology to fit into our plans? Do we choose to be in the moment playing ball with our children or choose to forego our humanistic experience in order to check our emails? On a lighter note, "Who let the dogs out?" The ones that come from out there in society telling us what to wear, what to eat, what to drive, what to do, what to say, what to buy, what to watch, what to hear, what to experience, and eventually what—or worse yet—whom to love? Who is in charge of you, anyway?

Every human being on earth is empowered with a bounty of God-given talents and resources. There is an infinite

Courage in Society

supply of human potential and natural resources. We have access to the abundance of all the treasures within the universe that have been discovered either through science or theology—both leading us to the same absolute laws of Infinite Intelligence or God.

We are asked by both science and theology to take certain leaps of faith regarding the unknown in our quest for meaning and purpose. This leap of faith requires great strength. We must harness this strength from within and not waste another precious moment of our lives.

The individuals who are honored in the following chapters have reached within themselves to a previously unknown cavern and sprung forth newly tapped resources of goodness. They did these things because they were urged to give of themselves from a place deeper than they even recognized. They, like you and I, were born with the capacity to love and make their lives fulfilling and complete. We have the ability to live each day to its fullest and become all that we were designed to become as we rejoice in our humanity and imperfections. At any given moment of life, we have the ability to alter our paths, if we steer our course on this magnificent journey toward the destiny that is calling our own unique name.

We can let go of our ego-driven desires, and trust our spirit-centered desires to lead us through our own mastery. When we let go and give unconditionally, the universe handsomely rewards us in unimaginable ways. Paradoxically, the more we give unconditionally through our spirit center, the more we will receive to nourish our ego to its precise nature and needs. This is so clearly exemplified by the heroes of history who have generously given of themselves either through ideas, tithing, ministry, work, politics, arts, humanities, battlefields, philanthropy, commerce, patriotism, or other numerous contributions to society.

Cheri Lutton

We can each bring an infinite proportion of service to society. The small acts of honor that we bestow upon our fellow neighbors will reflect the great acts of love that we possess for our Creator, our universe, and our humanity.

When it is all said and done, I have to conclude that I always come back to the same place in my heart—Love. In closing, I share with you Corinthians 13, 14:

LOVE

What if I could speak all languages of humans and of angels?
If I did not love others, I would be nothing more than a noisy gong…
What if I could prophesy and understand all secrets and all knowledge?
Moreover, what if I had faith that moved mountains?
I would be nothing, unless I loved others.
What if I gave away all that I owned and let myself be burned alive?
I would gain nothing unless I loved others.
Love is kind and patient, never jealous, boastful, proud or rude.
Love isn't selfish or quick-tempered.
It doesn't keep a record of wrongs that others do.
Love rejoices in the truth, but not in evil.
Love is always supportive, loyal, hopeful, and trusting.
Love never fails!
When we were children, we thought and reasoned as children do.
Nevertheless, when we grew up, we quit our childish ways.
Now all we can see of God is like a cloudy picture in a mirror.

> Later we will see him face to face. We don't
> know everything, but then we will,
> Just as God completely understands us. For now there
> are faith, hope, and love.
> Nevertheless, of these three, the greatest is . . . Love.

Indeed, it takes the emotional commitment of love to become a true hero of courage within society. It takes the utmost generosity of mind, body, spirit, work, and family altogether to move our passions of personal purpose into the larger purpose of humanity. Sometimes, this may mean saying no to those who tug at us to move against our grain. Do it and do not look back! For you, my friends, are the true heroes that your children and society are all seeking. I hope that you will recognize your soul as you read the following chapters on the fine individuals who are honored for their . . . Courage in Society.

Courage is knowing what you stand for and not being afraid to stand up for it.

—Scot Keranen

Scot Keranen

CHAPTER THIRTY-THREE
Courage In Society

Scot Keranen
The Courage to Step Up to God's Calling

Courage is knowing what you stand for and not being afraid to stand up for it.
—Scot Keranen

"I am serving God by loving his people—my friends, family, and everyone. I am a source of light as a positive example to my peers, friends, family, and to the whole world. I am living a happy, healthy, productive, and meaningful life." This is Scot Keranen's purpose in life.

So, what prompts a young man at sixteen years of age to spend his leisure time creating his missions in life with promises to love and help others?

I wondered about this question with amazement because this young sensitive lad has touched my life in just this way.

Standing athletic, handsome and 6'2" with eyes so blue, blonde hair, and a heartwarming smile, Scot has not only captured the heart of his proud mom, but just about every other lady who meets him. Yet, in spite of his attractive looks, Scot represents a growing genre of teenagers who would prefer to be self-actualizing than self-promoting. Scot's family has earned tremendous success in their careers, affording him the opportunity to attend a private school and enjoy an affluent lifestyle. Life has been sweet for Scot, but the journey has not always been easy.

I met Scot in 1998 during an international conference on health and wellness innovations. Scot's dad created the marketing arm for the company, offering Scot a solid venue in which to develop relationships with talented mentors. Scot and his siblings were visible forces in their parent's lives since family values naturally stood out as a priority for the Keranen's. Consequently, Scot became a gifted leader at a very early age. He displayed style, leadership, and class—a true gentleman on the verge of greatness.

Scot and I befriended through the Youth Mentoring International foundation (YMI), which held a simultaneous summit within the firm's health and wellness conference. Scot was the youth leader for YMI and I was a volunteer in support of the organization. Scot appeared as if he were naturally calm and confident all his life. As we became friends, I realized this was not the case. I discovered that the YMI founder Bob Proctor had become such a mentor for Scot that it changed the course of his life from struggle to ease. In fact, that is precisely how YMI was born . . .

As a young boy, Scot suffered from frequent bouts of asthma, which greatly hindered his freedom of sport, health, and spirit. In seventh grade, Scot was out of commission for twenty-eight days due to his respiratory attacks and distress. Frequent medications and allergy shots had become a way of life for this young man, and it was not fun.

Scot Keranen

When I consider how I take a relaxed breath for granted, it is daunting to comprehend what a teen with chronic asthma must experience every day. Add to the scenario the severe impact of peer pressure and ridicule during adolescence—and what would normally appear easy and enjoyable in life—suddenly becomes difficult and uninviting even for the most positive person.

It is said that luck occurs when preparation and opportunity meet. For Scot, that life-changing opportunity knocked on his door several years ago: enter Bob Proctor, a reserved, intriguing gentleman of slender stature. On a conscious level, they had no clue what was to happen. However, on a deeper subconscious level, they were both well prepared for each other. "My parents host quite a few hot shots, and I just thought this person (Bob Proctor) would be another," Scot describes about the man who would change the course of his life and . . . vice versa.

"Scot, I'd like you to meet Bob Proctor," Scot's mom, Jan, warmly spoke as she invited her son to engage in conversation with Bob. She knew Bob as a very successful speaker in personal development. Jan believed that Bob could help her son overcome his breathing challenges.

Although Scot admits he was initially reluctant, he could not help but at least become enchanted by Bob's uniquely resonating voice. (A must for everyone!) Soon Scot became fascinated with Bob's teachings about the higher powers of the mind and began to expand his levels of awareness. Throughout the evening, Scot deepened his understanding about his own choices in directing his life. Once Scot made the decision to commit himself to Bob's suggestions, providence moved forward, and his world began to shift. Through several mentoring sessions, a paradigm shift, and a fresh outlook on life, Scot successfully overcame his physical challenges. Gradually, Scot significantly reduced his reliance on medications and allergy shots permanently.

This fearless young leader subsequently became an instrumental force in the new Youth Mentoring International foundation. Once Scot's dad, Al Keranen, spurred the idea for both of them to mentor other teens, Bob and Scot were on a roll in developing and implementing the plan. Bob Proctor; world-renowned speaker, writer, and coach would become the founder of the YMI. Scot would be the leading catalyst, igniting curiosity in other teens for years to follow. This is how YMI began.

While some teenagers are more concerned about peer acceptance and sensory stimulation, Scot sharpens his mind using his memory, perception, will, reason, and imagination. He dares to dream big visions, desiring to build genuine relationships with teens around the country by sharing his experiences. He dreams of modeling a servant-based leadership style that is inspired by his deep and openly fervent faith in God. His dreams have arrived.

I spoke with Scot about his perspectives on leadership and courage. "To be a youth in today's society, one is faced with enormous pressures not only from our peers but also from the media. Especially critical is the sophomore year that I call 'Sophomore Syndrome.' This is where pressures can be overwhelming and the individual emerges with the decisions on which path they will choose for their life's journey," Scot comments as he chuckles with enthusiasm.

"I'd say the most awesome opportunity we have today is the option to discover Christ in the business and social world," remarks Scot, speaking on the world's shift toward spiritual growth. Scot concludes, "I have a dream of starting my own outdoor summertime seminars for youth and sharing what I have learned . . . do you want to help me?" "Of course," I reply.

Scot Keranen

Scot conveyed genuine candor, courtesy, and confidence in his voice. Scot is also mastering the art of public speaking, especially amazing since he was so nervous about speaking to audiences just a few years ago.

Yet, it is in the quiet acts of selfless interest that Scot's bravery speaks to my heart. A few years ago, my family was facing tremendous strife, centering on our then fourteen-year-old daughter's struggles. I shared some of my feelings with Scot since he displayed such a mature sensitivity, evident in his frequent telephone messages of solace and prayer. When I finally had the energy to return Scot's calls, he made me feel as if my concerns were the most important issue to him in that moment. Scot offered me words of warmth, respect, and empathy about our daughter Crystal. He endeared a mom who simply felt helpless and hopeless in that period of our lives. I remember hanging up the telephone with Scot and thanking the Lord for bringing such a pure soul into my heart. To this day, I know that Crystal also feels Scot's encouragement and warm rapport. She enjoys Scot's spontaneity and admires his unstoppable quest for goodness. I know, too, that Scot has touched Bob's life, as well as, many others. I close with a prayer for both of them.

Dear Lord, I thank you today for crossing the lives of Bob Proctor and Scot Keranen. So many lives—young and old alike—have been uplifted through their combined energies and efforts . . . through their synergy. I am happy and grateful to call both of them my friends and I appreciate that my family and home reflect a little bit more of who we are for having met such fine human beings. Amen. Go get 'em, Scot!

◆ ◆ ◆

AP/High Society

Little flower, you're the lucky one; you soak in all the lovely sun; you stand and watch it all go by; and never once do bat an eye; while others have to fight and strain; against the world and its every pain of living. But you too must have wars to fight; the cold bleak darkness of every night of a bigger vine that seeks to grow and is able to stand the rain and snow; and yet you never let it show on your pretty face.

—Grace, Princess of Monaco

AP

*Royal Rainier
Wedding, Monaco*

CHAPTER THIRTY-FOUR
Courage In Society

Grace, Princess of Monaco
The Courage to Lead from the Heart

Little flower, you're the lucky one; you soak in all the lovely sun; you stand and watch it all go by; and never once do bat an eye; while others have to fight and strain; against the world and its every pain of living. But you too must have wars to fight; the cold bleak darkness of every night of a bigger vine that seeks to grow and is able to stand the rain and snow; and yet you never let it show on your pretty face.
—Grace, Princess of Monaco

O the luck o' the Irish, to have the heritage of a beauty so graceful and, yet, so strong and steadfast. The quietly saucy woman of the Irish Catholic faith was determined to make her own movie . . . her own kingdom . . . and her own legend. Who, you ask? Why, there is truly only one . . . America's classic beauty, Grace Kelly, Princess of Monaco, affectionately known to her loved ones as . . . Gracie.

Make a movie she did—of her own life and many more, in spite of her dominant and successful father. Her movies became timeless classics, including one for the highest of all cinematic honors, an Academy Award. Not only did Grace imitate life through art, but she also became one of those rare human beings whose art imitated her life. Grace created a reality for herself of "the stuff that only dreams are made up." Our spitfire from Philadelphia made Cinderella look like a dull, black and white movie compared to her Technicolor romance with royalty. Her best role was still in her future as all of her fans awaited her next command performance, which would become legendary. Wake up America and Europe—we are going to have a party! The award-winning actress of Hollywood is going to France to become the Princess of Monaco.

Living only fifty-two years, the princess reflected her first name like no other. Grace epitomized the essence of courage with poise, especially in the face of rocky career beginnings and many tough roadblocks along the way. Grace's parents were not overflowing with support and enthusiasm about her acting quest. They actually favored Grace's sister, Peggy. "My older sister was my father's favorite," Grace would recall in her later years according to the book *Grace*. From her mother's perspective, in the same book, "She was nobody's Princess Charming."

Grace admitted, "I was terribly shy when I was young. I almost crawled into the woodwork. I was so self-conscious . . . I was so bland, they kept having to introduce me again and again before people noticed me. I made no impression."

I first saw Grace Kelly co-starring with Cary Grant in the great movie *To Catch A Thief*. The highly entertaining plot features witty dialogue, international intrigue, and glamorous on-location European settings. Grace's role takes her to Monaco for a costume party where she dresses up, yes, as a Princess. Talk about a life that eventually imitates art!

The sometimes nice, sometimes naughty, but always "in the role" Grace, was described by the film's famous director, Alfred Hitchcock, as a "snow-covered volcano." Grace had a demure style that blended wit, fortitude, ingenuity, and individuality.

It certainly took one independent gal in the forties to leave home with such a socially prominent and aristocratic Kennedy-like heritage. Grace's brother, Kell, once described her earlier life remarking on why Grace turned out differently, explaining that "she got away from home early—none of the rest of us managed to do that."

Breaking through movie stardom has never been an easy task. Yet, Grace careened her way around filmmakers with considerable aloofness. She was, even by Hollywood's critical standards, a natural-born actress. Sure, we say, it's easy for someone like her with all of her beauty, talent, money, and connections. What is so courageous about that?

Aaah the craft of myth, the magic of cinema! So clever, even we fell for it. The mythmaker herself, Grace Kelly, had us all fooled. However, Grace did not fall from the stars into a life of theatrical privilege. Her only inspirational asset was the influence of her Uncle George and his passion as a playwright and actor. Her uncle would become her primary role model during childhood.

"Whatever he talks about, he makes you understand all its beauty and hidden meaning. . . . You could sit and listen to my Uncle George all night long," she once reminisced. Grace developed a sense of purposeful will and a "go out and get it" spirit from both of her parents, along with a broader appreciation of the need for philanthropy.

Grace first began making waves in New York City through the highly competitive field of professional modeling, using her skill, beauty, and poise. Soon, her photogenic appeal began to emerge upon society as she was discovered and featured on the covers of *Redbook* and *Cosmopolitan*.

As an actress, Grace was able to captivate and tantalize her new audiences through her natural skill in the art of the tasteful seduction of life. She starred in eleven full feature films, winning the Oscar award for Best Actress in 1954. Grace had arrived in style.

So, why did she leave her real life of fame, fortune, and courtship in Hollywood for the surrealistic pomp and circumstance of Monaco? Surely, it was not because of any character flaw, which might have swayed her toward an illusionary, fairy tale life. Instead, Grace accepted royalty because of genuine affection and love for her husband-to-be, Prince Rainier III.

Crossing the Atlantic on the USS *Constitution* in April 1956, Grace set sail on a 4,000-mile journey to marry her prince, and the world followed her every move. This event would become the wedding of the century, complete with filming by MGM. As the transatlantic ship entered the charming harbor of Monaco, nestled in the Mediterranean waters of the French Riviera, the crowds watched as the royal yacht slowly motored toward the liner. Soon, Prince Rainier would greet and claim his princess. Grace stepped out in style adorned with a long dark silk coat, a white round hat, and a beautiful smile. After a week of festivities in the sunny picturesque town, the prince would marry his swanlike princess in a lavish royal ceremony on April 18, in the palace of Monaco, and again, on the following day, in the Cathedral on the rock.

Cynics may argue that Grace was only exchanging one surreal lifestyle, namely Hollywood glamour, for another, European royalty. On Rainier's side, the critics inferred that the romance was purely an arranged marriage for political reasons. This view was based on the ruling that required the prince to marry and produce heirs in order for the principality of Monaco to remain a tax-free haven for its citizens. Otherwise, without any heirs, Monaco would revert to France with their laws and higher taxation system.

Grace and Prince Rainier proved them wrong. Grace's love for the prince was genuine as was his love for her. She desired to give of herself fully in marriage . . . to her future family . . . to her newly inherited monarchy. Like all courageous women of history, Grace had actualized herself into this destiny, and she realized her evolving purpose in life. She showed us, by her own example, how to dream the big life, and, then, live the big dream.

Her Serene Highness would still encounter all of the ordinary nuances related to marriage, intimacy, and parenthood, that all human beings discover in their journey of self-fulfillment. Grace, like all wives and mothers, would be required to deal with her own weaknesses, her husband's, her children's, her principality's, and her occasionally not-so-charming circumstances of life. However, Grace continually transcended the emptiness that could beset the life of a princess. She faced her demons and accepted many tough compromises in her quest to be true to herself and to her chosen role in society.

Truly, what was most captivating about Grace was her genuine desire to fill her position as Princess of Monaco. It took sheer acts of solid focus, will, and determination to transform herself from an image of an American movie star —an outsider—to a woman of dedication to her husband, Prince Rainier, and to her people, the citizens of Monaco. Grace had to surrender to a life of unfamiliar protocol and enormous responsibility while still holding dear in her heart her love for her prince. The intimacy and romance of her royal courtship would soon become fading memories. Now, she had to immerse herself into a life of paradox filled with

Courage in Society

loveliness and loneliness, ritual and splendor within her royal marriage and royal duties. She was determined and serious about her new role as a princess, teaching herself how to speak fluent French. She walked on without regret and said good-bye to a thriving acting career that she had earned with true merit and talent.

The princess with snow-white skin, silky blonde tresses, and big brown eyes soon mesmerized new audiences around the world. Grace would gain respect for much more than her pretty face and talents. Monaco quickly became a principality with panache. Soon, it would be known to the world as the gateway for high-class politicians and celebrities alike to mix and mingle. Monaco's commerce prospered as one of the diplomats of the century courted the world in regal class. Prince Rainier had never captured the world's attention, yet his wife cast an enchanting spell on her newly devoted international fans. She became at home in her role as princess, devoted in every way to her prince, her children, and the good citizens of Monaco. Princess Grace of Monaco ruled her land with a blend of graceful elegance and strength. She was a vibrant force within the community. Her Serene Highness also worked on behalf of her adopted country in expanding Monaco's foreign trade and stature in international relations. With a growing sense of political savvy, the princess carried on in ways beyond the scope of most leaders destined to royalty. To this day, Monaco remains a thriving, independent country because of Grace's legacy of generosity.

In constant touch with her own passion for the creative, Grace delighted European society with her contributions to poetry, theatre, film, ballet, fashion, and even flowers! Chosen by the BBC in 1976 as the Pick of the Year for her excellence in poetry reading, the princess would, again, find another avenue to touch the hearts of many others.

Spiritually, Grace continued to develop her faith through

her work with her church. A lifelong Roman Catholic, she produced a television documentary at the Vatican in Rome. Director Barry Chattington praised Grace by stating, "She was just great to work with. I mean, it was funny—lots of jokes. She was just a natural, genuine tell-it-like-it-is human being. She was an amazing professional."

Diplomatically, this feminist archetype led the way for women's rights in the workplace. Grace also actively participated in the Red Cross, became a regular visitor in the local homes for the elderly and the orphaned, and founded a new hospital and daycare center within Monaco. Eventually, Grace became the honorary president of the World Association of Friends of Children (AMADE). Through AMADE, she would become instrumental in lobbying for education on medicine and against violence on television.

As Princess of Monaco, Grace actively supported the youth of her principality through a strong education program for Monaco's schools. More personally, she nurtured the children through parties and planned events. In fact, the Monégasque children enjoyed a special tradition with the princess—an annual Christmas party at the palace—complete with sticky buns, soda, a movie, a magician, clowns and, best of all, no parents.

Privately, she was a hands-on mother until the end. An avid storyteller at bedtime, Grace and the Prince took their child-rearing responsibilities to heart for all three of their children, Albert, Caroline, and Stephanie. Perhaps spoiled and indulgent amidst the good things in life, these three children were, however, always loved and respected by their parents. Grace commented at one time, "Whatever happens, you must always leave a door open."

All of this abruptly halted on September 13, 1982, in a disastrous automobile crash and ended in complete surprise and surrealism—the next day. Grace spent her last day with her daughter, Stephanie, tending to her teenage needs by driving her about town . . . just like any other mom. A little while later, Grace was gone. The world would mourn the tragedy and loss of a great woman. Deep sadness and controversial calamity would surround the princess's death after this fateful car drive. Ironically, Monaco's La Turbie Road, was the same hairpin curve that we saw the actress driving along as she captured our hearts in *To Catch a Thief*. Although the alluring princess was gone, her timeless beauty would remain in our hearts and memories through film. The wind-swept hair under a scarf with eyes hidden by sunglasses, the cool demeanor, and the illusive character of steel—all added to Grace's enigmatic appeal to the world.

Grace is remembered poignantly by Judith Quine, one of her closest friends, in *The Bridesmaids*. Touched personally by Grace, I gave this book to my own bridesmaids before my wedding. The author remarks that she asked the prince if there was anything else he wished he could have had with Grace. More time is all that he wished for with the princess. He missed the time for more meaningful conversations, the exchange of ideas and feelings—for the intimacy between husband and wife. At Grace's funeral, her Mass card read, "Lord, I ask not why you took her away. I thank you for having given her to us."

Maybe, you knew how much you were admired . . . maybe not . . . but, either way, Grace, you blazed a trail for all the young-at-heart to realize that . . . anything is possible! Your graceful touch of class will remain alive forever through all your lovely contributions. The Princess Grace Foundations are indeed flourishing. You will always be loved!

◆ ◆ ◆

Liz Mostov and Father

Courage is being able to accept change and challenge in your life.

—Elizabeth Mostov

*Cheri and Liz during
Lutton Wedding Festivities*

CHAPTER THIRTY-FIVE
Courage In Society

Elizabeth Mostov

The Courage to Show Compassion for All

Courage is being able to accept change and challenge in your life.
—**Elizabeth Mostov**

The waves rush to and fro, over the mighty waters of Mother Earth while the shoreline sparkles with brilliant colors amidst the sun's reflective smile. Our Heavenly Father sends the angels off to create one of the loveliest imprints in the sands of humanity. It is that of my dear friend, Lizzie, a delightful portrait of warm-hearted dauntlessness—a true lioness.

Liz's unwavering faith in the benevolent spirit of life has fueled her mission to protect the weak and enlighten the strong. Liz moves perpetually in an ocean of motion, constantly helping others. A ball of fire, this woman has an endless supply of energy—that needs no caffeine or alcoholic aperitifs of any kind—to propel her on her way.

A striking and slender 5'8" goddess of heart, Liz's radiance emanates through her deep blue eyes, which draw one invitingly into her soul. One house rule is clear for all those who desire entrance: sincerity. Liz can look into a person's eyes, catch an immediate glimpse of their inner being, and gently or boldly, call a spade—in its own name.

Animated and sensuous, Liz's love for life and laughter expresses itself vividly through her lovely smile, her blonde or brunette locks (depending on her mood), and her gregarious nature. A warm blend of humor and dimension, Liz sometimes reminds me of Joan Rivers and Barbra Streisand wrapped into one. Yet, her own uniqueness really prevents me from typecasting her at all. Most of all, what impresses me about my dear friend is her tenacity to effect change in herself, in her environment, and, eventually, throughout the universe. Weathering storms of resistance, rejection, and sometimes ridicule, Liz adapts and grows better with time, while others simply grow older.

Her love for animals has probably inspired her stuffed toy collection, and the animals at the local zoos have been known to clamor for her presence frequently. She devotes much of her free time advocating for animal and environmental concerns. On Saturdays, one can usually find Lizzie volunteering her time at the Central Park Zoo.

Liz has also enjoyed a repertoire of accomplishments in the fields of fashion, music, tourism, and the arts. In her newest desire to build her own business, Liz appeals to people from all walks to open their minds in seeking a balanced lifestyle. She attracts wealth into her clients' pocketbooks as

Elizabeth Mostov

well as into their mind, body, and spirit so that they are able to give more of themselves back to their families and society. Having received enormous benefit herself from alternative therapies, Liz is an enthusiastic proponent of self-empowerment in health and wellness.

Although Liz was raised in Ohio, she has lived in New York City for most of her adult life. As a Big Apple gal, she has graduated from life's school of hard knocks and has developed the necessary eye for surviving . . . and thriving. A staunch residential fan of Manhattan, Liz Mostov could start her own training camp for cabbies in the city. Her partisanship for the camp would, of course, lean toward the passengers and not the shrewd tactics of some of the current-day taxicab drivers.

I have now known Liz for twenty years after we met in Boulder, Colorado, through a group excursion hosted by a mutual acquaintance filled with fun, sun, and water-skiing. Afterwards, Liz's inviting gesture of "look me up if you ever come to New York" was the beginning of an almost annual tradition between us.

I'll never forget my first trip to the Big Apple in which I took Liz up on her offer of hospitality. At the time, I was going to New York for a business trip. I decided to spend a few extra days with my local acquaintance and catch the true flavor of the city that never sleeps. In time, I discovered that . . . neither does my new friend.

Catching a cab from LaGuardia Airport just before sunset, I was off in a whirl over the Triborough Bridge gazing at the glimmering skyline of Manhattan, which seemed to tease onlookers with hints of come and play. Parading south along the waterfront on the East Side, I enjoyed the sights along the highway—laced with trees and a stream of residential brick buildings—so different from the way that life looks back in Colorado.

Heading west across Central Park, past Park and Fifth Avenues, I could almost taste the diversity from one block to the next. Taking in the scent of nature and the lush greenery of this infamous garden, I could sense a world here on its own accord—filled with both the rich and the poor—all taking in their share of nature's gift in peaceful harmony. By day, Central Park truly is the level playing field where humanity can be enjoyed in its simplicity. This is the fulcrum where nature, the animals, and mankind can all come together for a better visit with themselves than, perhaps, we, as humans, embrace in our daily exchanges with the modern high-tech and status-oriented world.

Through the park and on the West Side of Manhattan, I saw a more relaxed atmosphere in comparison to the East Side's busy shopping district. The grand museums, standing tall on both sides of the park, appeared as majestic reminders of the cosmopolitan stature that this fascinating city claims for the world.

Upon arriving at the brownstone of my host, I had to chuckle at the vast difference in lifestyles between here and where we met at the health club nestled against the foothills of the Rocky Mountains. After taking a few deep breaths, I ventured up the very steep flights of stairs on the outside—as well as the inside—of the building. I stopped for a moment wondering whether this was such a good idea at all since I hardly knew Liz. Would she still be as warm and friendly? I thought. Would these stairs ever end?

Just as I turned the last corner, catching my breath again, I looked up and I was suddenly bedazzled by the shower of twinkling lights outlining my new friend's door. Approaching a bit closer, I noticed the huge sign with a big red apple and words that appeared to scream in big letters, "Welcome to the Big Apple and my home, Cheri!" I smiled, knocked, and felt glad that I had listened to my heart. "Hi, Cheri. Welcome to the city and my home!" Liz invited with

Elizabeth Mostov

a friendly smile, so unexpected in a culture known for its guarded cynicism.

Once inside—after our exuberant greetings, a huge hug and an introduction to Liz's cat, Kyoto—Liz pampered me with a freshly baked cake, making me feel right at home. From that moment forward, I knew that my relationship with New York City would always be blessed with warmth and genuineness—because of this woman.

Over the years, as we have visited each other back and forth from New York to Colorado, I have experienced the many bold, brave, and beautiful faces of this loving lioness. One time she confronted an irritable and hurried New Yorker who was pushing me into the doorway at Sak's Fifth Avenue. Another time, she was bargaining a deal with the clerk at the local delicatessen. There she was, again, a loyal friend, smiling at me during my wedding in downtown Boulder, Colorado.

As kind as I see her, however, Liz is not a woman to be crossed. She can be as tough as the situation requires. Liz has the gift of truly calling anyone on their actions in a graceful manner so that growth and change become a possibility. In fact, after all these years of friendship from such a heroine of strength, I have one recommendation: more New Yorkers need Liz in their lives! On the other hand, if the residents of Manhattan are actually like her, then, alas, I have uncovered the myth. I see now that the tough exterior in many people only serves to protect their gentle souls. Like many, they are tired of going unnoticed, undervalued, and overspent.

Like Liz, many New Yorkers have transplanted themselves either as immigrants from faraway places or as pioneers back from the West; here to create their own destinies in the land of golden opportunity. I can only imagine what courage it took Liz to venture away from her cozy home in Ohio to plant herself in NYC and brave the warriors in the fashion industry. All on her own, weathering the objections of a world filled with varying perspectives on human beauty, Liz eventually succeeded at becoming a professional model.

Enjoying the benefits of a life filled with fashion and culture, however, also had its price. Time and wear took its physical toll, and Liz was besieged with chronic joint disorders, which disabled her at times to the point of being bedridden or stricken to walking with a cane. The agony she endured in the simple acts of living would cause her to drastically limit the adventures she loved through tennis, biking, dancing, and running. Swimming became her primary form of physical self-expression and exercise. Fortunately, she has since gained back much of her activity through the help of more innovative and non-invasive technologies.

So, I ask her in a candid telephone conversation, "Liz, how do you remain so positive and strong in the face of the adversities that you have experienced?" Liz reflects and finally replies with a passionate tone, "Cheri, all of life requires courage. Fear seems to show up along the way. Actually, I think it is okay to be a little frightened. Our survival instinct naturally requires it, and we can learn so much from our feelings. We must listen to hear the source of these fears; be honest with ourselves; recognize these fears; and then free them—like a bird. We must follow our heart and believe that we can go out and do it . . . then act on it right away!"

On tips for anyone interested in pursuing a career in fashion, Liz reflects, "For me, I came into my looks around sixteen years of age, and I loved the flair of fashion. I was actually shy, and modeling was a way to push myself in front of people without talking too much. It helped me learn how to recognize my internal qualities, and become centered with strong values and boundaries. Nowadays, modeling is more about being a celebrity. I say, keep it all in perspective. Follow your dream, yet remember; it is just a career, and not the secret to your life's happiness. Have fun

Elizabeth Mostov

with it and develop your inner, as well as, outer beauty."

"How do you succeed at living in such a tough city with such warm and friendly inner qualities?" I ask. She pauses then whispers, "It's about the golden rule of respecting other people, Cheri, as I would want to be respected. I really love this city because I love people and being at the center of everything. Of course, I am careful, and a little bit of common sense and courtesies can go a long way. Yet, all in all, I really enjoy every day as another gift of life. A new day to treat myself. . . to make others feel good about themselves . . . and to make others laugh!"

I laughed, knowing it is one of Liz's favorite pastimes. It is also one of her greatest sources of inner strength. She confides, "I put a lot of importance on humor and imagination in developing the mental attitude that follows my inner spiritual guidance. Of course, I count all of my blessings, including my wonderful parents, my sister, my brother; and, last, but not least, my lovable cats, Bonzai and Kiwi. I enjoy being needed by them . . . they make me laugh!"

Liz lets out a spontaneous giggle, continuing, "People make me laugh over the silly things they do. I make myself laugh! The human side of us where we err can be enjoyed rather than criticized. We can turn our lemons into lemonade." She then whispers as if telling me a secret, "I use my mind to create a funny scene rather than worrying about a problem and being so hard on myself. Then, I always seem to find my way and create a better solution. In the worst of times, I try to think of something or someone good. Day-by-day, I eventually move in the direction of that good," she exclaims confidently.

On her boundless love and enthusiasm for all animals, Liz comments, "I've always had a great fascination with the thousands of animal species, and the delicate balance between nature and man. It's very important to be sensitive to all living creatures. The difference between animals and

Courage in Society

humans is that our animal friends are not able to speak up for themselves. I try to help them in any way that I can." She does. Liz volunteers her time to numerous organizations and is also a member of the likes of Delta Rescue, Best Friends, The Humane Society, Defenders of Wildlife, Doris Day's Animal League, Fund for Animals and more! She closes, "I have lots of fun in all that I do—isn't that what it's all about anyway?"

◆

Yes. For I will always savor the laughter and inspiration, that Liz has brought into my life. I am certain that the angels in heaven are smiling proudly and with giggles looking her way!

◆ ◆ ◆

AP/Bourdier

Life is mostly froth and bubble,
Two things stand in stone:
Kindness in another's trouble,
Courage in your own.

—Diana, Princess of Wales

AP/Stillwell

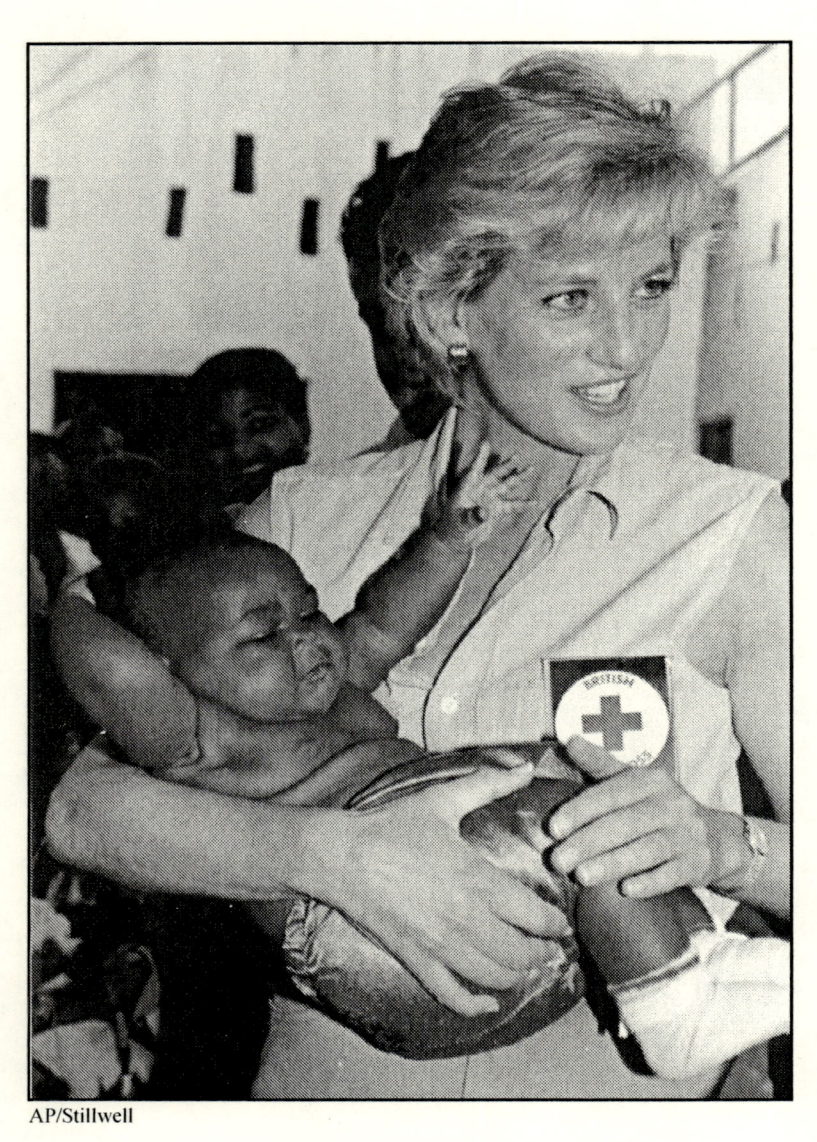

Diana, Princess of Wales holding baby on Luanda Red Cross visit

CHAPTER THIRTY-SIX
Courage In Society

Diana, Princess of Wales
The Courage to Find Goodness in Everything

> Life is mostly froth and bubble, Two things stand in stone: Kindness in another's trouble, Courage in your own.
> —Diana, Princess of Wales

What beckons an illuminating shower of meteors to fall? What troubles the mighty waters of the ocean to crash and roar? What brings our Lady Di, our queen of hearts, to a pinnacle of radiance, shining from north to south and east to west for the entire earth's delight, then . . . overnight, physically extinguishes her from us . . . forever?

Courage in Society

She brightened our hearts as the exquisite Diana, Princess of Wales, known to the world simply as Di. She was an enigma and a paradox. She was and continues to be one of the most photographed women in the world. A true beauty without effort, her unique look remains a timeless standard in fashion and style. Princess Diana's wispy blonde hair cradled her soft blue eyes and accentuated her attractive facial features. Her sinewy slender figure was always in demand by the world's top fashion designers. Whether in casual or formal wear, Princess Diana's natural elegance caught everyone's attention. Yet, her inner beauty is what truly drew her to eternal celebrity. Even after death, the princess remains a popular icon, and her mystique only continues to grow with time.

So, what is it about this shy young lady that perpetually captures our attention? Does she intrigue us because she was a princess? Certainly, this must be so, as international royalty becomes such a diminishing, yet, still, fascinating breed. Yet, of all the regal figureheads in the modern world, truly Princess Diana stands apart as a brilliant beacon of light. Why? What acts of courage did this legendary icon of the twentieth century accomplish that would propel me to include her in these writings?

Pondering this question, I thought about the courage of a soldier in battle and what is expected of him. In the face of possible death, he persists unwaveringly in his quest to defend his people and his country. A courageous soldier is willing to trade his life for his beliefs, regardless of outcome. Princess Diana, regal as she may have been, embodied this spirit as a true heroine. Undoubtedly, she has earned the title of a woman of great courage, a fierce warrior for . . . Love, Truth, and Beauty.

In her short life, Diana faced tremendous pressure and adversity. She had the heartbreak of a fairy tale marriage that did not turn out to be "the stuff that dreams are made of" as was celebrated during her spectacular wedding ceremony. I remember waking up in the wee hours of July 29, 1981, to enjoy this historical moment on live television, highly viewed around the world. I admired Lady Di for her sincere interest in caring for children, and could not help but wonder how her life would change once she became a princess. On the one hand, Diana seemed so down-to-earth that, like many women, I felt that I could identify with her as a young single professional finding her way in the world. On the other hand, however, I believe her royal courtship was so surrealistic in this modern world that vicariously many of us simply crossed our fingers for Diana, hoping that she could make it all work out—somehow. Sadly enough, the monarchy's true hand would be revealed all too soon in Diana's young marriage. A sobering reality would soon dawn on the new bride. The young princess would come to realize that, for her husband's sake, the stage had been set through her marriage for the proper heir to follow and become king. To Diana's dismay, "another woman" was already in the prince's life, even before Diana was actually the "other woman."

Alas, the beautiful Princess's tale did not include a marriage that was happily ever after. As Diana grew more estranged from her husband, Prince Charles, she suffered greatly. From her own accounts, the Princess would experience waves of turbulence and animosity in her days with the royal family. Motherhood would become both a deep source of love and tension, as Diana's maternal rights would become challenged by the monarchy. Yet, throughout the highs and lows, Diana remained the very epitome of grace, class, and courage. Photographers never ceased to capture her charismatic smile, demeanor, and bravado. Diana was simply too alluring to ever forget.

Oddly enough, Diana's most significant battle, however, was not with the strife of royalty or marriage. Diana's

Achilles' heel was the preservation of her personal freedom. Certainly, one would assume that a Princess could simply command privacy by virtue of her wealth, power, or easy access to royal properties of seclusion, i.e. a palace. Ironically, Diana preferred to be among the common folk. Consequently, this princess of the people would continually sacrifice her privacy as the media followed her every footstep all over the world. Never before had there been such an invasion of privacy than in the life of shy Di, as she was called during her initial courtship with the prince—and the press. She became a daily figure in the tabloids. Insensitive reporters and paparazzi photographers pursued Diana day and night. They crossed the fine line of public newsworthiness and professional journalism.

Could we even dare to imagine what she faced on a daily basis once she said "yes" to the eligible prince? I remember the photograph in those days of Lady Diana, politely and innocently at the side of her husband, Prince Charles, as they announced their plans to marry. Would it be possible to even think clearly when one is being photographed even during that thought? And the next . . . and the next . . . and the next. . . .

In spite of this constant surveillance, Diana learned that a professional leader—in any field—is at her best at all times, regardless of the circumstances. She serenely moved through her destiny and affirmed her power, using it as an instrument for constructive change even amidst all of the scrutiny. Diana chose to rise above the struggle and take charge of her notoriety rather than flee from the press in fright. Paradoxically, it was through the clear thinking of respectable journalists worldwide that Diana was able to make all of us so keenly aware of the causes that were so dear to her heart. The princess's work supporting animals, children, the sick, the needy, especially in her campaign against landmines, had a tremendous influence on many lives. Through Diana's sheer desire for goodness, she was able to make an enormous difference. Diana realized how profoundly her charisma could effect change in social issues of much greater importance than mere fame, fashion, and fortune.

Hence, the modern-day princess developed a uniquely personal style of courtly etiquette. Diana honored her regal obligations with an added touch of sincerity and compassion, not often demonstrated by others in the royal family. Diana, eventually known as the People's Princess, was the first royal to be photographed tenderly holding the hands of an AIDS patient, and a leprosy patient. She was the princess pictured holding the hands of Mother Teresa. Diana was photographed cradling a young child with cancer at a hospital in Pakistan. It was the Princess of Wales that we watched tirelessly supporting the cancer-stricken in America, the hungry in Zimbabwe, and the homeless everywhere. As a humanitarian, Diana explored landmine sites with British peacekeepers in Bosnia. As a friend, she comforted the bereaving rock star Elton John with a hug at the funeral of their mutual friend and one of her designers, Gianni Versace. As the people's princess, Diana made a wise decision and then acted on it. Princess Diana used her fame and fortune to draw attention to people in need, and raise social awareness toward improving the quality of many lives.

As "Mummy," Diana became self-empowered in her most treasured role for her two children, Prince William and Prince Harry. Motherhood gave her great joy, and what fun she brought to her boys! Running a relay race with the moms of her children's schoolmates, Diana was always willing to express her love and affection for them spontaneously. Full of hugs, kisses, laughter, and tender loving care, Diana showed her boys how to be more of themselves.

She walked her talk and followed her heart in voicing true feelings and personal inadequacies. Diana's honesty in revealing her own eating disorders brought to light the conflicts she was facing in her new lifestyle. As difficult and embarrassing as it must have been for the princess to be so candid about her vulnerabilities, she did it anyway. Through her courage, Diana gave others the permission to be more open about their own secret fears and battles.

Moreover, Diana did much more than simply speak about social issues. She also acted upon her words. Diana showed true compassion for the weak, the humble, and the needy. Attracted to like-minded Mother Teresa, Diana used her stature to enlighten the opulent and powerful toward lending a pocketbook or hand for people in crisis. Diana stated in a famous BBC interview, "I would like to be a queen in people's hearts . . . someone's got to go out there and love people and show it." This interview attracted the largest audience for any television documentary in broadcasting history. Shortly before she died, she expressed her true nature again, "My purpose is simple—to heighten global awareness of the human suffering . . . I am only trying to help—to highlight problems going on all the world. I am not a political figure but a humanitarian figure—always have been, always will be. . . . I'd like to be an ambassador for this country to every country in the world; I'd like to represent this country abroad in the best way possible—by showing the essential tolerance and concern that is the best of England, the best of any people."

In July 1997, a month before her death, the British parliament defended Diana in a poignant statement. Prime Minister Tony Blair publicly supported her although she was no longer married to Prince Charles, the future king of England, or entitled "Her Royal Highness" by expressing, "I think it is very important that Princess Diana is allowed to carry on the work that she is doing. She earns a lot of respect and admiration from people all around the world. I'm very happy for that to continue. She has done an immense amount for the causes she supports—as has the Prince of Wales."

Prime Minister Tony Blair was equally eloquent in his expression of high esteem for Princess Diana after the sudden news of her death caused by a tragic automobile accident in Paris.

". . . We are today a nation in Great Britain in a state of shock and in grief that is so deeply painful for us. . . . She touched the lives of so many others in Britain and throughout the world with joy and comfort. . . . They liked her. They loved her and regarded her as one of the people. She was the people's princess and that is how she will stay and how she will remain in our hearts and our memories forever. . . . "

Sadly enough, Diana was followed and photographed in times when the world really did not need to be there with her. She endured a life without privacy; yet, she remained sincere and true to herself. On September 6, 1997, Earl Charles Spencer expressed his final words of honor in a memorable eulogy to his beloved sister:

"I stand before you today the representative of a family in grief in a country in mourning before a world in shock. We are all united not only in our desire to pay our respects to Diana but rather in our need to do so. For such was her extraordinary appeal that the tens of millions of people taking part in this service all over the world via television and radio who never actually met her, feel that they too lost someone close to them in the early hours of Sunday morning. It is a more remarkable tribute to Diana than I can ever hope to offer her today.

"Diana was the very essence of compassion, of duty, of style, of beauty. All over the world, she was a symbol of selfless humanity. All over the world, a standard-bearer for the rights of the truly downtrodden, a very British girl who transcended nationality. Someone with a natural nobility who was classless and who proved in the last year that she needed no royal title to continue to generate her particular brand of magic.

"Today is our chance to say thank you for the way you brightened our lives, even though God granted you but half a life. We will all feel cheated always that you were taken from us so young and yet we must learn to be grateful that you came along at all. Only now that you are gone do we truly appreciate what we are now without and we want you to know that life without you is very very difficult. We have all despaired at your loss over the past week and only the strength of the message you gave us through your years of giving has afforded us the strength to move forward.

"There is a temptation to rush to canonize your memory; there is no need to do so. You stand tall enough as a human being of unique qualities not to need to be seen as a saint. Indeed, to sanctify your memory would be to miss out on the very core of your being, your wonderfully mischievous sense of humor with a laugh that bent you double. Your joy for life transmitted wherever you took your smile and the sparkle in those unforgettable eyes. Your boundless energy which you could barely contain.

"But your greatest gift was your intuition and it was a gift you used wisely. This is what underpinned all your other wonderful attributes and if we look to analyze what it was about you that had such a wide appeal we find it in your instinctive feel for what was really important in all our lives. Without your God-given sensitivity, we would be immersed in greater ignorance at the anguish of AIDS and HIV sufferers, the plight of the homeless, the isolation of lepers, the random destruction of land mines. Diana explained to me once that it was her innermost feelings of suffering that made it possible for her to connect with her constituency of the rejected. And here we come to another truth about her. For all the status, the glamour, the applause, Diana remained throughout a very insecure person at heart, almost childlike in her desire to do good for others so she could release herself from deep feelings of unworthiness of which her eating disorders were merely a symptom. The world sensed this part of her character and cherished her for her vulnerability whilst admiring her for her honesty.

". . . It is a tribute to her levelheadedness and strength that despite the most bizarre-like life imaginable after her childhood, she remained intact, true to herself.

"There is no doubt that she was looking for a new direction in her life at this time. She talked endlessly of getting away from England, mainly because of the treatment that she received at the hands of the newspapers. I don't think she ever understood why her genuinely good intentions were sneered by the media, why there appeared to be a permanent quest on their behalf to bring her down. It is baffling.

"My own and only explanation is that genuine goodness is threatening to those at the opposite end of the moral spectrum. It is a point to remember that of all the ironies about Diana, perhaps the greatest was this—a girl given the name of the ancient goddess of hunting was, in the end, the most hunted person of the modern age.

"She would want us today to pledge ourselves to protecting her beloved boys, William and Harry, from a similar fate and I do this here, Diana, on your behalf. We will not allow them to suffer the anguish that used to regularly drive you to tearful despair.

". . . I pledge that we, your blood family, will do all we can to continue the imaginative way in which you were steering these two exceptional young men so that their souls are not simply immersed by duty and tradition but can sing openly as you planned.

"... I would like to end by thanking God for the small mercies He has shown us at this dreadful time. For taking Diana at her most beautiful and radiant and when she had joy in her private life. Above all we give thanks for the life of a woman I am so proud to be able to call my sister, the unique, the complex, the extraordinary and irreplaceable Diana whose beauty, both internal and external, will never be extinguished from our minds."

Diana's spirit of light shines brilliantly through the living tribute of her legacy. The Work Continues . . . is a project that has carried on the torch of her causes through The Diana, Princess of Wales Memorial Fund. Since its inception in 1997, the Fund has pledged over 47 million to over 300 organizations in the UK and internationally. "Diana, Princess of Wales set a wonderful example of breaking down stigma and treating neglected or unpopular people as fellow human beings. It is an honour to try to use that inspiration to change lives and attitudes today and in the future—and there's no better memorial to her than that," expresses Andrew Purkis, Executive Director for the Memorial Fund. Today, Diana would be proud and her heart warmed by the caring staff, countless benefactors, and tireless volunteers who have carried on her spirit of compassion with great deeds of contribution toward a better world for all. Diana would smile upon her brother Earl Spencer for the tender loving care he has provided to The Althorp House, her resting place and the Spencer Family Estate, and also to The Althorp Charitable Trust Fund that continues to support many of her projects. Diana would be proud of her handsome young sons, the once and future kings . . . of her legacy of love.

"**G**oodbye England's Rose," as Elton John sang in moving tribute during Princess Diana's funeral. We

Diana, Princess of Wales

will always love and cherish you in our hearts and the spirit of all of your many courageous acts of kindness will indeed live on forever

◆ ◆ ◆

AP/Selby

Courage is stepping out into the unknown for the unknown with sheer intent to contribute yourself to the greater cause of life . . . regardless of the risk.

America's Finest in the Wake of Tragedy

Depot Music Productions

"You Made A Difference"
CD Cover

CHAPTER THIRTY-SEVEN
Courage In Society

America's Finest in the Wake of Tragedy

The Courage to Face Evil and Fight for Good

Courage is stepping out into the unknown for the unknown with sheer intent to contribute yourself to the greater cause of life . . . regardless of the risk.

April 19, 1995, began as a fine day. It was one of those spring days filled with the season's best greenery and flowers peeking about on our lawn. My children were both in school now and my husband, Steve, was settling into his workday as he managed the commercial printing company that he co-owned, Renegade Press, Inc. I smiled while driving by Steve's office as I

397

Courage in Society

returned to my home office after dropping Crystal and Steven off at their school. With his company only four miles from our home, I felt a sense of comfort as I passed by my husband's office and saw his car while on my way back home. Once home, I would start my entrepreneurial day. It was going to be a fun day, I thought to myself, because I was developing strong business relationships as an independent sales consultant with a few promising firms. I enjoyed the daily possibilities that came along with working from a flexible home-based business.

I brewed some freshly ground espresso coffee and sat at my desk to organize my day's agenda. I loved the aroma of French roast. I felt relaxed and turned on the radio to National Public Radio for background music and news. I quickly recognized breaking news. An explosion had gone off in Oklahoma City at the Federal Building. No, there seemed to be more to it. It was not an accidental misfortune. I sipped on my coffee and turned up the volume on the radio. It appeared to be a bomb. All that I could think about was that my sister-in-law Anita and her family lived in Oklahoma. I had no idea how close she might be to this crisis. Wait a minute—this was the heartland of America—could this really be happening? I called my husband and he assured me that Anita's home and army base were far enough away from the crisis to be out of danger. Still, we left a message at Anita's and called on Steve's parents in Ohio just to make a connection. Still, even the comfort of our family's safety did not diminish the anguish and helplessness growing inside each of us as we thought about the people in Oklahoma. It did not erase the real loss of loved ones that many Americans were experiencing at that moment.

Surely, there was a mistake. I left my office and turned on the television in our family room. Catastrophe was blasting all over the networks. Apparently, the Murrah Federal Building was demolished, and many people were dead or

America's Finest

injured, while others were running for their lives. My heart sank to the floor in a sudden rush of compassion and despair. I heard the somber voice of Janet Reno, the U.S. Attorney General, and eventually realized that this was an intentional act of terrorism. Then, I caught the news of the daycare center that was inside the building so that the federal employees would be closer to their children. This was such a tragic irony. In the end, there would be 168 deaths, innocent victims of all ages, from babies to seniors, who gave their lives as heroes. A young white American McVeigh committed this tragedy in a decision to choose evil over good, and harm his fellow countrymen. Soon, this act would become known as homegrown terrorism. What was his goal? Whatever it was, he was virtually living hell on earth, violently expressing his negative opinion about previous events—unrelated to these folks and unrelated to this town—by causing harm and death to innocent American people—young and old— who were just going about their business of leading productive lives. Sadly, the law of cause and effect was in action as a dark example of negative thoughts expressing negative results. "By their fruits, you will know them."

Thankfully, by their fruits we will also know the true American spirit, which cannot be encumbered by the evil forces of life. Love, compassion, and the idealistic spirit of humanity rose quickly to render countless acts of valor and miraculous bravado. New heroes were emerging every minute beyond those that had just transcended into Heaven, as rescue workers, police, firefighters, and ordinary citizens worked courageously to save countless lives trapped in rubble. The angels would take care of the heroes we lost. We on Earth would take care of the rest.

Many more heroes came forth in the following years of reconciliation and restoration in Oklahoma City. Wisdom, patience, empathy, generosity, gratitude, perspective, and humility swelled in the hearts and minds of Americans as we rushed in to our grieving southern belle to wipe away her tears, renew her hopes, and restore her dignity. Embedded in the minds of most will be the tender photograph of the firefighter at the Oklahoma catastrophe leaving the scene with a dying baby in his arms. The citizens of Denver became very involved when the trials of McVeigh and cohort Nichols were relocated to Denver. Without hesitation, the people of Denver opened their hearts and homes to visitors for the days of trial and justice to be served over this inequity toward humanity. Ethnicity, creed, and cultural lines did not matter as Americans flocked to listen and reach out in pocketbook, handiwork, and heartfelt need to stop, wait, and pick up our fellow neighbor before we all carried on with life on earth—the American way—the human way. The sounds of respect, freedom, and brotherly love rang loud and clear throughout our land of democracy. Good prevailed and justice was served.

Now, four years and one day have passed with springtime, once again, here in the Rockies. My son has just turned seven and Crystal was well into the earliest of the teen years. Renegade Press, Inc. my husband's firm, was going strong, although the printing industry was experiencing turbulent times with the onset of digital software and the computerization of printed materials. The industry's standards for quality were deteriorating because of desktop publishing and stiffer competition. To Steve's credit, he had stayed his ground and maintained a solid local reputation for quality and professionalism.

My entrepreneurial spirit was also still strong, yet it was tough. I wore many hats, and, some days, they would all come tumbling off my head at once. Nonetheless, I was cherished with kisses, hugs, and "I love you" sentiments by my endearing husband, and blossoming son and daughter.

Steven was becoming an avid soccer player, and Crystal sang Back Street Boys' songs all the time.

"Gotta go, honey," my husband whispers in my ear along with soft kisses on my cheeks. I ran downstairs after Steve in my robe to remind him, "Don't forget, honey, tonight, we're going to a meeting in Boulder." With a reticent smile, he replies, "Okay, have a good day." I wave as the burgundy Probe rolls out the driveway.

The drive to school began and we approached the drop-off circle. One had to be pretty calm and clever to master the circle with all of the minivans, parents, teachers, students, and little ones parading in and out of this tight area. I wondered how the right people ended up in the right places. "Bye mom, have a nice day!" shouts my daughter. "Ouch, you shocked me," yells my son after a static kiss. I'll never understand that concept of electricity, I thought. I drove away, admiring the school's principal, Mr. Glabb. He was faithfully outside with his coffee mug in hand while talking with students, parents, and teachers, yet, always with the other eye and ear watching over our children. Monarch was a unique K-8 school, so he definitely had his hands full of—variety. Rain or shine, he was a man of all seasons—on arrival and departure, dedicated to all of our sons and daughters. Mr. Glabb is one of those rare leaders who stood for fairness and firmness, regardless of trends and public opinion. My husband and I grew to truly respect him over the years, even if he was not always popular among the students. He was always well understood and respected for his consistent message of values and character by everyone. We knew that we were fortunate. I felt that we were very blessed. Both children had great teachers, and I felt safe with them at this school. I did have my concerns about where to send Crystal for high school, but for today, that was not on my mind.

Afternoon came all too quickly, and I still had to go to K-Mart to return some items and shop for a recording device

Courage in Society

in the electronics department. It was yet another gorgeous Colorado day with wide blue skies and a warm breeze in the air. How fortunate we all were to enjoy such a naturally beautiful and down-to-earth state. Some days, I thought it was all too good to be true, and Coloradoans were a lucky folk. However, today would not turn out that way at all. We would not be going to Boulder that evening. Life's lessons were coming.

"Hi, Mom," shouted Steven and Crystal as I picked them up after school, confirming that all three of us were accounted for and soon at K-Mart, roaming through the department store. Once at my destination in the electronics department, I happened to notice that all of the televisions were a blur of commotion. With partial attention on the TV screens and partial concentration on shopping for a recorder, Crystal and I eventually caught a scene on the television of a row of students walking frantically outside of their school with their arms up in the air as if they were suspected of something. Worse yet, a bloodstained student was dangling from an upper level window. Worse yet . . . Crystal looked up at me as if to ask "Mommy, what's wrong?" I knew that in some ways I would not be able to soothe her concerns. Soon, other shoppers were staring at the televisions, and, finally, all three of us [Luttons] were aware that an unreal event was actually real, and taking place right before our eyes. It still had not quite registered completely in my mind, although the scene was a high school, not too far, in Littleton, Colorado.

Dear God again, something was terribly awry in America, I thought. Now, closer than ever—less than an hour away from our home and school—our youth were experiencing the havoc of life's choices on the farthest side of evil . . . at Columbine High School.

The nightmare that I never imagined could happen in America was dramatically unfolding right before my eyes.

America's Finest

By day's end, fourteen youths and one teacher would be dead. Two of those youths, Klebold and Harris, would eventually be known as the apparent perpetrators of this destructive act toward humanity. The emotions of loneliness, hate, and bitterness managed to root their insidious vines into the hearts of those two young men, and, ultimately, impressions become expressions—both the good and the evil.

On April 20, 1999, Colorado would be changed forever —just as Oklahoma had experienced four years earlier. No longer immune to the wrath of terror, we would be forced to reckon with this darker path that tempts all too many individuals, without discrimination.

By next evening, the news was sinking in to the world's consciousness. My family, like so many in Colorado, felt the need to help and offer comfort. We attended the mourning ceremonies at Denver's Capitol Hill led by Mayor Wellington Webb. It was a cold, dreary, and rainy evening. Hundreds of people flocked to the ceremony and many young teenagers were pouring their tears out in anguish. What struck me tenderly was that most of these youth were here without their parents. They seemed to be lost in their own emotions and yearning for arms to cradle their sorrows. We just walked around after the formalities, offered hugs to these youngsters. . . and wept with them.

Throughout the week, we would travel back and forth to the Columbine area to participate in the spontaneous gatherings at the many shrines that were being created by the thousands of good people who felt just as we felt. We all hurt for those innocent young students. We hurt for their families. . . their moms and dads, brothers, sisters. . . their pets. . . their friends. . . their teachers, and other loved ones. We hurt for the lone teacher who died in the act of saving other students. We hurt for all the individuals who were in that high school and survived with these memories in their hearts and minds forever. We hurt for those parents of the assailant boys. We even hurt for those boys. We had so many anguishing questions. How could we have helped them better understand the differences between good and evil? As the adults leading the way, what could we learn from this wake-up call from the troubled youth in America? What could each one of us do in our own small daily acts of goodness to show our children the way to the light?

It was one of the darkest moments in Colorado history. I knew however, deep in my heart, that the heavens were in grand welcome of these young heroes.

With God's grace, we eventually moved from grieving to healing. Slowly, the light began to shine and warm our shattered Colorado hearts. The world sent us compassion, generosity, and much love. My family humbly did our parts by baking cookies and making blue ribbons near Columbine High School at Light of the World Church, where we observed our Almighty God in motion. So many unsung heroes showed their valiant colors—whether they were police, governmental, or school authorities, lay persons, or the clergy. Ordinary acts of kindness and justice were being demonstrated in extraordinarily painful times. The American heart was broken, and we came together as a nation to reckon with the times. It was the American way to pause and reflect on our state of being and learn how we can carry on toward our ideals for freedom, liberty, justice, and the pursuit of happiness for all. We are not a nation that ignores our troubled and needy; we care, and we wait to see how we can best help our brothers and sisters. We pick up our pieces, quietly, openly, and together—without further violence or escalation of evil. We, as a people, have a spirit for brotherly love that can never be destroyed. Our American spirit only grows stronger with each new growing pain of life.

America's Finest

It is now 2001, and, at nine years old, Steven has become a talented and enthusiastic football player. He yearns to become just like many of the professional football players that he admires these days. How important those football heroes become to our youngsters. He is also an enthusiastic reader now, thanks to J.K. Rowling and the fables of Harry Potter. Crystal, now, sixteen years of age, enjoys singing more than ever and has become a serious student of her Catholic faith and academic courses at Holy Family Catholic High. She draws leadership and inspiration from professional artists like Celine Dion and Rachael Lampa. As a mom, I am so proud of her. I am, also busy, working on creative literary and music projects with both Steven and Crystal. They are happy kids, and for that, Steve and I are happy parents.

Steve has continued to cultivate his expertise in gardening, cooking, carpentry, and family life. He has taken to raising our little rabbit, June, as well as a colony of chinchillas. Renegade Press is growing slowly but steadily while many other printing shops are flailing in the winds of bankruptcy. As for me, I have taken to the passion of this book and mission while leaning on my professional business and nursing skills as a means of livelihood. I receive great joy in honoring other people and offering our youth a source of inspiration for true character guidelines. It is more than I could have imagined in my wildest dreams. I love to write and long to create a multi-media business of my own with my own television show. Creative freedom has become a valued asset that allows me to grow and share more of myself with others. We [Lutton family] all love the country setting that our home life offers more and more with each growing day of these turbulent, modern times. We have grown fond of many old and new family and friend relationships.

On this particularly sunny Tuesday morning, September 11, 2001, I slept in a few minutes longer than usual. Steve left for work early, as usual, and now, I was awakened by a bright little greeting by my son, "Good morning, Mommy, can I take a little snoozy with you?" I looked at the clock and saw that it was 7:00 AM. "Alright, Steven, come on in," I reply as I indulge in five more minutes to cuddle with Steven. "Okay, let's get movin' here," I cheer five minutes later as I scurry our teenage singer and fourth grade wizard out of bed, into their school clothes, and finally outside to the car. The drive to school was fun. We prayed, as was our routine now for many years. We laughed. Yet, mostly we visited. I wanted to send my kids off to school in a positive vibration. Our drive became very pivotal to how we would all approach our days. Life's tough times would come and go; yet, we could count on these moments to be nourishing and consistent. How little did we know how much we would come to love nourishment and consistency?

First stop: Holy Family High and Crystal races off to meet her friends before beginning her classes, starting with Choir or French, depending on the day. "Bye, mom, I love you," and then she's gone. I smile. Second stop: Monarch K-8 with sloppy kisses and hugs as Steven grabs his backpack, and darts off to catch a bit of sports before the school bell rings. "Have a nice day, Mom, see ya!" shouts Steven while waving at me. I smile again.

Now, I just have to get out of the circle, I thought to myself, and then I can start my business day. I decided I would run first today. I enjoyed running or cycling everyday. It was a welcome routine to me for many years now. I used this time to reflect, pray, create, and energize myself for the goals-at-hand. On the way out of the circle, I turned on the radio to catch the morning news. I was listening to a Christian radio station, when the broadcaster broke his own conversation in a confusing tone, announcing, "Wait . . . I am hearing that the World Trade Center has been hit." By then, the terrorists had already committed their horrific acts causing

America's Finest

unimaginable damage and many of us were just catching on . . . even him.

I forgot about running, drove home, turned on the television . . . and the rest is history. Once again, America was under attack, and this time, it was New York, Pennsylvania, and our nation's capital, Washington, D.C. This time the day would end as an unprecedented nightmare of disproportionate magnitude.

Televisions around the world would show constant scenes of disaster. Smoke, screams, tears, airplanes, fire, imploding buildings, craters in the ground, firefighters, dogs, police, FBI agents, military, doctors, nurses, frightened youth, humanitarians, rescue workers, and every day people just trying to make sense out of the chaos, and just help . . . help anybody in need that could be reached. Throngs of people were killed by anti-American terrorists who decided to take life into their own hands. These, criminals, spearheaded by terrorist bin Laden, thought they could control the Spirit of America by destroying our innocent people. Soon, the entire world would come to our aid with compassionate bonds of universal goodwill. Once more, the common threads of humanity would reveal the essence of overpowering love and goodness that is available within each individual as an inherent gift of choice.

That very day, I went to a funeral for the mother of Renee Sisney. Renee, herself, is portrayed in this book for her own quiet acts of courage. On this day, she would again display her strength, as she not only grieved for her mother, but now also for America.

The day in Colorado remained warm and sunny with blue skies. It was actually a beautiful day. The funeral was complete with military honors for a veteran family. There was a modest pond in front of the cemetery with a flock of birds skimming the water surface. I could hear them singing during the ceremony. I could feel the heat of the sun on my

Courage in Society

arms. In fact, the sun was shining at that moment, casting a brilliant reflection across the water. With such beauty beaming around us, it was as if God and his lovely angels were sending us a message from Heaven.

It felt so surreal to be a part of such a fitting memorial in celebration of one individual's wholesome life, when so many thousands of individuals lay slain on the East Coast, lost in the rubble of someone's acts of destruction toward humanity. These victims of terrorism—close to three thousand innocent heroes—also deserved a fitting memorial for their wholesome lives. I knew that God was preparing just such a welcome for all of them in Heaven. The choir of angels would be gloriously embracing all of those sweet heroes who lost their lives on American soil that September 11, 2001, just because they were going about their business of leading productive lives. I know they were all blessed and that the trumpets were gloriously sounding for the new angels lifted from Earth.

It would be those of us left on Earth who would be lost for a while. Our hearts were broken, and for many . . . their family units completely shattered to pieces. The tears on many days would be unbearable, and the pain unreachable. We would find it difficult to concentrate on our own productivity and be too sad to think about our leisure. However, we did not give up or give in to the terrorist's fears and threats. Americans would rebuild their country and their dream. We would give tirelessly of our blood, sweat, time, money, clothes, food, entertainment, patriotism, cards, candles, and most of all, our prayers. Flags would wave everywhere and churches, synagogues, mosques, and all other holy institutions would open their doors for all. Comedians would cry, politicians would pray, children would console other parentless children. Investors would become charitable. Firefighters, police, humanitarians, health professionals, rescue workers, and animals would continue to serve and protect us—as they demonstrated so valiantly before, throughout, and after that day.

Our beloved President George W. Bush and First Lady Laura Bush would be ready to lead us—the American way, the brotherly way. "Let's roll" would become a poignantly, remembered slogan used by the president in memory of one of the heroes from the ill-fated flight that crashed in Pennsylvania. Certainly, we Americans can be very proud of the leadership of this fine First Couple at the helm of our government. I am confident that their past preparation in life has brought them to this purposeful mission in service of America.

Our leader of New York City, Mayor Rudolph Giuliani, would also become the man of the year. As the real deal, Mayor Giuliani's visionary wisdom would lead the Big Apple out of the dark aftermath and guide the rest of the world onto a triumphant path. Secretary Colin Powell and Secretary Donald Rumsfeld would become household names, calming the world's nerves. The American spirit to pursue justice and freedom would roar ferociously into the days and nights ahead.

In solidarity, we would wear our heartache openly and honestly because we are lovers of humanity. The American spirit is the melting pot of the world. We stand for freedom, democracy, and brotherly love. We fight proudly and bravely for human life and the pursuit of individual happiness, regardless of race, creed, or culture. As we grow as a nation, we are determined to emulate justice and equality for all. The world looks upon us as "the land of the free and the home of the brave." The world shares in our grief for we are part of a United Nations that dignifies all of humanity. We, as Americans, are always responsive to our international neighbors in their times of dire need and strife. We take our founding fathers seriously in the foundation that rang true throughout our homeland when we declared our independence with the belief that "all men are created equal".

In all three of these destructive events, individuals chose to terrorize us as a people, a tactic as old as time. Terrorism is an insidious evil, tempting individuals under very subtle disguises. Yet, it is what it is. By its very nature, terrorism is a choice brought about by evil forces. Where evil serves only to destroy life through disintegration, good serves only to support life through growth. Evil is on the side that leads one on the low road away from God to hell. The line in the sand is clear and each of us is bestowed with the choice of free will while we move through our human journey. Because of these events, our nation has learned much about our ideals and ourselves. As a people, we are stronger than ever in our love for America . . . and our love for life! The American spirit continues to grow on the side of good. The light is beaming within our hearts. Above all, Love continues to lead our way.

We, the Lutton family, are proud to be Americans. We, as American parents, are grateful for the blessings and gifts that we have to offer our children in this society. We, as freedom lovers, know that God is watching over us, and we know that the American spirit is the Spirit of God. We know all of this because the spirit within all forces of life is always for expansion and fuller expression. We know that greatness in humanity is always shown through humility and gratitude. We know that the high road of good is the road that leads us to Truth…to the Light of God . . . to Heaven. It is, after all, in God we trust.

God Bless America!
God Bless the World,
Homeland for Humanity.

◆ ◆ ◆

AFTERWORD

By Don M. Green
Executive Director
Napoleon Hill Foundation

Cheri Lutton has written a book that is a delight to read, but the great value in the book is to spur the reader to take action to make the world a better place in which to live.

The list of people for which the author gives an insight portrays to the reader that having good ideas or studying others is helpful, but only when one takes action.

What is so important is to realize that once a passion or worthwhile purpose is formulated, the how-to can be learned by obtaining information that is available through our own background or the experiences of others.

The story of President John F. Kennedy and the positive impact he had on society is very important, and it took courage for him to make the statement that the United States would land a man on the moon in this decade. Courage is not in just saying but also doing. Even though President Kennedy was assassinated before the moon landing occurred, the courage that he projected in making the statement and then seeing technology developed that allowed the venture to become a reality, portrays courage at its finest point.

It is extremely important to realize that having courage is more than thinking or even talking about situations that are difficult or frightening, but requires action. I am not a psy-

Afterword

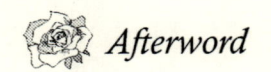

chologist, but I have read enough, and experiences will show that fear is not easily dispelled by thinking; however, taking action will work.

The many individuals of which Ms. Lutton writes, tells us again and again of people that had the courage to take action when they saw problems that needed correcting or of great opportunities that were available to the person with courage.

An excellent reason to study success and to continue to repeat it over and over, whether it be reading books of Cheri Lutton's or *The Life of Helen Keller*, Wilma Randolph and others, is that it helps the reader to realize that if others facing such odds can have the courage to overcome difficulties, the reader should be able to realize that he/she can take the courage and act out solving whatever affronts them.

To be successful, an individual needs courage, and if courage is lacking, then it must be developed. Studying the lives of successful individuals is an excellent way to learn. Any worthwhile skill can be learned by studying others. If you want to learn or improve at golf, just study Tiger Woods. If you want to study success, read Napoleon Hill's *Think and Grow Rich*.

If you truly desire to be successful, you must decide for yourself what success means to you. To some people, it may be acquiring a million dollars or more. To someone else, success may be writing a book, raising a family, or working for disadvantaged youths. In whatever way, a person defines success for himself or herself, each should remember Ben Sweetland's quote that "success is a journey and not a destination." It is what we become while we are on the success journey that is important.

To me, success is being in a position to help someone who is less fortunate in life. I believe that most people that are genuinely happy are not this way as a result of a goal, but are happy as a result of being successful while helping others.

Don M. Green

AUTHOR'S COMMENTS

When I look back to the time I started writing this book, I realize that I was naïve. I plunged into this project, wanting to make a difference by honoring individuals for their acts of courage. I had no idea how daunting of a task it is to write a book of this nature. I certainly had no idea how much I would grow from the entire experience. Today, I am forever changed and humbled by this act.

I have become tremendously close in spirit to all of the individuals that I have profiled in this book. I have learned so much from each one of these great human beings. I have studied courage from all aspects of life: spirit, mind, body, family, work, and society. I have shared with you the centered qualities of courage that both celebrated and private individuals can possess and act upon in their lives.

Courage has no prejudice toward the rich, the famous, or the privileged. In fact, the measure of a great person is marked from the inside and knows no boundaries from the outside. True character in a human being far outweighs the pleasantry of personality. Inner beauty will always outshine outer beauty. Great human beings remain in a constant state of humility and gratitude, which perpetuates their cycle of success. Over the years, we begin to appreciate the leaders in life that bring out the inner beauty within us all.

It is my hope, indeed, to create a positive movement toward celebrating the centered qualities of humanity. Through *Mirrors of Love*, I hope to spur others around the

Author's Comments

world to join me in my quest to honor individuals—both celebrated and private—in all aspects of life who deserve to be recognized for their inner beauty.

I hope to attract other writers, singers, and artists to join me in collaboration as we move forward to bring the good news of those who have touched all of our lives to the rest of the world. I hope that through *Mirrors of Love* and CCQH, Inc., our youth will have true guidelines on character and leaders who can show them the way!

Together, we can make a positive difference! Please visit and contact us with your interest at mirrorsoflove.com, ccqh.com, or cherilutton@mirrorsoflove.com. Also, please feel free to send me any positive messages that you may like forwarded to any of the living individuals honored in this book.

REFERENCES

Courage in Spirit

American Bible Society. Holy Bible:CEV. New York, New York: American Bible Society, 1995.

Bloch, Douglas. *Listening To Your Inner Voice*. Center City, MN:Hazeldon,1991.

Collier, Robert. *The Secret Of The Ages*. Oak Harbor, WA: Robert Collier Publications 30th Printing, 1999.

Mayhall, Carole. *When God Whispers*. Colorado Springs, CO: NavPress, 1994.

O'Hearn, Bill. *Life More Abundant*. Wilsonville, OR: Book Partners, 1999.

Pope John Paul II

Bernstein, Carl & Marco Politi. *His Holiness*. New York, New York: Doubleday, 1996.

John Paul II. Edited by Vittorio Messori. *Crossing the Threshold of Hope By His Holiness*. New York, New York: Alfred A. Knopf, Random House, 1994.

John Paul II. *Gift & Mystery: John Paul II*. New York, New York: Doubleday, 1996.

Kwitney, Jonathon. *Man of the Century: The Life and Times of John Paul II*. NewYork, New York: Henry Holt & Co.,1997.

Malinski, Mieczyslaw. *Pope John Paul II: The Life of Karol*

415

References

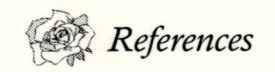

Wojtyla. New York, New York: The Seabury Press, 1979.

Szulc, Tad. *Pope John Paul II: The Biography*. New York, New York: Scribner, Simon & Schuster, 1995.

Weigel, George. *Witness To Hope: The Biography of Pope John Paul II*. NewYork, New York: Cliff Street Books, Division of HarperCollins, 1999.

Mother Teresa

Mother Teresa. *A Simple Path*. New York, New York: Random House, 1995.

Mother Teresa. *Mother Teresa – Nobel Lecture, Nobel E Museum*. Stockholm, Sweden: The Nobel Foundation, 2002.

Sanness, John, Norwegian Nobel Committee. *The Nobel Peace Prize 1979 – Presentation Speech, Nobel E Museum*. Stockholm, Sweden: The Nobel Foundation, 2002.

Scolozzi, Angelo. (compilator) for Mother Teresa. *Thirsting for God*. Ann Arbor, MI: Servant Publications, 2000.

Steve Barnhill

Barnhill, Steve and Father Wm. Breslin. *Bridges International Manual*. Denver, Colorado: Bridges International, Ltd., 2001.

Lutton, Cheri. Personal interview. November, 2001.

Crystal E. Lutton

Lutton, Cheri. Personal interview. July, 2001.

Courage in Mind

Allen, James. *As A Man Thinketh*. White Plains, New York: Peter Pauper Press, 1998.

Frankl, Viktor E. *Man's Search for Meaning*. New York, New York: Touchstone edition, Simon & Schuster, Inc., 1984.

References

Hill, Napoleon. *Think and Grow Rich*. New York, New York: Pauper Press, Columbine Book, Division of Ballantine Books, 1983.

Hill, Napoleon. *Grow Rich With Peace of Mind*. New York, New York: Fawcett, Columbine Book, Division of Ballantine Books, 1996.

President John Fitzgerald Kennedy

Kennedy, John F. *Profiles in Courage*. New York: Harper & Row Publishers, 1955.

Reeves, Thomas C. *A Question of Character*. Roseville, CA: Prima Publishing, 1992.

Salinger, Pierre. *With Kennedy*. New York: Doubleday, 1966.

Schlesinger Jr., Arthur M. *A Thousand Days*. Boston, MA: Houghton Mifflin Co., 1965.

Bob Proctor

Lutton, Cheri. Phone interview. June, 2001.

Proctor, Bob. *You Were Born Rich*. Cartersville, GA: LifeSuccess Productions, 1997.

Proctor, Bob. *Bob Proctor's Mentor Study Manual*. Cartersville, GA: LifeSuccess Ventures, 2000.

Proctor, Bob. *The Liberty League*. Phoenix, Arizona: LifeSucceess Productions, 1999.

Larry Wilson

Lutton, Cheri. Phone interview. May, 2001.

Wilson, Larry & Hersch Wilson. *Play To Win*. Austin, Texas: Bard Press, 1998.

Wilson, Larry with Hersch Wilson. *Changing the Game: The New Way to Sell*. New York, New York: Fireside Book, Simon & Schuster, 1987.

References

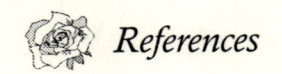

Wilson, Larry with Hersch Wilson. *Stop Selling, Start Partnering*. New York, New York: John Wiley & Sons, 1994.

Mark Victor Hansen

Canfield, Jack & Mark Victor Hansen. *Chicken Soup for the Soul*. Deerfield Beach, FL: Health Communications, 1988.

Canfield, Jack & Mark Victor Hansen. *Dare To Win*. New York: The Berkley Publishing Group, 1994.

Canfield, Jack; Hansen, Mark Victor & Les Hewitt. *The Power of Focus*. Deerfield Beach, FL: Health Communications, 2000.

Lutton, Cheri. Fax & phone interviews. February, 2001.

Steven H. Lutton II

Lutton, Cheri. Personal Interview. October, 2000.

Courage in Body

Boreyko, Jason. *Making The Impossible Possible*. Tempe, AZ: JBE, Inc., 1999.

Glover, Bob and Pete Schuder. *The New Competitive Runners' Handbook*. New York, New York: Penguin Books, 1988.

Schaller, Bob. *The Olympic Dream and Spirit: Volume One*. Grand Island, NE: Ex-Husker Press a Division of Cross Training Publishing, 2000.

Steven H. Lutton

Lutton, Cheri. Personal interview. October, 2000.

Steve Siebold

Gove-Siebold Group. Website: Steve Siebold. Bradenton, FL: Gove-Siebold Group, 2001.

Lutton, Cheri. Phone interview. July, 2001.

Siebold, Steve. *The Call 10 Tiger Program*. Bradenton, FL:

References

Gove-Siebold Group, 2000.

Rachael Lampa

Lutton, Cheri. Personal interview. March, 2001.

Buc, Michele. *Rachael Lampa Press Kit*. Nashville, TN: Word Entertainment, 2001.

Robert Troch

Lutton, Cheri. Phone interview. December, 2000.

Steve Immer

Lutton, Cheri. Personal interview. December, 2000.

Courage in Family

Covey, Sean. *The 7 Habits of Highly Effective Teens*. New York, New York: A Fireside Book a Division of Simon & Schuster, 1998.

Narramoree, Bruce. *Parenting with Love & Limits*. Grand Rapid, MI: Pyranee Books a Division of Zondervan Publishing House, 1987.

Omartian, Stormie. *The Power Of A Praying Parent*. Eugene, OR: Harvest House Publishers, 1995.

Vannoy, Steven W. *The 10 Greatest Gifts I Give My Children*. New York, New York: Fireside Book a Division of Simon & Schuster, 1994.

Jacqueline Kennedy Onassis

Anthony, Carl Sferrazzo. *As We Remember Her: Jacqueline Kennedy Onassis, In The Words of Her Friends & Family*. New York: HarperCollins Publishers, 1997.

Gallagher, Mary B. *My Life with Jacqueline Kennedy*. New York: David McKay Co, 1969.

References

Klein, Edward. *All Too Human: The Love Story of Jack & Jackie Kennedy*. New York: Simon & Schuster, 1996.

Klein, Edward. *Just Jackie: Her Private Years*. New York: Ballantine, 1998.

Van Rensselaer Thayer, Mary. *Jacqueline Kennedy: The White House Years*. Boston: Little Brown & Company, 1967.

Yvonne Kalench

Kalench, John. *Being the Best You Can Be in MLM*. San Diego, CA: Millionaires in Motion, 1990.

Lutton, Cheri. Phone interview. November, 2000.

Doc Moody

Lutton, Cheri. Personal & phone interviews. October, 2000.

Renee Sisney

Lutton, Cheri. Personal interview. January, 2001.

Missy Montoya

Lutton, Cheri. Personal & phone interviews. March, 2001.

Courage in Work

Biro, Brian. *Beyond Success*. Hamilton, Montana: Pygmalian Press, 1997.

Gross, Daniel. *Forbes Greatest Business Stories Of All Time*. New York, New York: John Wiley & Sons, 1996.

Hendricks, Gay, Ph.D and Kate Ludeman, Ph.D. *The Corporate Mystic*. New York, New York: Bantam Books, 1996.

Lowe, Tamara. *Peter Lowe's Success Workbook*. Tampa, FL: Success Events International, Inc., 2001.

Wattles, Wallace D. *The Science Of Getting Rich*. Cartersville, GA: LifeSuccess Productions, 1996.

References

Robert Francis Kennedy

Goldfarb, Ronald. *Perfect Villian, Perfect Heroes, RFK's War.* New York: Random House, Inc., 1995.

Guthman, Edwin & Richard Allen. *Collected Speeches: RFK.* New York: Viking/Penguin USA, 1993.

Harrison, Barbara & Daniel Terris. *A Ripple of Hope: The Life of Robert F. Kennedy.* New York: Lodestar Books, 1997.

Heymann, David C. *RFK: A Candid Biography of Robert F. Kennedy.* New York: Dutton Book, Penguin Group, 1998.

Kennedy, Maxwell T. *Make Gentle The Life of This World: The Vision of RFK.* New York: Harcourt Brace & Co., 1998.

Dean Nixon

Lutton, Cheri. Phone interview. February, 2001.

Anita Sanders

Lutton, Cheri. Phone interview. October, 2000; November, 2001.

Secretary of State Colin Powell

America's Promise Website and Portfolio, 2001.

Powell, Colin with Joseph E. Persico. *My American Journey.* New York, New York: Ballantine Books, Random House, 1996.

U.S. Government. *Department of State Website: Secretary of State.* Washington, D.C.: State Dept., 2001.

Patricia Krown

Lutton, Cheri. Personal interview. January, 2001.

Courage in Society

Kersey, Cynthia. *Unstoppable.* Naperville, IL: Sourcebooks, Inc., 1998.

References

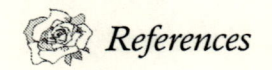

Shapiro, Steve. *Listening for Success*. Laguna Beach, CA: Chica Publications, 1999.

Scot Keranen

Lutton, Cheri. Phone interview. November, 2000.

Grace, Princess of Monaco

Lacey, Robert. *Grace*. New York: Putnam, 1994.

Princess Grace Foundation USA and Monaco Web Sites.

Quine, Judith Balaban. *Grace Kelly & Six Intimate Friends, The Bridesmaids.* New York: Pocket Books, Division of Simon & Schuster, 1990.

Liz Mostov

Lutton, Cheri. Phone interview. April, 2001.

Diana, Princess of Wales

Althorp House Website.

Campbell, Lady Colin. *Diana In Private*. New York: St. Martin's Press, 1992.

Diana, Princess of Wales Memorial Fund Website.

Spoto, Donald. *Diana - The Last Year*. New York: Harmony/Crown, 1997.

America's Finest in the Face of Tragedy

Websites about Oklahoma City Bombing, Columbine School Shooting, and September 11 Attacks on America.

ABOUT THE AUTHOR

A multidimensional visionary, Cheri Lutton has earned degrees in theatre and nursing, and an MBA in marketing. With careers as a leader in neonatal clinical research, international marketing, and now as founder of CCQH, Inc., Cheri has launched her visions as an author, lyricist, speaker, media host, thinker, and marketing executive for the Mirrors of Love™ multi-media series. Cheri enjoys living in Lafayette, Colorado, as a devoted wife to Steve, and mother to Crystal and Steven. She is an avid runner, cyclist, and gardener; loves people and her Catholic faith. Cheri is available for interviews, speaking engagements, seminars, and multi-media performances. She can be contacted at www.mirrorsoflove.com, www.ccqh.com, or at cherilutton@mirrorsoflove.com.

ABOUT...
CCQH

"Celebrating the Centered Qualities of Humanity"

The overall mission of CCQH, Inc. is to create a positive movement toward celebrating the centered qualities of humanity through a multi-media series. These centered qualities such as courage, compassion, integrity, humor, wisdom, and patience—when put to action—not only serve in building human character, but also in making the world a better place for all. CCQH is dedicated to building a reference series that explores these inner qualities of humanity in depth for the enhancement of leadership in youth and adults. CCQH plans to honor individuals—private and celebrated individuals—for their diverse acts of goodness through books, television, radio, the Internet, performing arts, marketing partners, and corporate sponsorships. *Mirrors of Love* is the first brand line owned by CCQH, Inc. designed to focus on a literary, musical, and merchandising series targeted on leadership development. Visit our web site at www.mirrorsoflove.com or email us at cherilutton@mirrosoflove.com

CCQH is also interested in creating marketing alliances to promote other like-minded businesses. Contact CCQH at ccqh.com with interest in participating as a potential writer, artist, musician, vocalist, benefactor, marketing partner, distributor, or corporate sponsor.

ABOUT...

Mercy Corps

Mercy Corps is a not-for-profit organization that exists to alleviate suffering, poverty, and oppression by helping people build secure, productive, and just communities.

Since 1979, Mercy Corps has provided more than $640 million in assistance to 74 countries. Mercy Corps is known nationally and internationally for its quick-response, high-impact programs. Over 91 percent of the agency's resources are allocated directly to programs that help those in need. The Diana, Princess of Wales Memorial Fund has been a supporter of Mercy Corps.

With headquarters in the United States and Scotland, Mercy Corps is an international family of humanitarian agencies that currently reaches more than five million people in over 30 countries. Established by Christian leaders, including Doug Wead, Pat and Shirley Boone, and President Dan O'Neill, incorporating their faith values into an agency that has developed into the broader vision of today, Mercy Corps provides assistance exclusively based on need, without regard to religion or politics.

Partial proceeds from the *Mirrors of Love* book series are donated to Mercy Corps. More information about Mercy Corps is available online at mercycorps.org.

About...

Diana

THE WORK CONTINUES

The Memorial Fund started with the donations at the time of the Princess's death in 1997. Five years on, it has built a global humanitarian organization, creating a living memorial to Diana, Princess of Wales and taking its inspiration from her global humanitarian work. The Fund helps people to change their lives for the better, by giving grants to charities in the UK and around the world, along with its sister fund in the US, championing causes and raising new money to support this work.
The Work Continues . . .

Values and Inspiration

Five powerful words sum up The Fund's values.

Excellent   Passionate   Special   Accessible   Transparent

Diana, Princess of Wales made people feel special, highlighted controversial issues and changed perceptions. The staff at The Fund hopes these values come through strongly in all the work they do. For a global organization, inspired by the humanitarian work of the Princess and which owes so much to the support of so many members of the public, nothing else will do. Visit online at www.theworkcontinues.org.

About...
The Princess Grace Foundations

The Princess Grace Foundation of the principality of Monaco was founded in 1964 with the aim of reaching out to those with special needs for whom no provision has been made within the ordinary social services. Since then the work of the Foundation has been chiefly directed toward children in need reflecting Princess Grace's passionate concern for children. The Foundation also plays a significant role in the sphere of education and training for the arts, both in Europe and in the United States. The web site address is www.fondation-psse-grace.mc/foundation.

The Princess Grace Foundation – USA was established by His Serene Highness Prince Rainier in 1982 as a tribute to Princess Grace's memory and her long-standing desire to create an organization for the support of aspiring artists in American theater, playwriting, dance, and film. As a public charity, this not-for-profit organization provides encouragement and recognition to young artists during their critical formative years. The Princess Grace Awards is a program of the United States Foundation dedicated to identifying and assisting young talent in theatre, dance, and film through grants in the form of scholarships, apprenticeships, and fellowships. The website address is www.pgfusa.com.

About...
The Missionaries of Charity

Mother Teresa received a calling from God to serve the poorest of the poor in 1945 and began by caring for one sick and dying person whom she found on the streets of Calcutta. She eventually formed the Missionaries of Charity, a religious order originating in Calcutta, that received the Vatican's blessing in 1950. Sisters and brothers of the Missionaries of Charity practice their life of poverty with the absolute faith that this will bring them nearer to God. Her mandate of mercy is to spread love into the world by relieving the suffering of others—through a Catholic sisterhood and brotherhood who serve a largely non-Christian community, and who do not compel those they help to convert to the Catholic faith. Mother Teresa encourages Christians and non-Christians to follow a simple path in life expressing small acts of love toward others so that we may bring dignity and value to each human being.

The Order is composed of eight branches with many facilities around the world: the Active Sisters, the Contemplative Sisters, the Contemplative Brothers, the Missionary Fathers, the Lay Missionaries, and the Volunteers and the Sick and Suffering Co-Workers. The Order is solely supported by the Love of God and through donations given by persons of all Faiths. The U.S. headquarter for contact is at:

335 E. 149th St. Bronx, NY 10451, phone: 718-292-0019.

> No act of kindness, no matter how small, is ever wasted.
>
> *Aesop*

Mirrors of Love
. . . A Human Rose in Bloom

Printed in the United States
746700003B